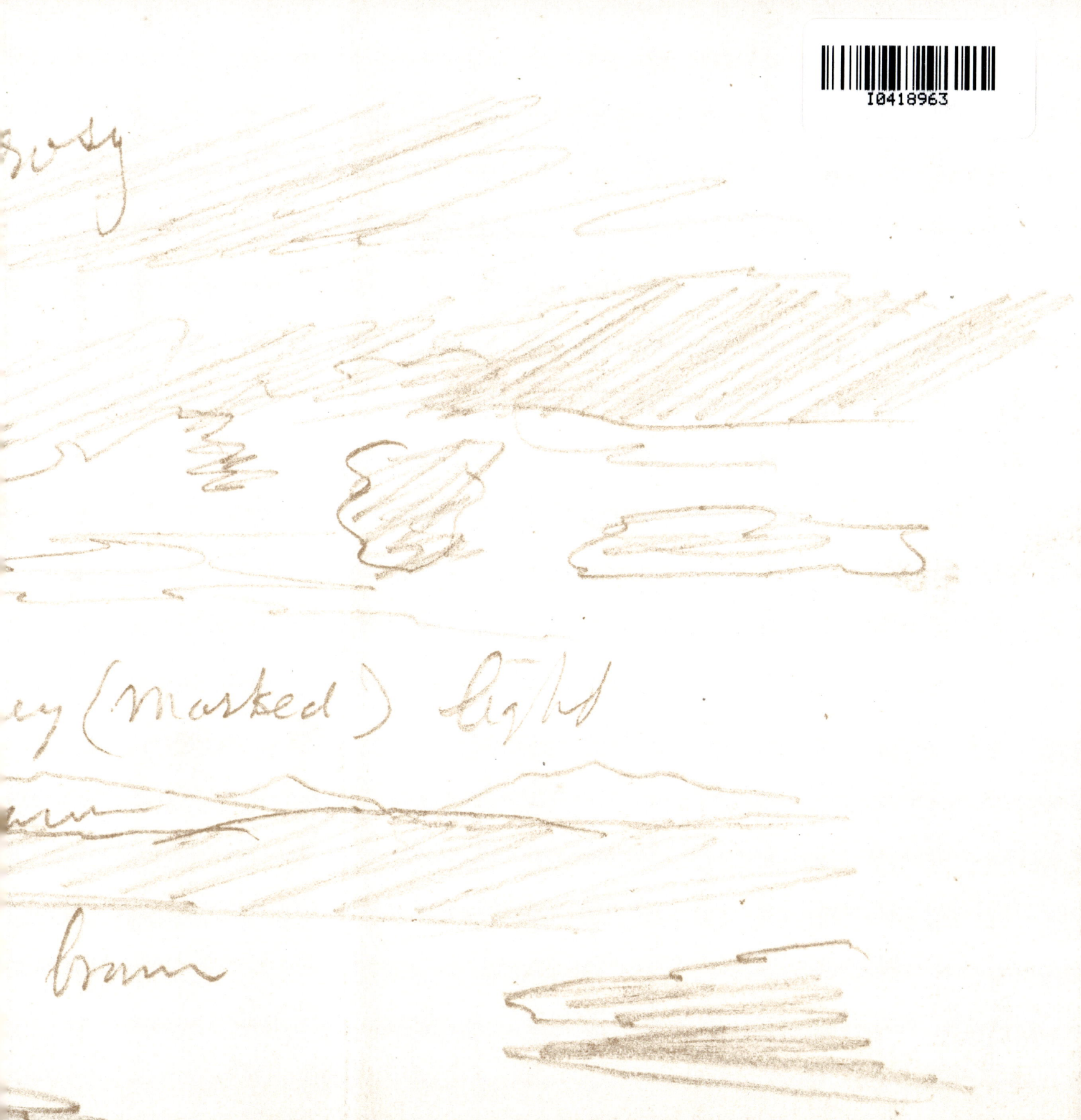

ey (marked) light

brown

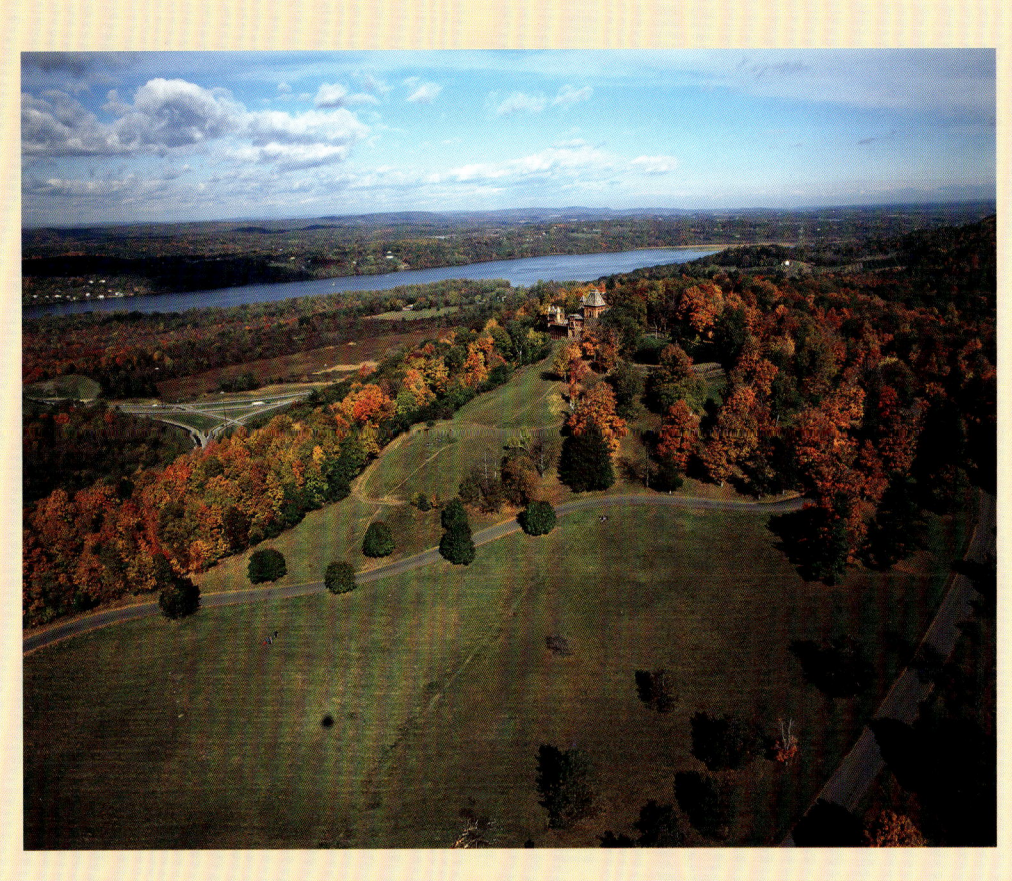

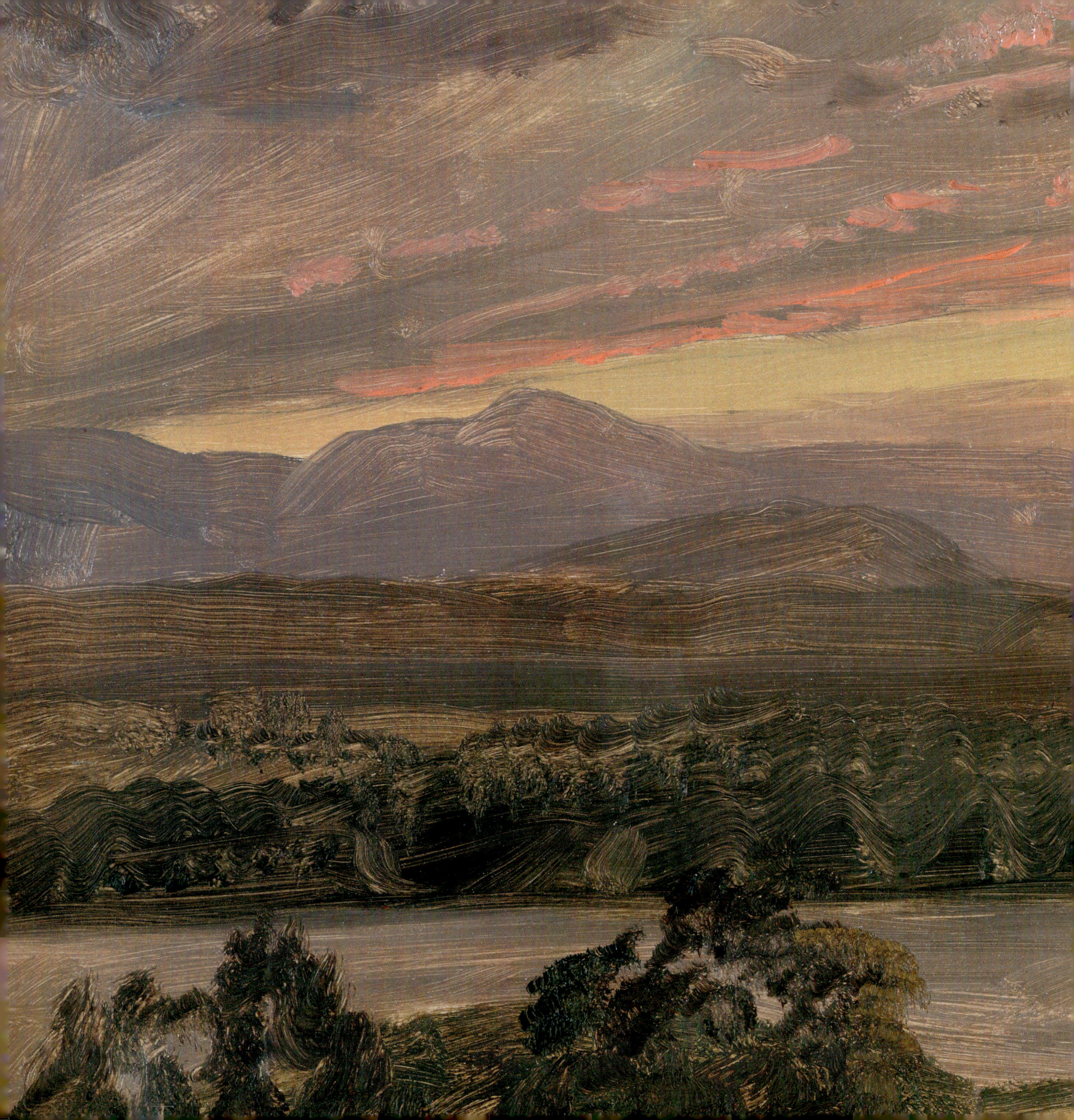

Glories of the Hudson

Frederic Edwin Church's Views from Olana

Essay by Evelyn D. Trebilcock and Valerie A. Balint

Introduction by Kenneth John Myers

Foreword by John K. Howat

Glories of the Hudson
is the inaugural exhibition in the
Evelyn and Maurice Sharp Gallery

The Olana Partnership
Hudson, New York

New York State Office of Parks, Recreation
and Historic Preservation
Albany, New York

Cornell University Press
Ithaca and London

This exhibition, *Glories of the Hudson*, was organized by The Olana Partnership and the New York State Office of Parks, Recreation and Historic Preservation, using predominantly objects from the collection of Olana State Historic Site, Hudson, New York.

A grant from Furthermore: a program of the J. M. Kaplan Fund helped in the publication of this catalogue.

Olana State Historic Site is one of 35 historic properties administered and operated by the New York State Office of Parks, Recreation and Historic Preservation: David A. Paterson, Governor.

Unless otherwise credited, all photographs and other visual images are courtesy of Olana State Historic Site, New York State Office of Parks, Recreation and Historic Preservation.

Library of Congress Control Number: 2009921382
ISBN: 978-0-8014-4843-0

First published 2009 by The Olana Partnership and Cornell University Press.

Endsheets: Frederic Edwin Church, *The "Bend in the River" from Olana*, detail, c. 1875–92, graphite on white wove paper, 4⁷⁄₁₆ × 6⅞ in., OL.1980.1502

Page 1: Stan Ries, *Aerial View of Olana*, photograph, 2001, © Stan Ries

Pages 2–3: Frederic Edwin Church, *Sunset from Olana*, detail, July 2, 1870, oil on off-white academy board, 11¹⁄₁₆ × 15⅛ in., OL.1976.8

Pages 4–5: Stan Ries, *Olana in Winter*, photograph, 2001, © Stan Ries

Page 6: Frederic Edwin Church, *Winter Twilight from Olana*, detail, c. 1871–72, oil on off-white academy board, 10¹⁄₁₆ × 13 in., OL.1976.4

Page 10: Frederic Edwin Church, *The Hudson Valley in Winter from Olana*, detail, c. 1866–72, oil on academy board, 11¾ × 18¼ in., OL.1980.36

Page 27: Nicholas Whitman, *View of the House from across the Lake*, photograph, 2008

Page 86: Nicholas Whitman, *Mexican Pot, Persian Tiled Fireplace, and Indian Carved Teakwood Mantel in the Studio of Olana*, photograph, 2008

Page 94: Nicholas Whitman, *Rustic Bench within the Olana Parkland*, photograph, 2008

Page 96: Nicholas Whitman, *View of the Hudson River and Catskill Mountains from Olana*, photograph, 2001

Edited by Lory Frankel
Proofread by Fronia W. Simpson and Barbara McGill
Designed by John Hubbard
Color management by iocolor, Seattle
Produced by Marquand Books, Inc., Seattle
  www.marquand.com
Printed and bound by CS Graphics Pte., Ltd., Singapore

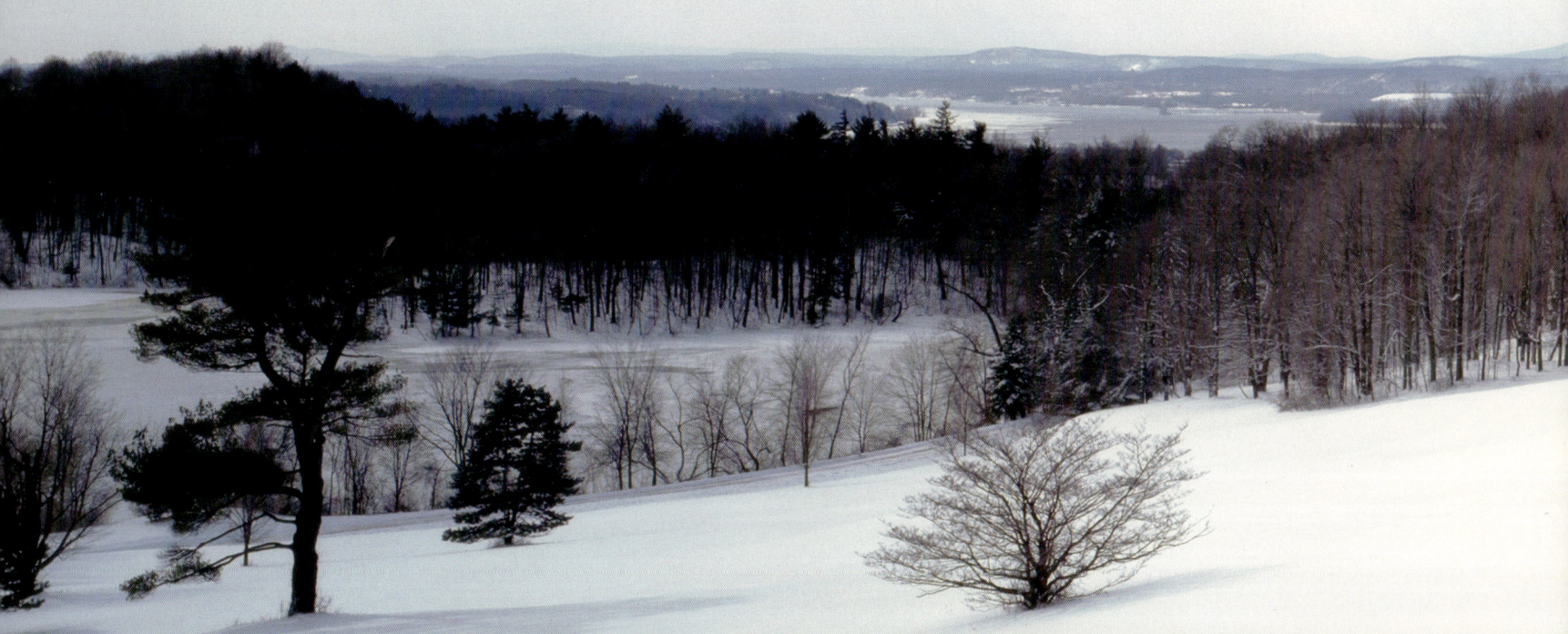

Contents

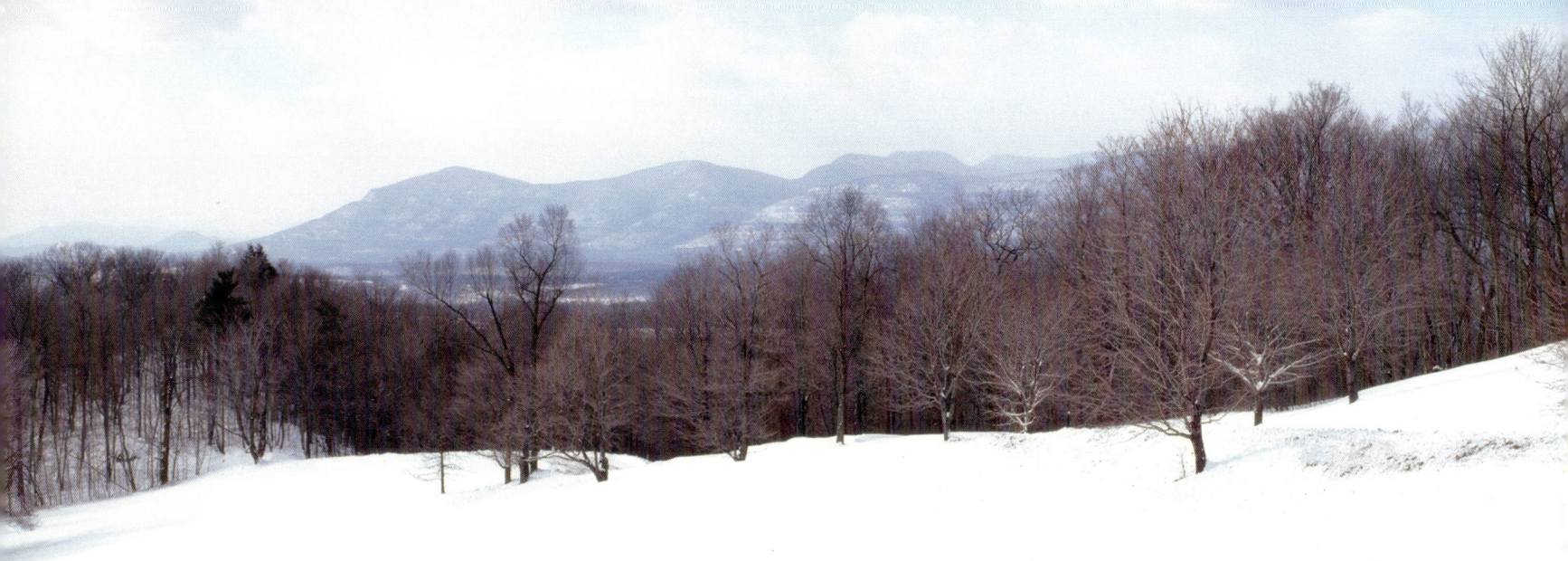

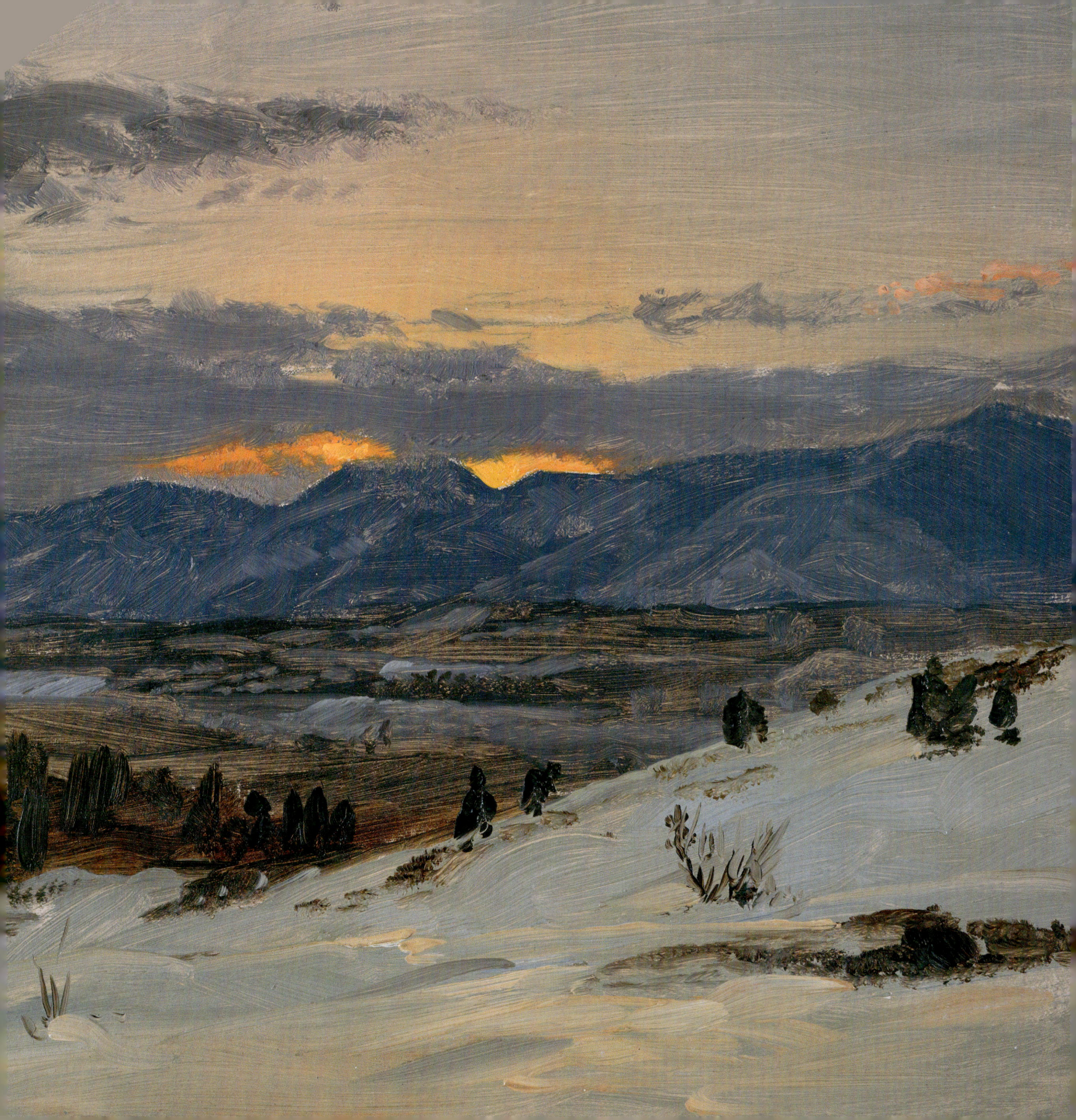

Preface and Acknowledgments

In this, the quadricentennial year of Henry Hudson's voyage up the river that now bears his name, The Olana Partnership and Olana State Historic Site celebrate the opening of the Evelyn and Maurice Sharp Gallery, a newly established exhibition space located in the main house at Olana. Our inaugural exhibition, *Glories of the Hudson: Frederic Edwin Church's Views from Olana*, highlights Church's sketches of the Hudson River from his home, Olana. The oil sketches chosen document his passion for the River as transformed by the seasons, weather, and light. Included in the exhibition is material never before seen by the public. Visitors will have the extraordinary opportunity to examine the sketches and then to look out the window at the view that inspired them.

Collaborative projects such as this exhibition and the creation of the Sharp Family Gallery represent a tremendous joint effort on the part of the New York State Office of Parks, Recreation and Historic Preservation and its nonprofit partner The Olana Partnership. Together, these two institutions are working to preserve and restore this vital Hudson River Valley asset. The many projects completed within the main house include the opening of restored second-floor bedrooms for the first time in forty years and the restoration of the studio and numerous objects, furnishings, and painted surfaces. In addition, extensive restoration of the artist-designed landscape has been carried out, resulting in acres of restored views, and the historic farm complex is now home to the newly reconstructed Wagon House Education Center.

We thank the following for their help with this exhibition: New York State Governor David A. Paterson; New York State Office of Parks, Recreation and Historic Preservation Commissioner Carol Ash; Deputy Commissioner for Historic Preservation J. Winthrop Aldrich; Regional Director, Taconic Region, Jayne McLaughlin; and at Olana State Historic Site, Site Manager Linda E. McLean and Interpretive Programs Assistant Carri Manchester. We are also grateful to The Olana Partnership staff members: Curator Evelyn Trebilcock; Associate Curator Valerie Balint; Librarian/Archivist

Ida Brier; Curatorial Intern Alyson Mazzone; President Sara Griffen; Vice President for Development Robert Burns; Director of Administration and Public Affairs Nelson Sterner; and Executive Assistant Mary Curran.

For providing their thoughts on painters in the Hudson Valley, we thank John K. Howat for his lovely foreword and Kenneth John Myers for his thoughtful introduction. For managing the loan and preparing the paintings, photographs, and printed material for display and photographic materials for this publication, we are grateful to the New York State Office of Parks, Recreation and Historic Preservation Peebles Island Resource Center staff: Former Director James Gold; Acting Director John Lovell; Collections Manager Anne Ricard Cassidy and her staff Erin Czernecki, Ronna Dixson, and Mary Zaremski; Curators Robin Campbell and Susan Walker; Paper Conservator Michele Phillips; Frames Conservator Eric Price; Paintings Conservator Joyce Zucker; and Photographer Rich Clauss.

The catalogue, which will serve to bring the story of Olana and Church's view of the Hudson Valley to new audiences long after the exhibition closes, would not have been possible without early support from Henry and Sharon Martin; a grant from Furthermore: a program of the J. M. Kaplan Fund; and the guidance of Ed Marquand and his staff at Marquand Books. For their continued support of Olana publications we are grateful to Cornell University Press, especially John Ackerman and his staff. For supporting images we thank: Allison Munsell at the Albany Institute of History and Art; Selina Bartlett at Allen Memorial Art Gallery, Oberlin College; Melissa McCready at the Baltimore Museum of Art; Trevor R. Weight at Brigham Young University Museum of Art; Patricia King at Colby College Museum of Art; Jill Bloomer at the Cooper-Hewitt, National Design Museum, Smithsonian Institution; Ila Furman at the Corcoran Gallery of Art; Elizabeth Weinman at Crystal Bridges Museum of American Art; Helena Grubesic at Debra Force Fine Art; Sylvia Inwood at the Detroit Institute of Arts; Marshall Field; Joel Garzoli at Garzoli Gallery; Colleen K. Zorn at A. J. Kollar Fine Paintings; Peter and Paula Lunder; Jamieson Bunn at the Metropolitan Museum of Art; Clara Pyo at the Museum of Fine Arts, Boston; Joanna Hanna at Springfield Museums; and Charles Hilburn at The Westervelt Company. For the contemporary images of Olana included we thank photographers Len Jenshel, Stan Ries, and Nicholas Whitman.

For their advice, support, and encouragement of the exhibition, the Sharp Family Gallery, and this publication we want to recognize the Olana Curatorial Committee: Susan Winokur, Chair; Armin B. Allen; Robin Campbell, Peebles Island Resource Center; Stephen Edidin, Curator of American & European Art, New-York Historical Society; Sara Griffen, The Olana Partnership; Mary Ellen Hern, Associate Director for External Relations, The Norman Rockwell Museum; Judith Hernstadt; Frederick D.

Hill; Paul Leach; John Lovell, Peebles Island Resource Center; Carri Manchester, Olana State Historic Site; Linda E. McLean, Olana State Historic Site; Amy G. Poster, Curator Emerita of Asian Art, Brooklyn Museum of Art; Richard T. Sharp; Carol Irish Strone, Carol Strone Art Advisory; and Karen Zukowski, Independent Scholar.

Finally, we wish to thank the generous individual and institutional donors; they provided the necessary funds that have made this important book and exhibition possible: anonymous; Furthermore: a program of the J. M. Kaplan Fund; Mr. and Mrs. Brock Ganeles; Frederick D. and Eileen Hill; Hudson-Fulton-Champlain Quadricentennial Commission; Mark LaSalle; Paul Leach and Susan Winokur; Henry and Sharon Martin; Chas A. Miller III; the Lois H. and Charles A. Miller Foundation, Inc.; The New York State Council on the Arts Museum Program; Open Space Institute, Inc. Barnabas McHenry Award; Eileen Patrick and Jeffrey Ervine; Lou Salerno, Questroyal Fine Art; and Richard T. Sharp.

The exhibition represents years of dedication and planning on the part of The Olana Partnership and Olana State Historic Site to make more of the vast collections and the story of Frederic Church accessible to the public. We hope this exhibition will serve as a springboard for many years of exploration of Olana's collections in the Sharp Family Gallery, bringing us ever new insights into and appreciation of the life and work of one of America's greatest artists.

Washburn S. Oberwager
Chair, The Olana Partnership

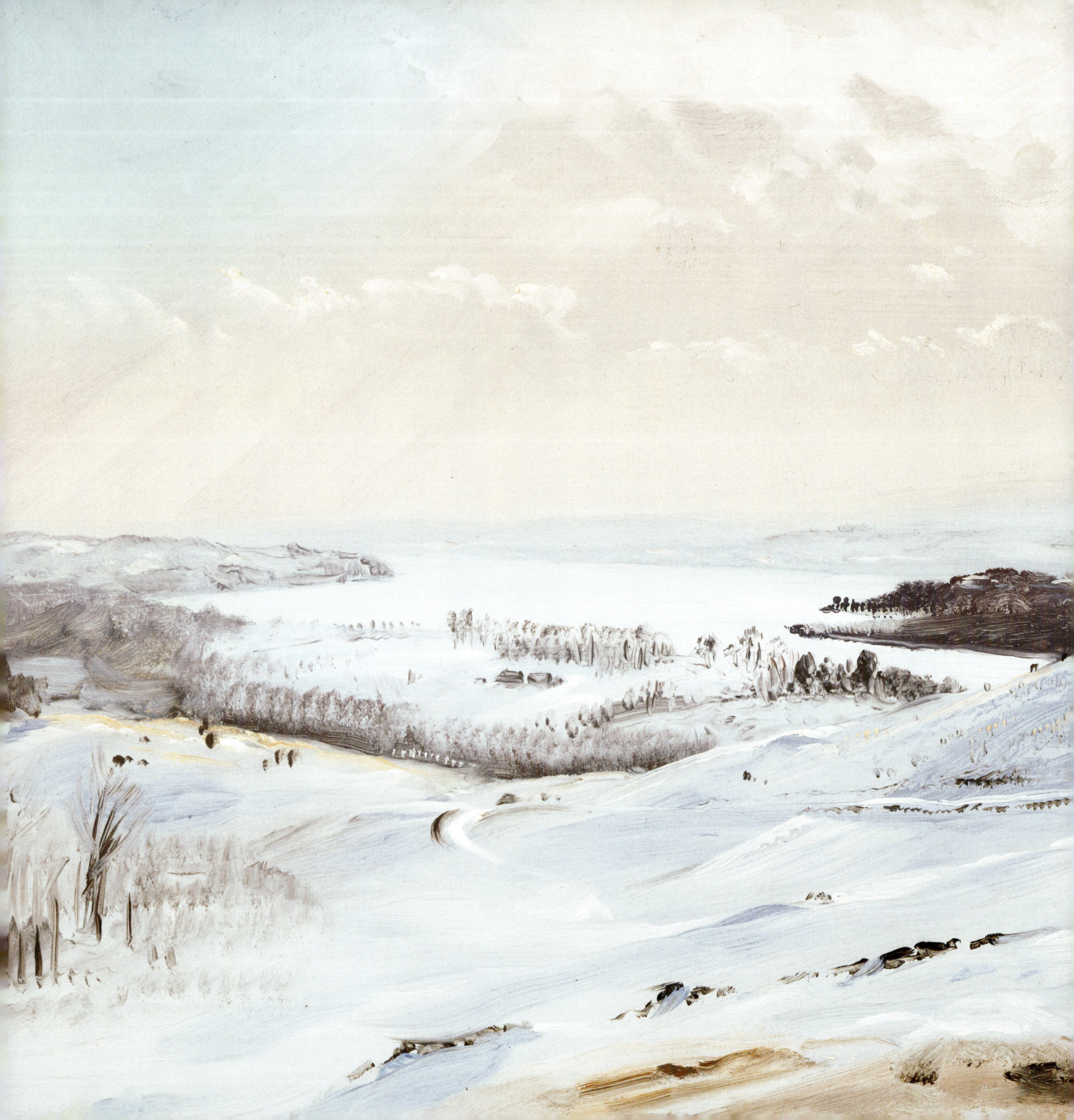

John K. Howat

The Hudson River, Its School, and Frederic Church

The Hudson River and its valley, following their discovery, have been the scene of many subsequent "discoveries" that have provided rich opportunities for the historical, economic, social, and cultural growth of the United States of America. The voluminous written history of the Hudson had its birth four hundred years ago with the entries in Robert Juet's journal covering late August through early October 1609. In those pages, not published until the nineteenth century, Juet recorded the troubled sail of Henry Hudson and his crew on the *Half Moon* up the Hudson River as far as the site of the future city of Albany and then back downriver to the Atlantic Ocean. So far as reliable European history is concerned, it was the first such voyage. Juet related encounters with the "people of this country" that were, by turns, friendly (eating, drinking, and trading), wary ("we durst not trust them"), and deadly (perhaps a dozen natives and one Englishman were killed in violent confrontations). Juet also described the riverine landscape as containing good anchorages, teeming fish, and "good ground for corn, and other garden herbs, with great store of goodly oaks, and walnut trees, and chestnut trees, yew trees, and trees of sweet wood in great abundance, and great store of slate for houses, and other good stones."[1] The beautiful and seductive grandeur of the Hudson Valley would receive fuller and more artful description countless times in later centuries.

Soon enough, in the seventeenth and eighteenth centuries, the Hudson Valley become a lure for settlers whose military, political, economic, and cultural activity furnished the stuff on which the folklore, literature, written history, and art of later times would be based. From the early nineteenth century, the works of Washington Irving and Thomas Cole spring to mind. However, at the time the United States struggled into existence, only a limited number of its citizens could maintain an interest in the visual arts or have access to illustrated books, prints, and paintings. Portraiture was the only art form to claim reasonable currency. Landscape imagery was available to a limited public through rare published sources like *Scenographica Americana* (London, 1768) and *The Atlantic Neptune* (London, 1774–81), both militarily inspired view and chart books; English-inspired prints by William Guy Wall, John Hill, and William J. Bennett; and sporadically exhibited paintings by a small group of artists, including William and Thomas Birch, John Trumbull, Washington Allston, and Thomas Doughty.

The visual arts in the young country, like almost every other aspect of its culture, grew rapidly from modest beginnings at the start of the nineteenth century so that by 1820 the evidences of an established art world were to be seen in institutions in eastern seaboard cities (New York's American Academy of Fine Arts, founded in 1802, and Philadelphia's Pennsylvania Academy of the Fine Arts, founded in 1807), which, with varying degrees of success, provided art instruction and exhibitions. The 1820s saw the establishment of two organizations that brought additional vigor to the American art scene: New York's National Academy of Design (an artists' association founded in 1826, the year of Frederic Church's birth) and the Boston Athenaeum (a library, museum, and exhibition facility founded in 1827).

The "discovery" of the impoverished Thomas Cole and several of his earliest views of Hudson River scenery in a New York City gallery in the fall of 1825 by John Trumbull, William Dunlap, and Asher B. Durand is one of the best-known, and most heartwarming, moments in American art history.[2] The trio of discoverers made sure that Cole became an instant success and a leader of the city's art community. Not many months later, in 1826, Cole was elected a founding member of the National Academy of Design, assuring his future role as head of what came to be called the Hudson River School. The early records of the academy cast light on the composition of New York's artist population (by then the largest in the country), as well as the criteria for election to the academy. Its original self-selected membership was divided into these areas of professional practice: painting (sixteen members), sculpture (one member), architecture (two members), and engraving (five members). Among the painters, only Thomas Cole was wholly devoted to the practice of landscape painting; of the other fifteen painter members, twelve were primarily portraitists.[3] Asher B. Durand, entered as an engraver, was yet to undergo his artistic metamorphosis from engraver through portrait and genre painter into landscape painter, later to succeed Cole as the doyen of American landscape painters. Following Cole and Durand, numerous ambitious young American painters became well-regarded landscape painters during the middle decades of the nineteenth century.

With the establishment of the Apollo Association in January 1839, later renamed the American Art-Union, which purchased large numbers of works of art for free exhibition and subsequent dispersal by lottery, the artist community was afforded substantially greater visibility and financial support. Frederic Church was among the happy recipients of this bounty, from 1847, when he sold his first pictures to the Art-Union, until the demise of the organization in 1851. Church was fortunate to sell 28 canvases to the Art-Union, while many of his fellow landscapists did equally well or far better: Thomas Cole sold 28; Jasper Cropsey, 46; Thomas Doughty, 91; Asher B. Durand, 50; Sanford R. Gifford, 27; Regis Gignoux, 61; George Harvey, 39; Daniel Huntington, 64 (of which 41 were landscapes); George Inness, 24; John F. Kensett, 49; William Rickarby Miller, 33; and T. Addison Richards, 36.[4] The final figures for the Art-Union are impressive. Over the years of its operation, 2,481 works of art were purchased, with a total expenditure of $226,516.67, a very large sum at a time when an artist could study, travel, and live in Europe for three to four hundred dollars per annum. In its last year alone, the Art-Union spent $41,321.58 on purchases.[5] The American Art-Union was not a limitless gold mine for the artists, but it supplied them a ready, dependable, and reasonably generous resource. These remarkable, and very welcome, benefits continued until 1851, when antagonists of the Art-Union, calling it an illegal lottery, caused it to be closed. Among the anti-Art-Union group were members of the Academy of Fine Arts, who objected that the annual *free* exhibition by the Art-Union, timed to overlap the spring annual *paid* exhibition at the academy, cut heavily into the latter's primary source of income. Thomas Seir Cummings, the combative treasurer of the academy, recalled the situation of spring 1851, when the academy's exhibition income had—again—fallen short: "the falling off was undoubtedly attributable to the Art Union Free Exhibition (open at the same time). It was scarcely to be expected that one Exhibition should be attended at *twenty-five cents* admission, if an equally good one was obtainable, at the same time and equally convenient, for nothing."[6] For members of the academy and others in the art community to encourage the disappearance of the Art-Union was a regrettable example of recipients of largess killing the golden goose or shooting themselves in the foot.

Frederic Church became probably the most famous of those artists whose works and patrons helped to transform the New York City art world into a warmly welcoming climate for landscape painters. In 1845, when Church first exhibited at the National Academy, among the twenty-six academicians were four full-time and eight part-time landscapists, but they were heavily outnumbered by portrait and genre painters. The four landscape painters were Cole, Durand, and the far more obscure John Evers and Andrew Richardson. However, in the exhibition that year were 369 items, of which 103, or 28 percent, were landscapes, a significant show of interest in that genre.[7]

The fortunes of American landscape painting were enhanced significantly in 1846 when the National Academy elected Durand to succeed Samuel F. B. Morse as its president. During Durand's tenure, which ended in 1861, the number of academicians rose, as did the number of landscape painter members. In 1860 there were 47 academicians, of whom 18 were either full-time or part-time landscapists. Among them were these who had "arrived" on Durand's watch: Albert Bierstadt, John Casilear, Church, Cropsey, Gifford, Richard M. Hubbard, Kensett, and Richards, men whose names stand high on the honor-roll of American landscape painting.[8]

Frederic Church enjoyed rapid success after beginning his exhibition career. He was elected an associate member (A.N.A.) of the National Academy in 1848 and academician (N.A.) in 1849. In 1850 Church was elected to the Century Association, a New York club for artists, writers, and amateurs of the arts, which Durand had helped establish three years previously. At the age of twenty-four Church had reached the pinnacle of New York art society, placing him within the grasp of a great career that would involve extensive domestic and foreign travel. The following decade was a time of wide-ranging exploratory expeditions by adventurers around the world, which became renowned through lectures, publications, and exhibitions of artworks like those by Church. His trips to exotic places and subsequent paintings of breathtaking panoramas shown with great panache, made him the nation's most famous living painter. In a regulated series, almost year after year, he offered his most recent triumphs to an eager public: *New England Scenery* (1851); *Mt. Ktaadn* (1853); *The Cordilleras: Sunrise* and *Tequendama Falls, near Bogotá, New Granada* (1854); *Niagara* (1857); *Morning in the Tropics* (1858); and *The Heart of the Andes* (1859). His exhibitions, the most successful being one-man events, and their associated business activity demonstrated to the art world how a gifted and very smart artist like Church could harvest what seemed to be immense sums of money. That Church also benefited from the support of a wealthy and generous father added to his financial comfort and the envy of his colleagues.

During the 1860s Church experienced the complexities of war (in his case, from a distance), marriage, establishing a family, which had to be reestablished after the death of his first two children, and the maintenance of a career soon to decline in public popularity. The meticulous design and construction of Olana, along with guarding an intensely private family life, became his primary interest in 1870. Although canvases came from his easel as the 1870s and 1880s went by, they were fewer in number. The very elderly Durand suffered a similar professional recession. He sent his final landscape to the National Academy Annual Exhibition in 1874, twelve years before his death at the age of ninety. Church exhibited his last academy picture in 1878, twenty-two years before his death.[9]

Younger artists appeared to fill New York City's galleries with work that looked to Europe, mostly France; names like William Merritt Chase, Winslow Homer, John La Farge, Homer Martin, and Thomas Moran replaced those of Durand and Church. The new state of art affairs was made clear when Durand died in 1886; in his death notice *Harper's Weekly* said, not unkindly, of his pictures:

[they] belonged to what has of late years been disparagingly called the "Hudson River School," and their manner has been rendered obsolete by works the painters of which had the advantage of a wider and deeper technical knowledge. But . . . we must acknowledge that with whatever technical weakness they may betray, they exhibit also a sincere love and study of nature, and a power of reproducing poetic impressions with delicacy and grace which the works of younger and better equipped men by no means always show.[10]

Church's final years, when he was afflicted with advanced arthritis, were mostly spent at Olana and in travel to Mexico. In both places he was able to make numerous small oil and pencil sketches that yet demonstrate his admirable sense and control of line and color. In particular, the oil sketches of the surrounding scenery executed at Olana, some of which grace the current exhibition, are marvels of a naturalistic gift not often seen in other hands. These late works by Church are yet another discovery to be made in the Hudson River Valley.

NOTES

1. *Robert Juet's Journal,* from the collections of the New-York Historical Society, 2nd ser., 1841, at www.newsday.com/community/guide/lihistory/ny-history-hs216a1v,0,919043.story.

2. William Dunlap, *A History of the Rise and Progress of the Arts of Design in the United States of America,* new ed., 3 vols. (Boston: C. E. Goodspeed, 1918), vol. 3, pp. 149–50.

3. Thomas S. Cummings, *Historic Annals of the National Academy of Design* (Philadelphia: George W. Child, 1865; facsimile ed., New York: Kennedy Galleries and Da Capo Press, 1969), pp. 28–29.

4. Many artists who are little celebrated today also fared well: De Witt Clinton Boutelle sold 71; Gustasvus Grünewald, 37; James Hamilton, 31; Walter Oddie, 64; Andrew Richardson, 49; Joshua Shaw, 33; and Jessie Talbot, 31.

5. Charles E. Baker, "The American Art-Union," in *American Academy of Fine Arts and American Art-Union,* by Bartlett Cowdrey and Theodore Sizer,

2 vols. (New York: New-York Historical Society, 1953), vol. 1, pp. 160–61.

6. Cummings, *Historic Annals,* p. 219.

7. *Catalogue of the Twentieth Annual Exhibition of the National Academy of Design* (New York, 1845), passim.

8. A list of members is given in Eliot Clark, N.A., *History of the National Academy of Design* (New York: Columbia University Press, 1954), pp. 247–75.

9. For a survey of Church's career, see John K. Howat, *Frederic Church* (New Haven: Yale University Press, 2005).

10. "Asher B. Durand," *Harper's Weekly* 30 (September 25, 1886), p. 619, quoted in Doreen Bolger Burke and Catherine Hoover Voorsanger, "The Hudson River in Eclipse," in *American Paradise: The World of the Hudson River School,* by John K. Howat et al. (New York: Metropolitan Museum of Art, 1987), p. 90.

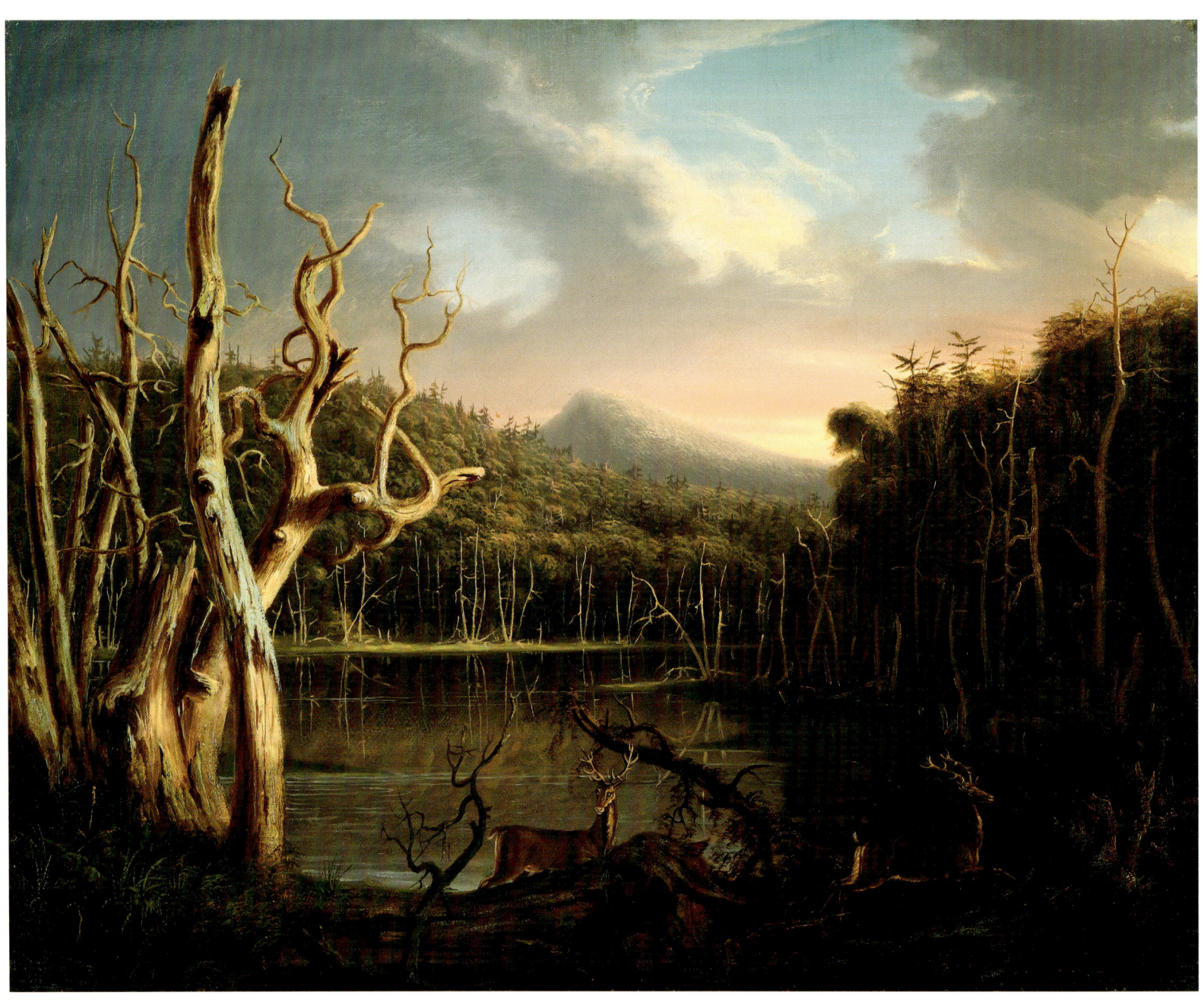

Kenneth John Myers

Hudson Valley Landscapes: Cole, Gifford, Church

Frederic Church did not invent the Hudson Valley as a subject for serious painters, but his teacher and mentor, Thomas Cole, did.

Although scholarly and popular writings about landscape art, literature, and tourism usually assume that the ability to appreciate physical environments as landscapes is intuitive or natural, available to all people in all cultures at all periods in history, both anthropological and historical evidence suggests that this is not so. Like other culture-specific mental abilities, landscape appreciation is learned. Today, in the United States and in much of the rest of the world, we take this ability for granted because landscape representations have become so commonplace in our society that we learn how to appreciate physical environments as aestheticized landscapes without even being aware of the fact that we are doing so. Unlike eighteenth- and early-nineteenth-century Americans, we live in an image-rich culture. From infancy we are bombarded with images in books and on television, in shops and on billboards, which show us parts of nature already transformed into formally pleasing pictures. Our parents give us our first camera, gently criticize us when we take pictures at odd angles that contain too much foreground or too much sky, teach us to hold the camera parallel to the ground and arrange the field of vision so that it captures a well-composed picture. In countless ways and on numberless unremarkable occasions we learn, generally without realizing that we are learning, mentally to step back from natural environments in order to objectify them as aesthetically satisfying pictures.[1]

In his pathbreaking exhibition *Views and Visions: American Landscape before 1830*, Edward J. Nygren demonstrated that almost no landscape art was produced in British North America before the American Revolution.[2] There was also little landscape writing and virtually no landscape tourism. The emergence and initial popularization of all three of these closely related forms of landscape experience did not take place until the 1820s, when the rapid growth of the economy, the unprecedented expansion of New

Fig. 1. Thomas Cole, *Lake with Dead Trees (Catskill)*, 1825, oil on canvas, 27 × 33¾ in., Allen Memorial Art Museum, Oberlin College, Ohio, Gift of Charles F. Olney, 1904, 04.1183

York and other northeastern cities, and the importation of landscape ideas from Europe created an initial audience of well-to-do agricultural producers, merchants, and professionals who had developed an interest in landscape and had the money, leisure, and desire to read landscape literature, or visit a landscape destination, or acquire a landscape print, or—if they were particularly well-off—buy a landscape painting. In the United States, no environment was more important to the initial popularization of landscape art, writing, and tourism than the mid-Hudson Valley. And no visual artist was more important to the popularization of the Hudson Valley as a destination for writers, artists, and tourists in search of the picturesque than Thomas Cole.[3]

Cole moved to New York City in April 1825. He arrived six months before the opening of the Erie Canal linked the Hudson River with the Great Lakes, enabling Manhattan merchants to take control of the rapidly growing markets in western New York State and the Midwest. Cole was twenty-four years old, largely self-taught, without reputation, and poor. That fall, he made a brief sketching trip up the Hudson, getting as far as Cohoes Falls on the Mohawk River. Back in New York, he completed paintings of three Hudson River scenes: a view of the Hudson from Fort Putnam, near West Point (Philadelphia Museum of Art); a view from the cavern behind Kaaterskill Falls in the Catskills; and *Lake with Dead Trees (Catskill)*, a view of one of the small lakes above Kaaterskill Falls (fig. 1). The fate of the Kaaterskill Falls painting is unknown, but it must have been very similar to the surviving variant Cole painted for the Hartford, Connecticut, collector Daniel Wadsworth in 1826 (Wadsworth Atheneum Museum of Art). In November 1825, Cole put his three new paintings on display in a Manhattan

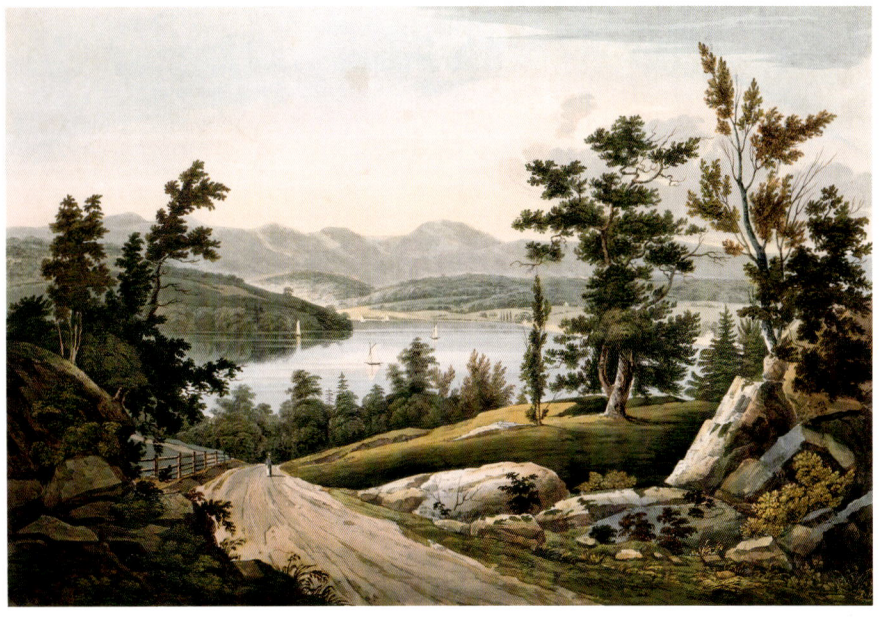

Fig. 2. John Hill, after William Guy Wall, *View near Hudson*, hand-colored aquatint, from John Hill and John Rubens Smith, *The Hudson River Portfolio* (New York: Henry Megarey, 1823–24), The New York Public Library, Astor, Lenox and Tilden Foundations, Spencer Collection

frame shop, where they, and Cole, were soon "discovered." Within weeks, all three of the paintings had been sold, all were on display at the annual exhibition of the American Academy of Fine Arts, and Cole was fast on his way to becoming the most influential landscape artist in the nation and the founder of the American landscape tradition.[4]

In the two or three decades preceding Cole's arrival in New York, a small number of watercolorists and itinerant painters produced a few images of the Hudson Valley, some of which included distant views of the Catskills. The most influential of these early views were the engravings after watercolors by William Guy Wall that appeared in the serial publication *The Hudson River Portfolio* (1821–25) (fig. 2). But Cole was the first painter to produce an important

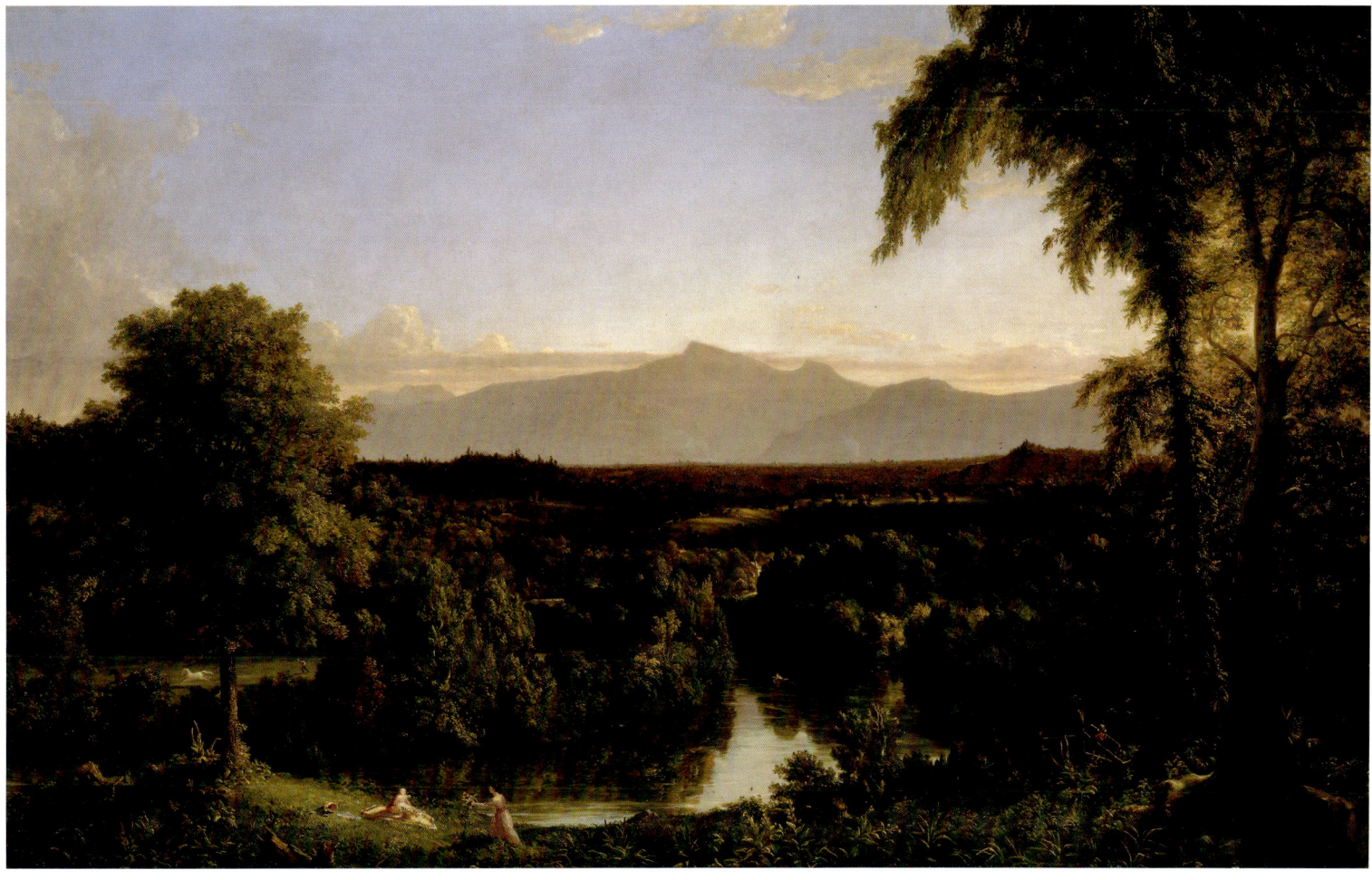

body of work celebrating the Hudson Valley. Between the fall of 1825 and June 1829, when he left New York for an extended study trip to Europe, Cole completed about fifty paintings, of which more than half were views of the Hudson Valley. When Cole returned from Europe in November 1832, he settled in Manhattan. For the next three years he spent most of each summer and fall in the Hudson River port village of Catskill. In November 1836 he married a young woman from Catskill and became a permanent resident of the village. From 1832 until his untimely death in 1848, Cole's bread-and-butter subject was the distant view of the Catskills from near his Catskill home, which he painted on more than a dozen occasions (fig. 3). Cole was so closely identified with the Hudson that when he died it was virtually inevitable that memorial paintings such as Asher B. Durand's *Kindred Spirits* and Thomas Charles Farrer's *A Buckwheat Field on Thomas Cole's Farm* would place him, literally or metaphorically, in a Hudson Valley landscape (figs. 4, 5).

Fig. 3. Thomas Cole, *View on the Catskill—Early Autumn*, 1836–37, oil on canvas, 39 × 63 in., The Metropolitan Museum of Art, New York, Gift in memory of Jonathan Sturges by his children, 1895, 95.13.3, Image © The Metropolitan Museum of Art

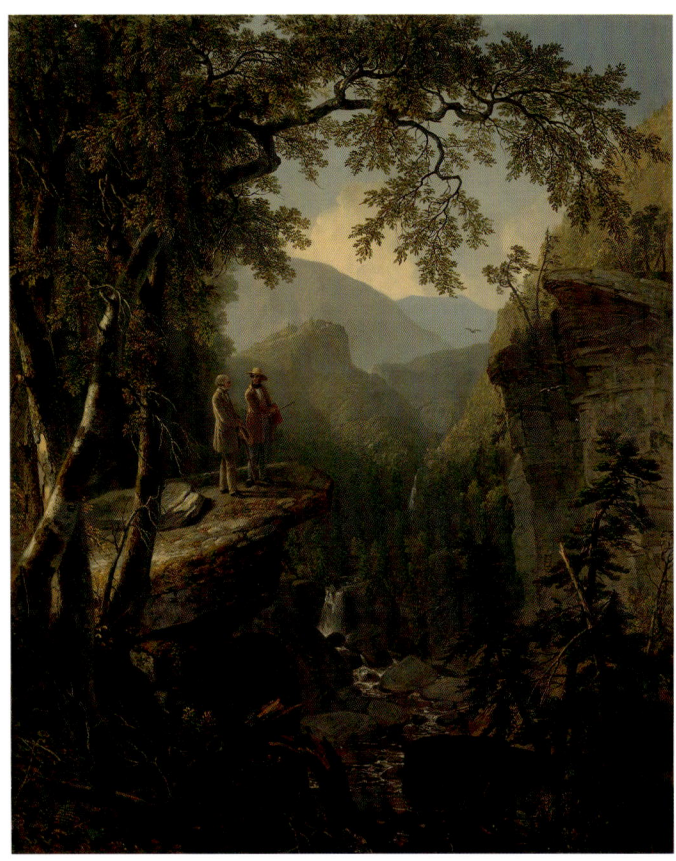

Fig. 4. Asher B. Durand, *Kindred Spirits*, 1849, oil on canvas, 44 × 36 in., Crystal Bridges Museum of American Art, Bentonville, Ark.

Cole died just as the taste for landscape art, literature, and travel was becoming commonplace among the rapidly growing middle and professional classes. Demand for all varieties of landscape experience spiked in the late 1840s and 1850s, as evidenced by the expansion of older landscape destinations, the establishment of many new destinations, the increased popularity of landscape literature, and the emergence of the nation's first large cohort of successful landscape painters. By the late 1850s, the market for landscape art had become so large that it had begun to segment, by quality (A-list artists, B-list artists, hacks), medium (paintings, engravings, colored lithographs), and style. Two styles dominated the prestige end of the market for landscape paintings. One was more subjectivist, putting a new stress on the need for each artist to develop a distinctive, individual way of representing the world, expressive of his or her unique experience of it. The other was more objectivist, assuming that artists should be primarily concerned with the accurate representation of natural facts.

The more expressive style began to emerge in the late 1850s. By the early 1860s, it was being championed by several prominent art critics who were aware of recent developments in French art. The most insightful of these critics was probably Eugene Benson, who argued that "the personality of a man is the most sacred thing about him," and that the work of an artist should be, "to a great extent, the supplement to his character."[5] For artists in the subjectivist branch of the American landscape tradition, the most important goal was not to show the ideal essence of a place, but to express his own individual and, therefore, unique experience of it. The object of representation mattered, but it mattered less, which may explain why these artists often stayed close to home, producing new images of already familiar subjects such as the White Mountains, Newport, the Connecticut shore, and the Hudson Valley. Most of the great midcentury paintings of the Hudson Valley were produced by subjectivists. Major examples include Martin Johnson Heade's *Lake George* (1862, Museum of Fine Arts, Boston), John F. Kensett's *View from Cozzens' Hotel near West Point* (1863, New-York Historical Society), Worthington Whittredge's *Twilight on the Shawangunk Mountains* (1865, Manoogian Collection), Kensett's *View on the Hudson* (fig. 6), and Jervis McEntee's *Indian Summer* (1867, private collection).

Like many twenty-first-century art historians and collectors, Benson thought that Sanford Gifford was the greatest of the landscapists working in the subjectivist style.[6] Born in Saratoga County, New York, but raised just a few miles north of Olana in the town of Hudson, New York, Gifford painted more great views of the Hudson Valley

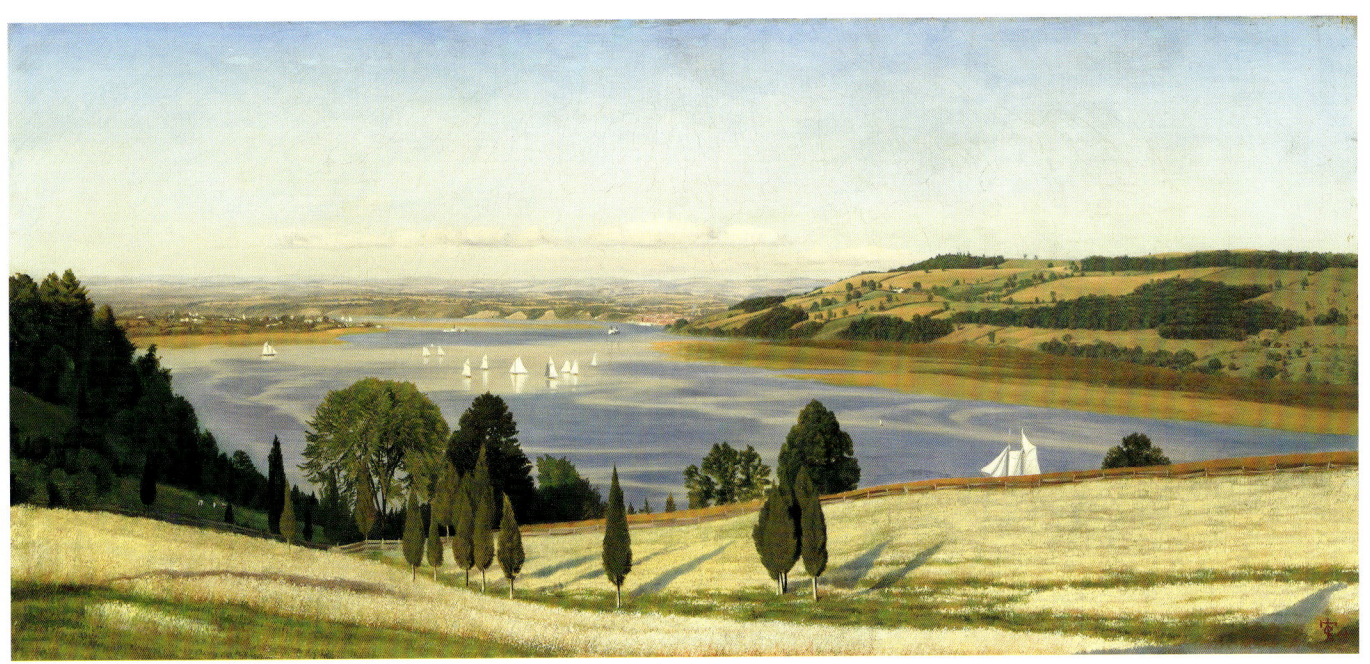

Fig. 5. Thomas Charles Farrer, *A Buckwheat Field on Thomas Cole's Farm*, 1863, oil on canvas, 11¾ × 25¼ in., Museum of Fine Arts, Boston, Gift of Maxim Karolik for the M. and M. Karolik Collection of American Paintings, 1815–1865, 62.265, Photograph © 2009 Museum of Fine Arts, Boston

Fig. 6. John Frederick Kensett, *View on the Hudson*, 1865, oil on canvas, 28 × 45 in., The Baltimore Museum of Art, Gift of Mrs. Paul H. Miller, BMA 1942.4

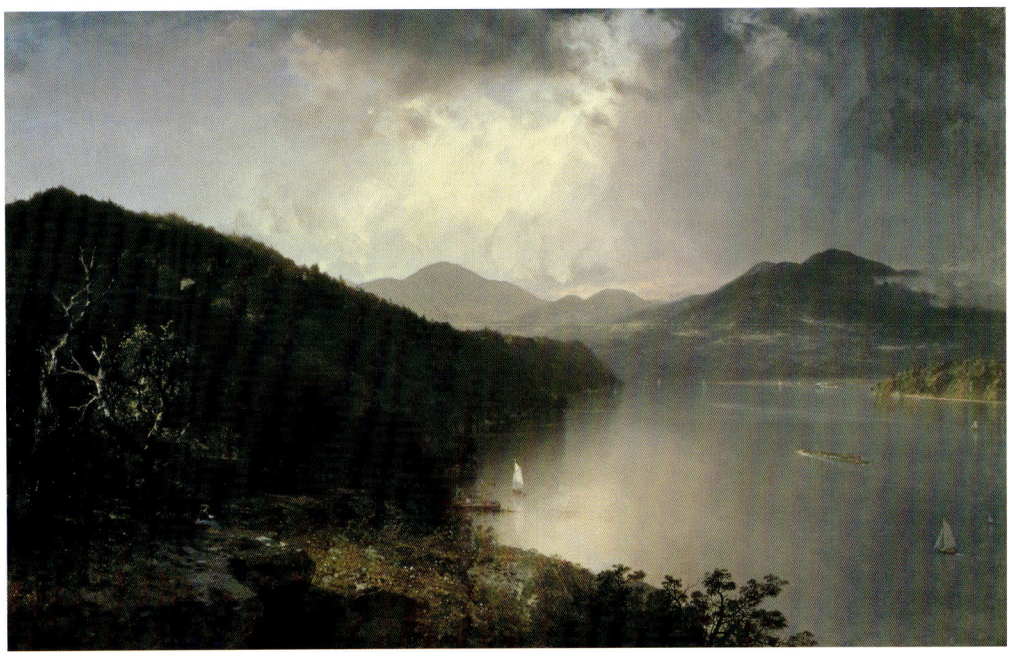

than any other midcentury landscapist. A partial list of his major Hudson Valley subjects would include *A Twilight in the Catskills* (1861, private collection), *A Gorge in the Mountains* (fig. 7), *Twilight in the Adirondacks* (1864, the Adirondack Museum, Blue Mountain Lake, New York), *Hunter Mountain, Twilight* (1866, Terra Foundation for American Art), *A Passing Storm in the Adirondacks* (1866, Wadsworth Atheneum Museum of Art, Hartford), *The View from South Mountain, in the Catskills* (1873, St. Johnsbury Athenaeum, St. Johnsbury, Vermont), and *A Sunset, Bay of New York* (1878, Everson Museum of Art, Syracuse, New York). In a brief memoir published shortly after Gifford's death in 1880, the painter John Ferguson Weir observed that "Gifford's art was poetic and reminiscent. It was not realistic in the formal sense. It was nature passed through the alembic of a finely-organized sensibility."[7] Gifford never tired of the valley of his youth because he sought to paint not places but his experiences of them. Where his colleagues working in the more objectivist style tended to paint light, Gifford painted atmosphere. Unlike light, which stands apart from the viewer, in Gifford's best paintings the light-filled atmosphere visually binds the foreground with the distances, becoming a palpable symbol for human consciousness, which conjoins the perceiving self with the objects of its experience, half creating that which it perceives. In *A Gorge in the Mountains* and Gifford's other mature canvases, the glowing atmosphere both expresses and embodies the artist's struggle to represent his experience of the unities of his world.

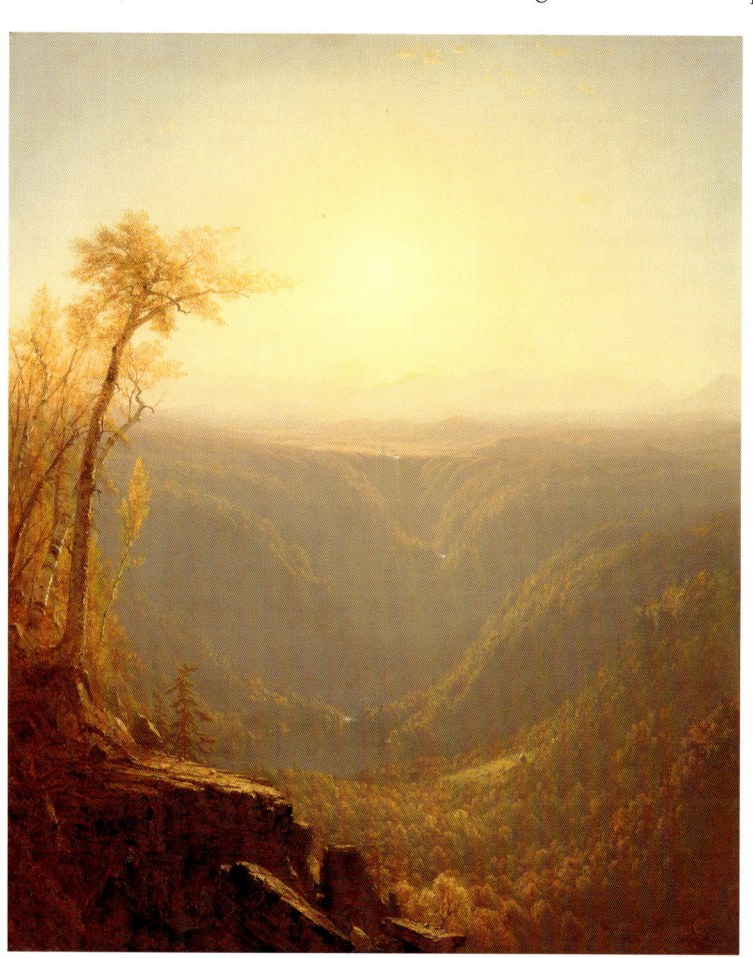

Fig. 7. Sanford R. Gifford, *A Gorge in the Mountains (Kauterskill Clove)*, 1862, oil on canvas, 48 × 39⅞ in., The Metropolitan Museum of Art, New York, Bequest of Maria DeWitt Jesup, from the collection of her husband, Morris K. Jesup, 1914, 15.30.62, Image © The Metropolitan Museum of Art

Painters working in the more objectivist style sought to combine the high moral seriousness of Cole's allegorical and historical landscapes with the naturalism of his straight landscapes. These artists sometimes produced explicitly allegorical landscapes. But they generally sought to organize the components of a scene so that the resulting painting—though infused with scientific, religious, or cultural significance—looked natural. Artists working in this tradition sometimes painted the Hudson, but because they were primarily interested in the meaning of the represented place, they tended to abandon locales once they had become familiar. To keep their work fresh, artists like Albert Bierstadt, William Bradford, Louis Rémy Mignot, Thomas Moran, and Thomas Hill needed new vistas. Not the Hudson or the White Mountains, but Maine, the Rockies, Yosemite, Labrador, the Andes.

Frederic Church was the most important and influential artist working in the more objectivist mode. Unlike the more subjectivist artists, who generally had to rely on the patronage

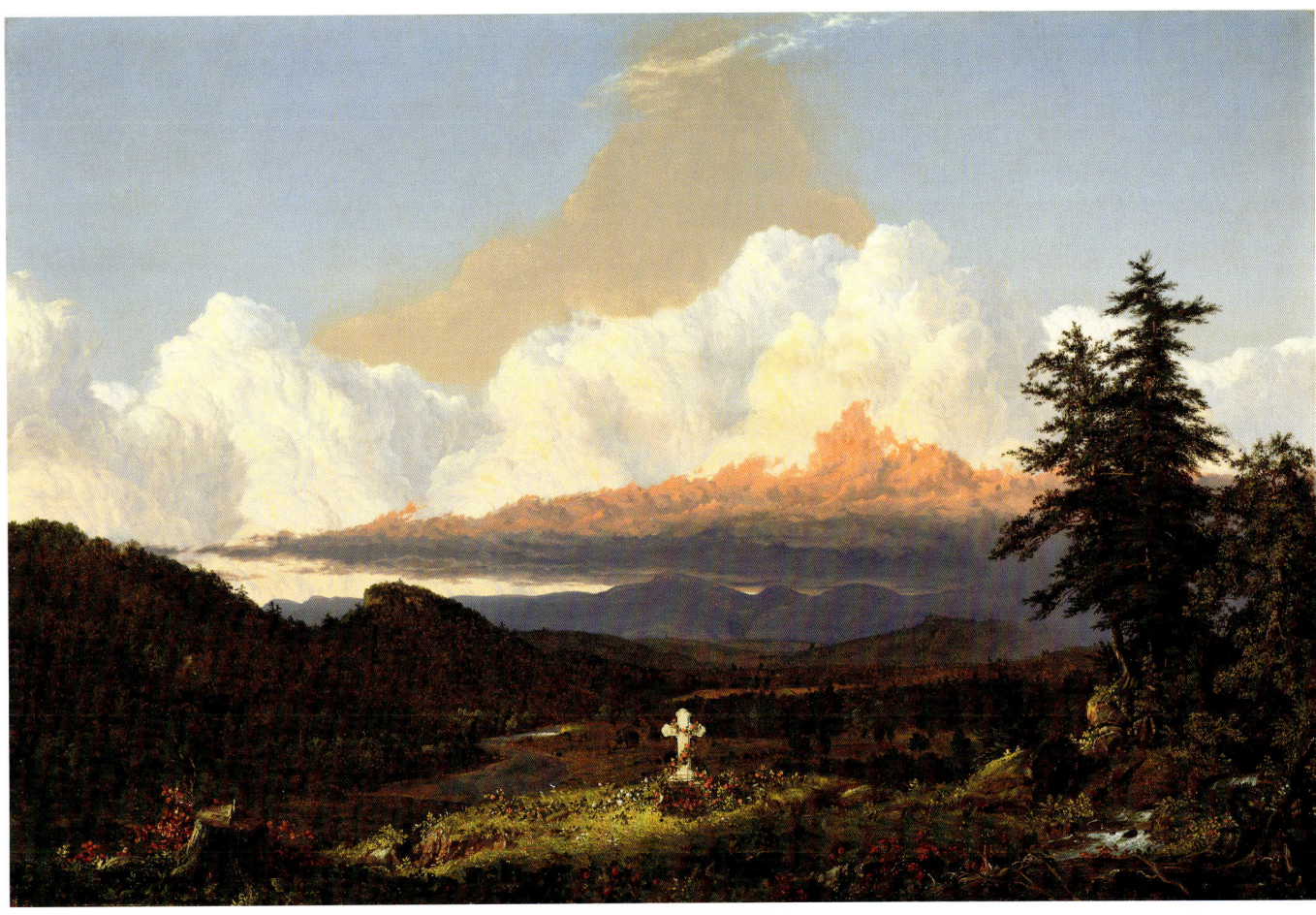

Fig. 8. Frederic Edwin Church, *To the Memory of Cole*, 1848, oil on canvas, 32 × 49 in., Image courtesy A. J. Kollar Fine Paintings, LLC

of a comparatively small group of private patrons, Church maximized profits from his major landscapes by turning their public exhibition into media-driven events that attracted a mass audience eager to see his visual reports from faraway lands. As Church's audience grew, so did demand for both his paintings and reproductive prints after them. By the late 1850s, Church was a major cultural figure and the best-paid artist in the nation.

Cole's only important student, Church studied with Cole in Catskill from June 1844 until June 1846. Church completed a dozen or so Hudson Valley paintings between 1844 and the beginning of 1849, ranging in style from the self-conscious ideality of *To the Memory of Cole* (fig. 8) to the apparently straightforward naturalism of *July Sunset* (1847, private collection). The greatest, and almost certainly the last of the Hudson Valley subjects that Church completed during these years is *Above the Clouds at Sunrise* (fig. 9). One of Church's first fully mature paintings, *Above the Clouds at Sunrise* works both as naturalistic representation of a morning sunrise over the Hudson Valley as seen from

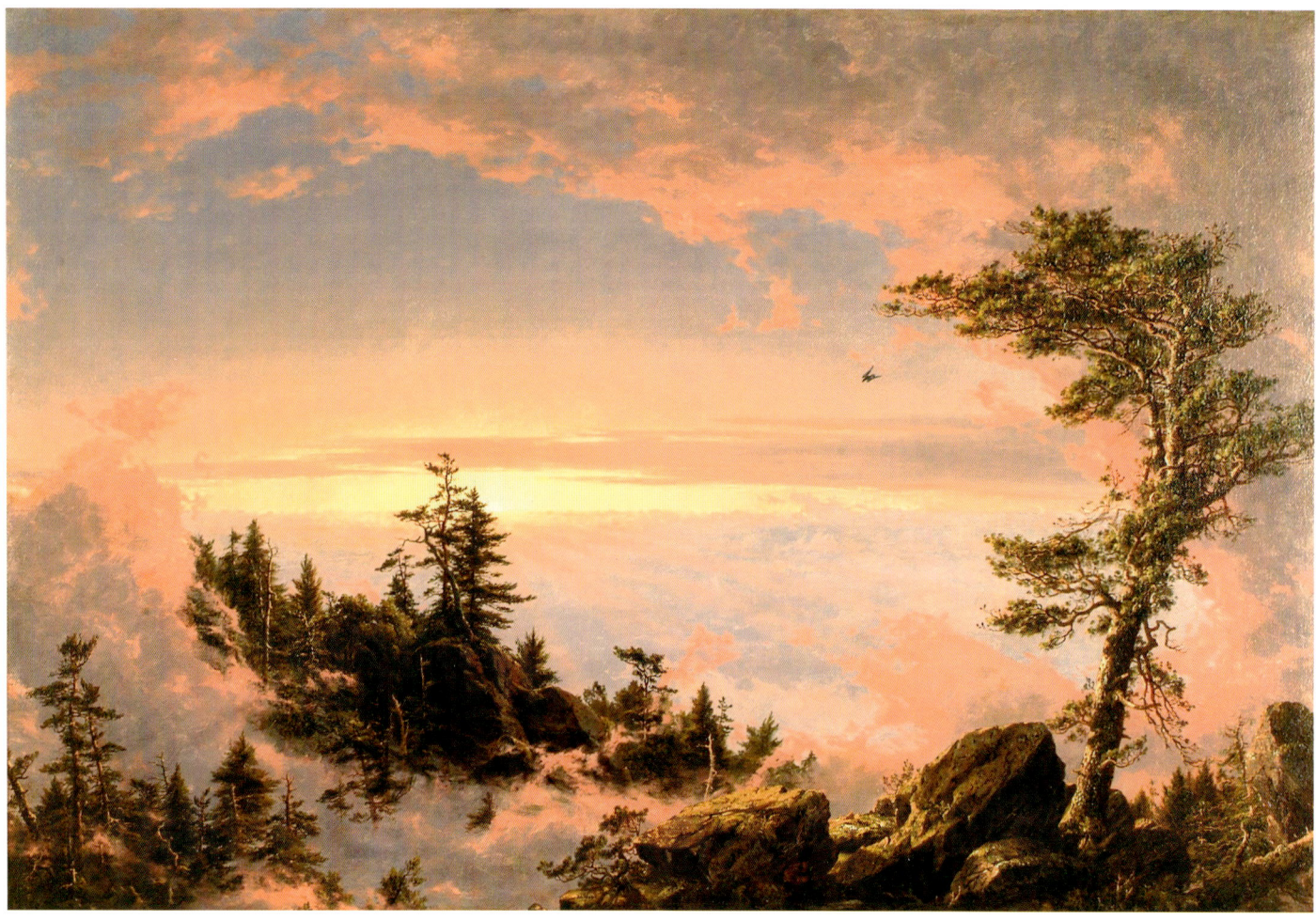

Fig. 9. Frederic Edwin Church, *Above the Clouds at Sunrise*, 1849, oil on canvas, 24¼ × 40 in., Property of the Westervelt Company and displayed at the Westervelt–Warner Museum of American Art, Tuscaloosa, Ala., 1983.0088

the escarpment near the Catskill Mountain House and as a didactic memorial to Church's recently deceased teacher, who had tried but failed to represent the sublime inchoateness of that then-famous scene.[8]

Eleven years after finishing *Above the Clouds at Sunrise*, and a few months before his marriage to Isabel Carnes, Church returned to Cole's old haunts and purchased the property that became Olana. Isabel and Church made their home on their hill, within sight of Cole's home in Catskill, and lived there until the end of their lives. During the late 1860s and early 1870s, Church produced dozens of often spectacularly beautiful oil sketches of the view from Olana. But he never attempted any large paintings of the gorgeous views he and Isabel lived with. Indeed, *Above the Clouds at Sunrise* was his last major treatment of any Hudson Valley subject. Church left no written explanations for this, but one supposes that, like the other major midcentury landscapists primarily interested in the meaning of the presented scene, he thought that the valley was too familiar—and

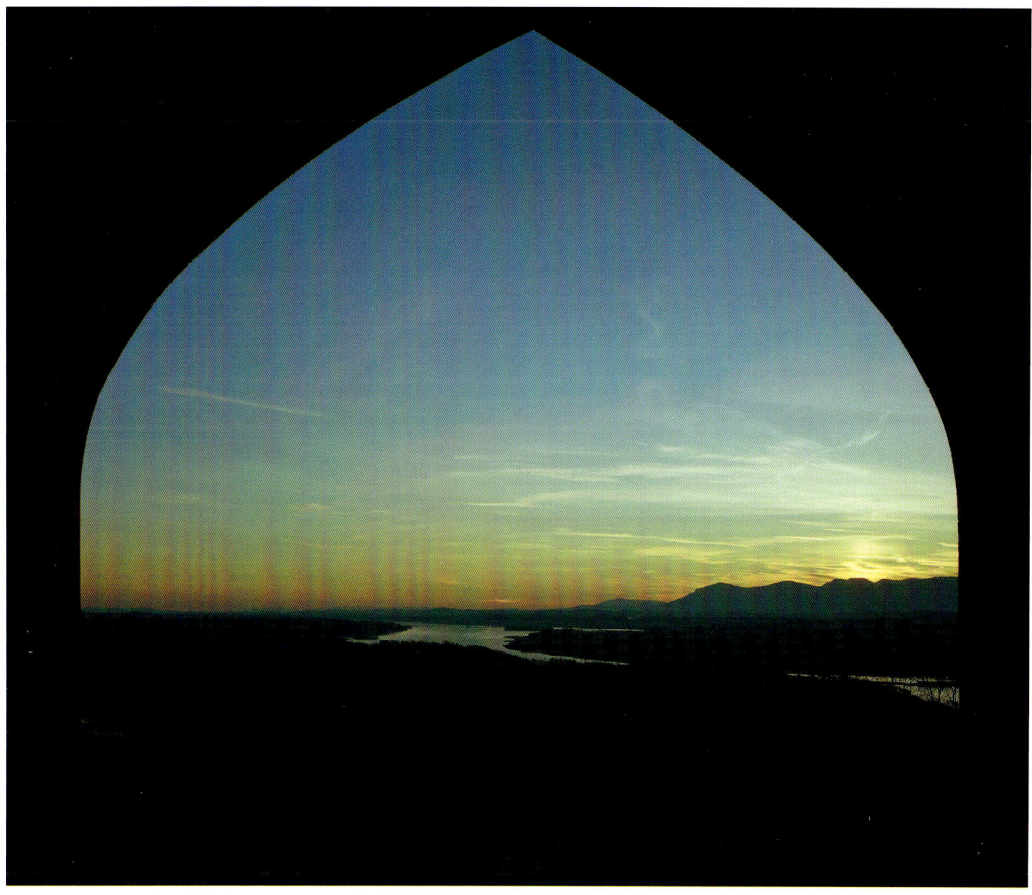

that, as a subject for art, the Catskills belonged too fully to Cole. In a recent essay on the painter Lucian Freud, the artist Julian Bell observed that "having stated that Freud was something of a father figure in my own life as a painter, it follows—as you may have realized—that I have a certain urge to kill him."[9] Perhaps this was the case with Church. Once he had painted *Above the Clouds at Sunrise,* Church may have felt that he had proved, to his peers and to himself, that he had both mastered Cole's lessons and superseded them.

But if Church gave up the Hudson Valley as a subject for painting, it remained at the center of his life as an artist. After 1870, Church's greatest aesthetic achievement was not a painting—it was his home, Olana (fig. 10). A Persian fantasy of a Hudson River castle, Olana commands spectacular views of both the Catskills and the mid-Hudson Valley. As Church intended, the drives, the walks, and the vistas from the house function as a series of moving panoramas, each filled with the ever-changing majesty of the grand valley that he shared with Cole, Gifford, and the rest of the great midcentury American landscapists.[10]

Fig. 10. Nicholas Whitman, *View from the Court Hall, South through the Ombra, Olana,* photograph, 2001

1. I have explored this shift in more detail in Kenneth John Myers, "On the Cultural Construction of Landscape Experience: Contact to 1830," in *American Iconology: New Approaches to Nineteenth-Century American Art and Literature*, ed. David C. Miller (New Haven: Yale University Press, 1993), pp. 58–79. My methodological and historical assumptions in that essay, as in this one, were influenced by the work of Michel Foucault, Raymond Williams, and Richard Rorty. See especially Michel Foucault, *The Order of Things: An Archeology of the Human Sciences* (New York: Vintage Books, 1973); Raymond Williams, *The Country and the City* (New York: Oxford University Press, 1973); and Richard Rorty, *Philosophy and the Mirror of Nature* (Princeton: Princeton University Press, 1979).

2. Edward J. Nygren, ed., *Views and Visions: American Landscape before 1830* (Washington, D.C.: Corcoran Gallery of Art, 1986).

3. For Cole and the beginning of picturesque tourism in the Hudson Valley, see Kenneth John Myers, "Thomas Cole and the Popularization of Landscape Experience in the United States: 1825–1829," in *America! Storie di pittura dal Nuovo Mondo*, ed. Marco Goldin (Treviso, Italy: Linea d'Ombra, 2007), vol. 1, pp. 67–79 (in Italian); vol. 2, pp. 50–61 (in English); idem, *The Catskills: Painters, Writers, and Tourists in the Mountains, 1820–1895* (Yonkers, N.Y.: Hudson River Museum of Westchester, 1987); and Roland van Zandt, *The Catskill Mountain House* (New Brunswick, N.J.: Rutgers University Press, 1966).

4. For Cole and his rapid rise to prominence, see Ellwood C. Parry III, *The Art of Thomas Cole: Ambition and Imagination* (Newark: University of Delaware Press, 1988), pp. 21–28; and Alan Wallach, "Thomas Cole: Landscape and the Course of American Empire," in *Thomas Cole: Landscape into History*, ed. William H. Truettner and Alan Wallach (New Haven: Yale University Press, 1994), pp. 23–24.

5. Proteus [Eugene Benson], "Our Artists: II, S. R. Gifford," *New York Commercial Advertiser*, October 17, 1861.

6. For Gifford, see Kevin J. Avery and Franklin Kelly, eds., *Hudson River School Visions: The Landscapes of Sanford R. Gifford* (New York: Metropolitan Museum of Art; New Haven: Yale University Press, 2003); and Ila Weiss, *Poetic Landscape: The Art and Experience of Sanford R. Gifford* (Newark: University of Delaware Press; London and Toronto: Associated University Presses, 1987).

7. John F. Weir, "Sanford R. Gifford: His Life and Character as Artist and Man," in *A Memorial Catalogue of the Paintings of Sanford Robinson Gifford, N.A.* (1881; reprint, New York: Olana Gallery, 1974), p. 8.

8. For Church's relationship with Cole, see Franklin Kelly, *Frederic Edwin Church and the National Landscape* (Washington, D.C.: Smithsonian Institution Press, 1988), pp. 1–21; John K. Howat, *Frederic Church* (New Haven: Yale University Press, 2005), pp. 9–16; Franklin Kelly, "A Passion for Landscape: The Paintings of Frederic Edwin Church," in *Frederic Edwin Church*, by Kelly et al. (Washington, D.C.: National Gallery of Art; Smithsonian Institution Press, 1989), pp. 34–38; and J. Gray Sweeney, " 'Endued with Rare Genius,' Frederic Edwin Church's *To the Memory of Cole*," *Smithsonian Studies in American Art* 2 (Winter 1988): pp. 45–72. For a fuller discussion of *Above the Clouds at Sunrise* as a memorial, see Kenneth John Myers, "Frederic Church's Memorials to Thomas Cole," in *Pittura americana del XIX secolo: Atti del convegno*, ed. Marco Goldin and H. Barbara Weinberg (Treviso, Italy: Linea d'Ombra, 2008), pp. 57–77.

9. Julian Bell, "The Way to All Flesh," *New York Review of Books* 55 (March 6, 2008): p. 24.

10. For Olana, see Gerald L. Carr, *Frederic Edwin Church: Romantic Landscapes and Seascapes* (New York: Adelson Galleries, 2007), pp. 111–23; and James Anthony Ryan, "Frederic Church's Olana: Architecture and Landscape as Art" in Kelly et al., *Frederic Edwin Church*, pp. 126–56.

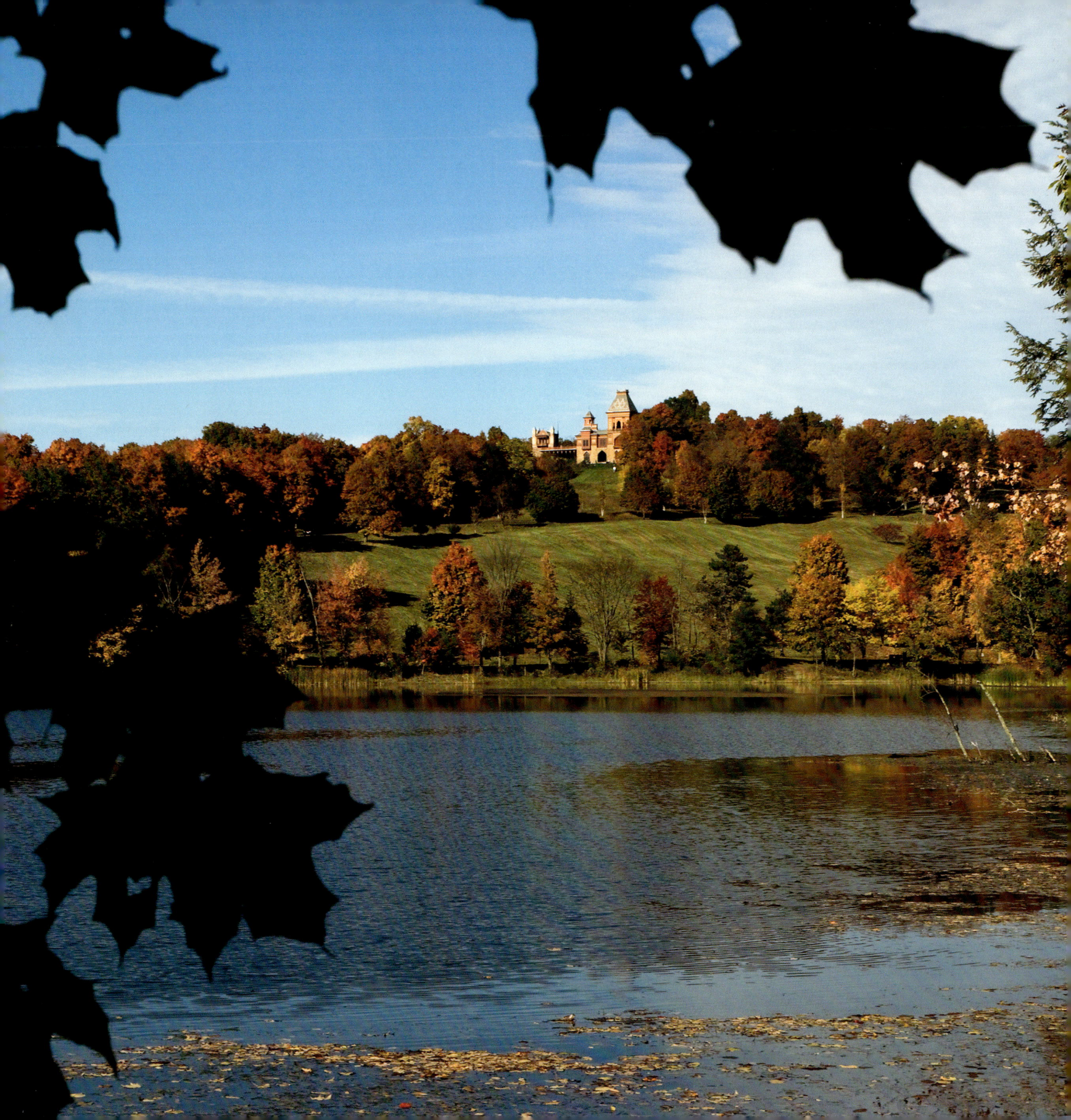

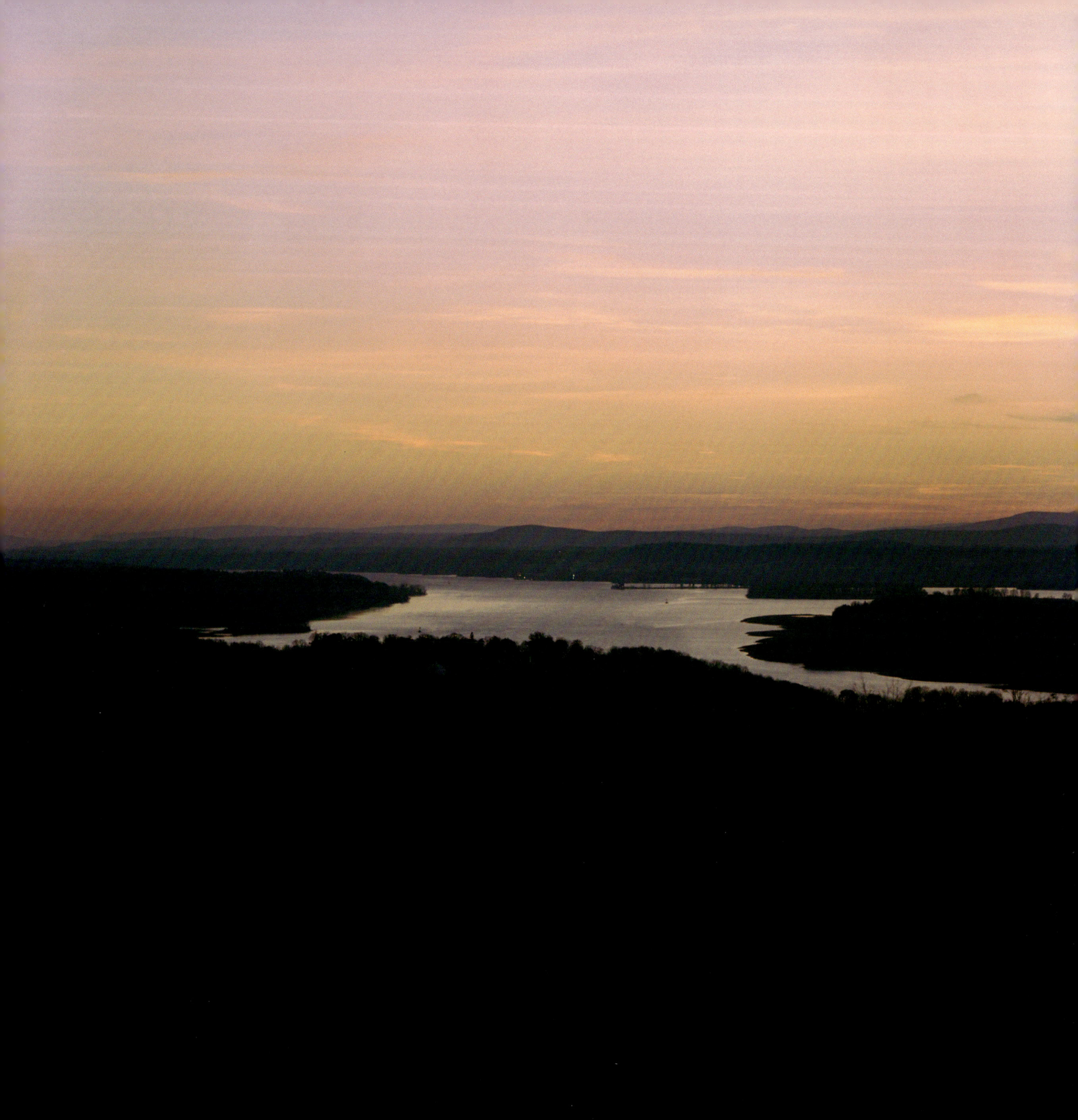

Evelyn D. Trebilcock and Valerie A. Balint

Glories of the Hudson: Frederic Edwin Church's Views from Olana

The site is the result of a careful study of the river-banks, and commands so many views of varied beauty, that all the glories of the Hudson may be said to circle it. — H. W. French, *Art and Artists in Connecticut*, 1879[1]

Everyone who visits Olana is transfixed by the breathtaking panorama of the Hudson River and the Catskill Mountains (fig. 1). At Olana, the home of Hudson River School artist Frederic Edwin Church (1826–1900), today a New York State Historic Site open to the public, rarely a day goes by without a tourist admiring the vista of the Hudson River or an artist portraying the profile of the Catskill Mountains. Church designed Olana—the property and the house—to take full advantage of these spectacular views. Documenting his passion are the numerous oil and pencil sketches he reserved for his own collection—not necessarily as an aide-mémoire, since certainly he could admire the same views from one of many arched windows or winding carriage drives, but as a celebration of his single largest and most personal artistic creation: Olana. Of it he wrote, "Almost an hour this side of Albany is the Center of the World—I own it—"[2]

For the Hudson Valley, the quadricentennial of Henry Hudson's voyage of discovery, up the river that now bears his name, signals an important milestone. It presents the ideal moment to explore Church's sensational depictions of the Hudson and, beyond these exquisite painted images, the artist's home and its grounds, which pay equal homage to the grandeur of the river (fig. 2).

Today the Hudson is treasured for its history and its beauty, sweeping New York State from its origin in Lake Tear of the Clouds in the Adirondack Mountains to Manhattan Island, where it flows into New York Harbor, mingling there with the Atlantic

Fig. 1. Nicholas Whitman, *Bend in the River from Olana*, photograph, 2004

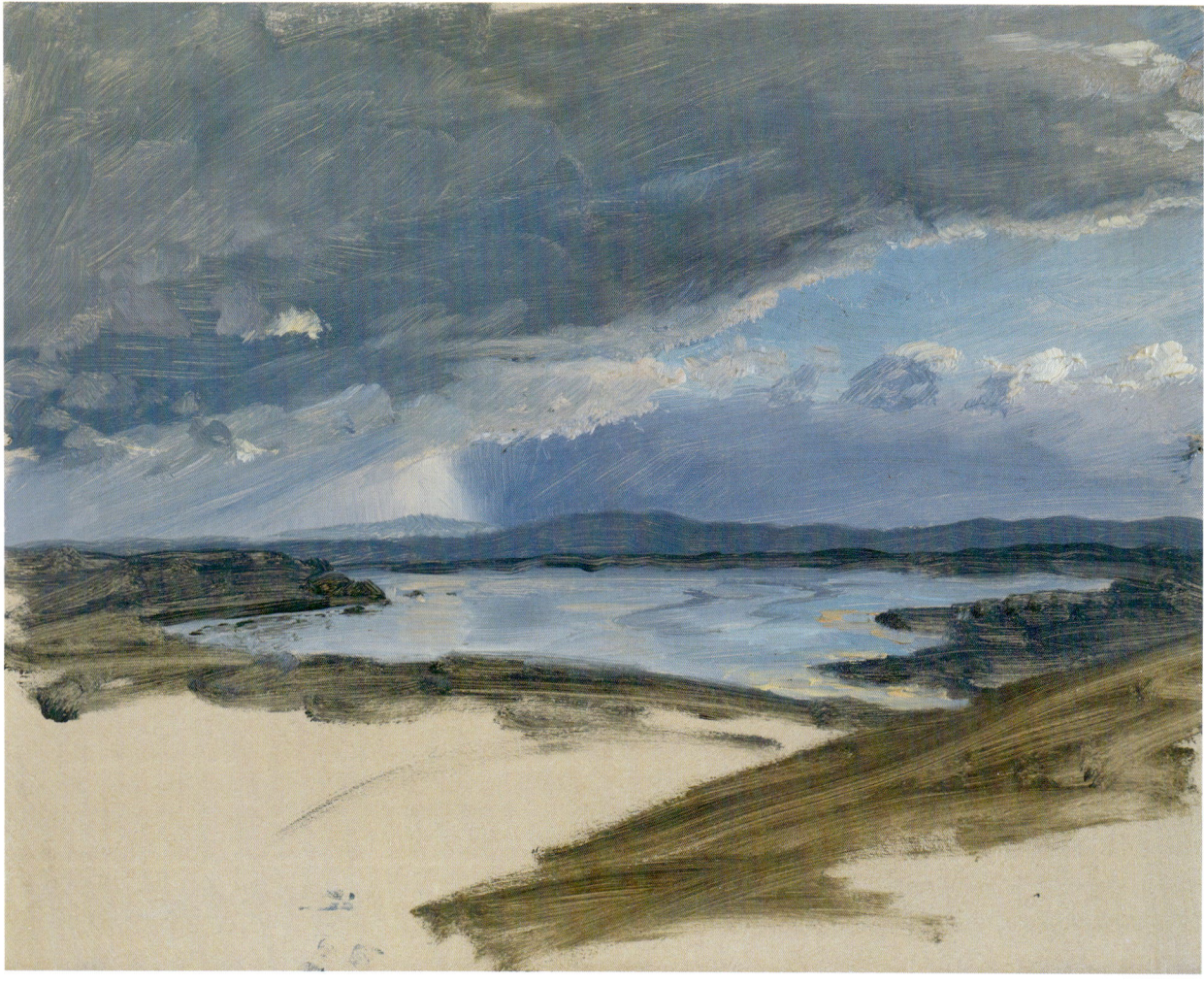

Fig. 2. Frederic Edwin Church, *The "Bend in the River" from Olana*, c. 1870–73, oil on off-white academy board, 10 1/16 × 12 7/8 in., OL.1977.209

Ocean. The river inspired Native American legends, facilitated early exploration, enabled New World trade, and was vital to military control of the colonies and, later, the young nation. In the early nineteenth century, with the political stability and increasing economic prosperity enjoyed by the American middle class, the Hudson could be experienced in new ways, oriented around artistic production and leisure pursuits.

The Hudson was scenic in itself and provided access to the scenic. In the nineteenth century, voyagers up the Hudson passed the Palisades, the Hudson Highlands, West Point, and the Catskills on their way to the Catskill Mountain House, the spas at Saratoga and Ballston, or Niagara Falls. These natural wonders and sites of historical significance became places of pilgrimage for citizens of a young nation searching for a cultural identity. Novelists, such as Washington Irving and James Fenimore Cooper, wove tales and fables inspired by the river, the valley, and the surrounding countryside, and artists' renderings of the Hudson adorned travel books. A visit up the Hudson River, made feasible by easy and affordable steamship travel, thus formed a key component of the nineteenth-century Grand Tour of the United States.[3] By the time Frederic Church made his first foray to the Hudson Valley, the river's significance was already firmly ingrained in the American consciousness.

Frederic Church (fig. 3) left his native Hartford, Connecticut, for the Hudson Valley in the spring of 1844 to study with Thomas Cole (1801–1848), then the most renowned landscape artist in the United States. In the summer of 1825, only months before the completion of the Erie Canal, the English-born Cole embarked on a sketching expedition in search of "magnificent" scenery. The adventure led him to various picturesque locales and historic points all along the Hudson River.[4] On his return trip to New York City, Cole stopped in the village of Catskill to explore the mountains in the vicinity of the newly opened Catskill Mountain House. The three paintings resulting from this enterprise, shown in a bookstore in New York City, led to his "discovery" as an artist and launched his career as America's leading landscape painter. By 1836 Cole had settled in Catskill, married Maria Bartow, and taken up residence in her family home, Cedar Grove, an extensive 110-acre farm bordering the Hudson River just northeast of the village.

The young Church, anticipating that his tutelage would include traipsing about the countryside sketching from nature, stated in his introductory letter to Cole, "it would give me the greatest pleasure to accompany you in your rambles about the place, observing nature in all her various appearances."[5] His first outing was to the Catskill Mountain House. This popular resort hotel at North and South Lakes, set at the very edge of an escarpment, providing a famous bird's-eye view of the Hudson River and the surrounding valley, became a site of frequent pilgrimage during his student years, and one he returned to throughout his lifetime.

Cole suggested to his young pupil numerous sketching destinations, including the hills on the east side of the Hudson River, across from Cedar Grove and a bit to the south. This locale offered a tremendous view of the Hudson bordered by the Catskills. In *Scene from Red Hill* (fig. 4), a graphite drawing on gray-brown paper, Church delineates trees and buildings in the foreground; the widening of the river at Inbocht Bay; the Shawangunk Mountains in the distance to the south; and the southern slope of Overlook Mountain.[6] In the top right-hand corner Church diagrams Overlook Mountain more accurately and in relation to the next mountain to the north, Plattekill Mountain, both peaks in the Catskills. The rendering, dated May 1845, was done from the land that later became Church's home.[7] It is the first evidence of Church walking and sketching from Red Hill, the land he purchased almost fifteen years later as the initial parcel for what became his extensive property.

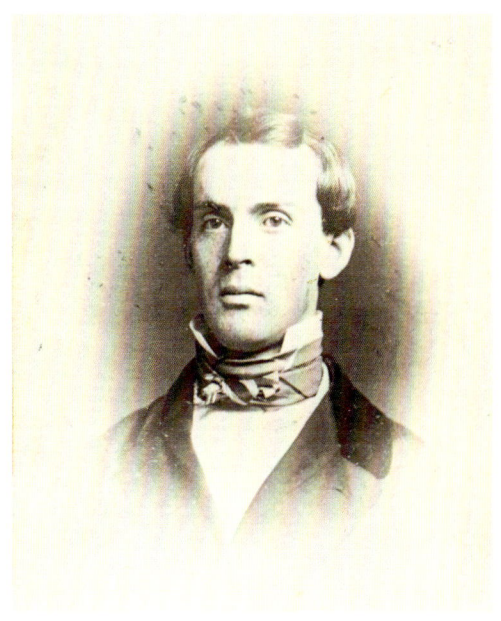

Fig. 3. R. S. De Lameter, *Frederic Edwin Church*, c. 1855, carte-de-visite, 4 × 2⅜ in., a photograph of a daguerreotype taken in 1844, OL.1992.57.1 – .6

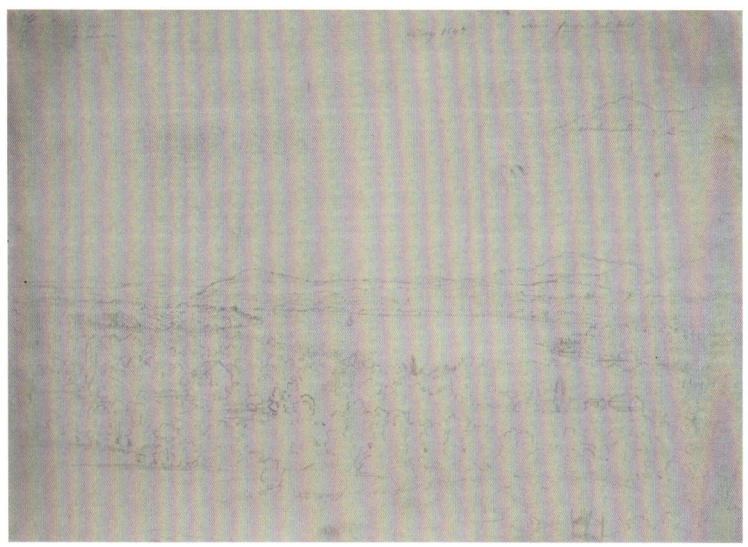

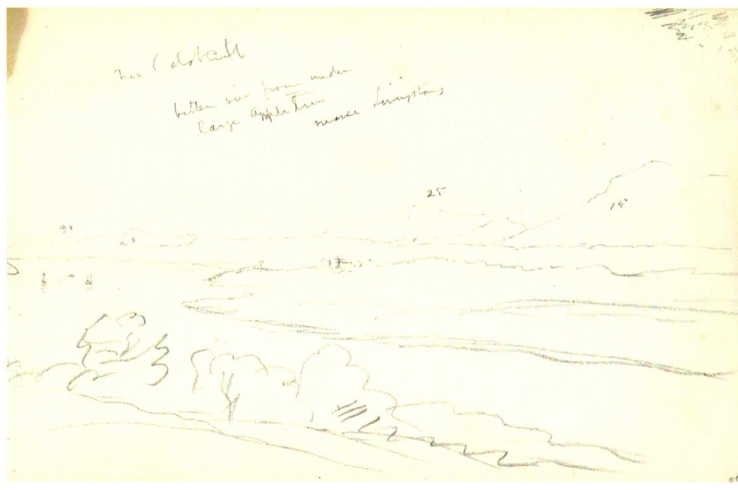

Fig. 4. Frederic Edwin Church, *Scene from Red Hill*, May 1845, graphite and chalk on light gray-brown paper, 10⅛ × 14⅜ in., OL.1980.1333A-recto

Fig. 5. Thomas Cole, *View from near Red Hill*, c. 1836, graphite on paper, 5⁵⁄₁₆ × 11⅞ in., The Detroit Institute of Arts, Founders Society Purchase, William H. Murphy Fund, 39.569.28, Photograph © 2002 The Detroit Institute of Arts

Thomas Cole, as early as 1836, had also drawn the view of the broadening of the Hudson from close to the same spot, as documented in a small red sketchbook now in the collection of the Detroit Institute of Arts.[8] *View from near Red Hill* (fig. 5) flows over two sheets and articulates in only a few lines of pencil the bend in the Hudson River bearing three vessels, the profile of Overlook Mountain, and the distant Shawangunk Mountains. The work is inscribed "near Catskill / better view from under / large Apple Trees / nearer Livingstons." This reference to other locales on the east side of the Hudson demonstrates his familiarity with the area and presaged future expeditions that are recorded in several sketchbooks.[9]

In addition to steering his student to various scenic views, Cole encouraged Church to focus on studies of specific elements in nature, such as trees, rocks, and clouds. *Rowboat on the Hudson River in Fog* (fig. 6), a student work by Church dated May 1845, depicts a two-man rowboat on the Hudson. The oil sketch shows Church experimenting with water, both the rippled surface disturbed by the moving craft and the still surface reflecting the far shore. Maximizing his painting surface, Church used the lower half to render the textures and colors of a moss- and lichen-covered boulder in the precise detail of one observing directly from nature.

Another small oil sketch reveals a very different aspect of life on the Hudson River. *Hudson River with Factory by Moonlight* (fig. 7), probably painted early in Church's career, illustrates a factory at night, most likely an iron foundry near the city of Hudson. Industrialization on the Hudson's banks and commercial traffic on the river were realities often excluded by painters and writers, who chose to exalt the virtues of a natural landscape, as if unadulterated by human intervention. By the 1850s there were already several industrial factories on or near the river bays just west of the city of Hudson. One, in fact, was owned by the family of Church's friend and fellow landscape painter Sanford Gifford (1823–1880).[10] In this small work Church concentrated on the dramatic effects created by the diffusion of smoke illuminated by the moon's cold light and reflected in the river. It foreshadows the erupting volcanoes of Church's later South American works and

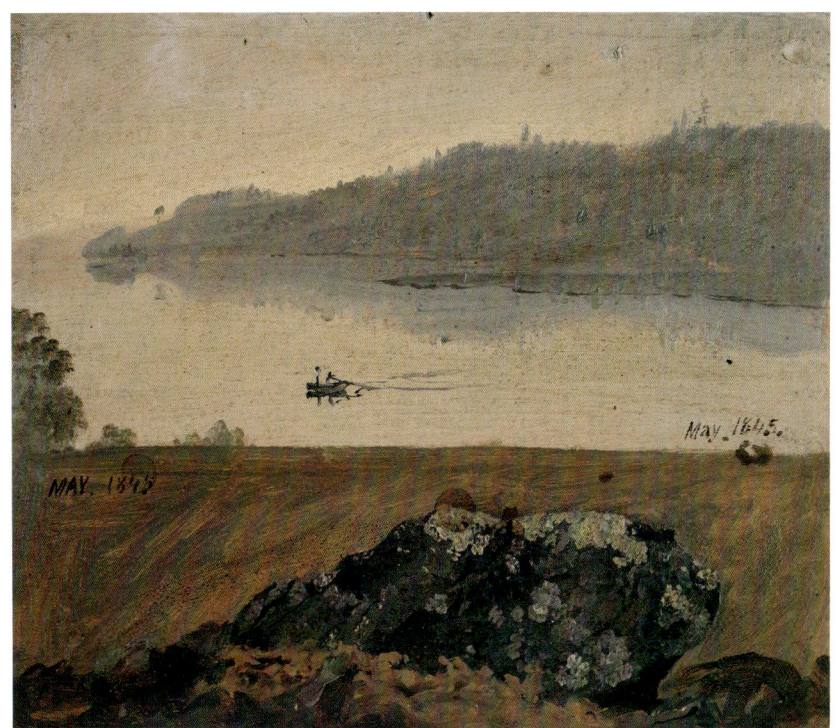

Fig. 6. Frederic Edwin Church, *Rowboat on the Hudson River in Fog; Moss-Covered Boulder, Catskill*, May 1845, oil on light brown cardboard, 8¼ × 9⁹⁄₁₆ in., OL.1977.234

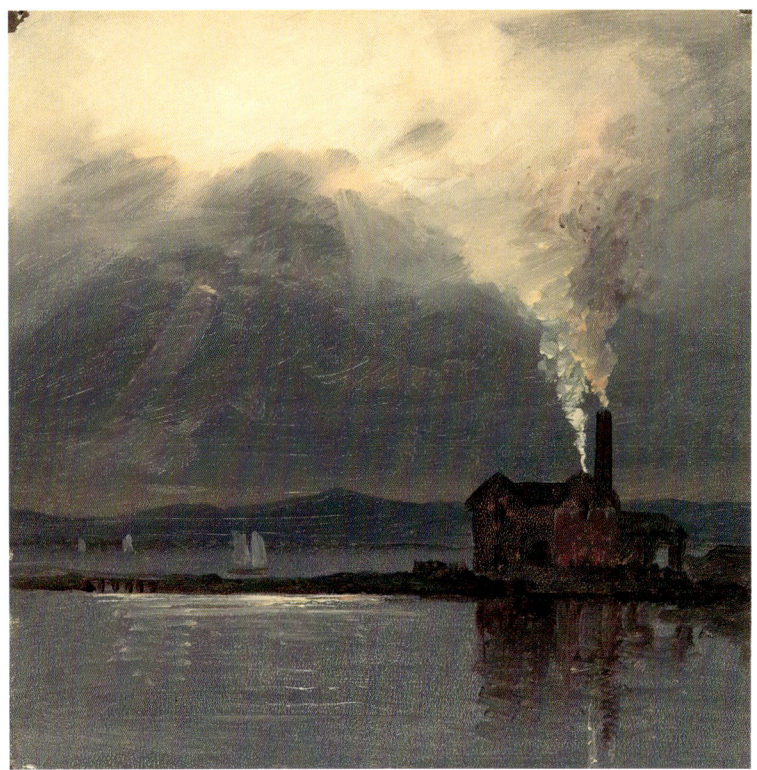

Fig. 7. Frederic Edwin Church, *Hudson River with Factory by Moonlight, South Bay, New York*, c. 1844–45, oil on paperboard, 8¹¹⁄₁₆ × 8¹⁵⁄₁₆ in., Cooper-Hewitt, National Design Museum, Smithsonian Institution, Gift of Louis P. Church, 1917-4-44, Photograph: Matt Flynn

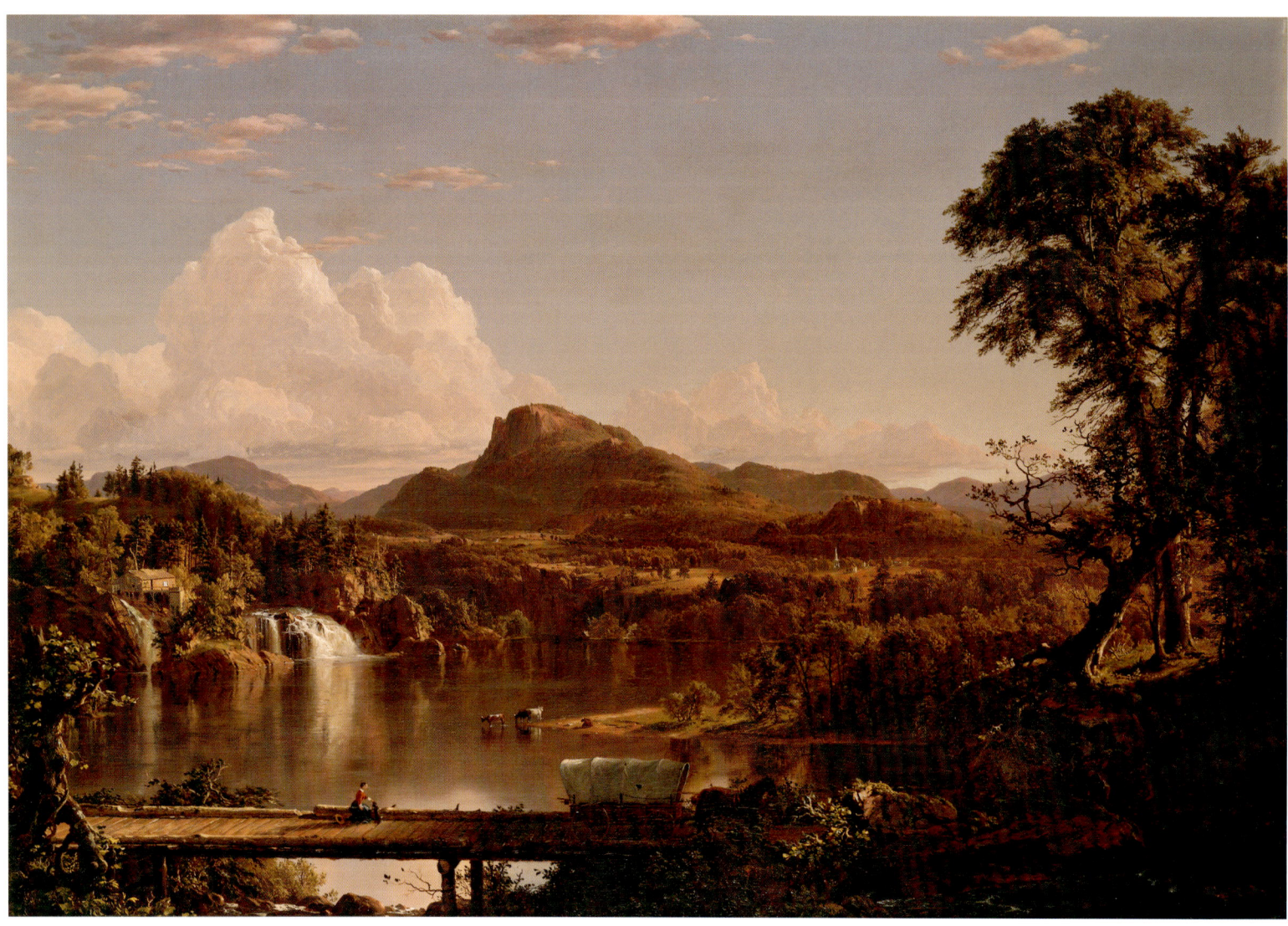

Fig. 8. Frederic Edwin Church, *New England Scenery*, 1851, oil on canvas, 36 × 53 in., George Walter Vincent Smith Art Museum, Springfield, Mass., George Walter Vincent Smith Collection, GWVS-1.23.24, Photograph: David Stansbury

exhibits the artist's early fascination with atmospheric effects, a signature quality of many of his works, regardless of their subject matter or date.

After two years of study with Cole, Church chose New York City—then the center of the American art world—as his base. His summer and fall travels throughout New York and New England inspired numerous paintings, bringing the young artist early success. In 1849, his achievements were recognized when Church was elected, at the age of twenty-three, a full member of the National Academy of Design, important for its annual spring art exhibition. *New England Scenery* (1851; fig. 8) brought a record price and heralded Church's more mature works, which sought to represent in one canvas an entire region rather than a specific location.

Venturing beyond the eastern United States, Church explored the more exotic locales of Colombia and Ecuador in 1853 and 1857 and Newfoundland and Labrador in 1859. Oil and pencil studies of lush foliage, smoking volcanoes, and electric green icebergs became the subjects for the monumental canvases that brought Church phenomenal success. His dramatic depiction of the American landmark and popular nineteenth-century tourist destination, *Niagara* (1857; fig. 9), presented in solo exhibitions throughout the United States and in London, made Church the most renowned artist in America. His expeditions to South America following in the footsteps of the German naturalist Alexander von Humboldt (1769–1859) culminated in *The Heart of the Andes* (1859; fig. 10), a tour de force of luxuriant tropical undergrowth, temperate forests, and snowcapped Mount Chimborazo—condensing all of Ecuador into one epic canvas.[11] This work, by the thirty-three-year-old artist, drew twelve thousand visitors in a mere three weeks while on exhibition in New York City.[12]

The adventure and romance associated with Church's art were mirrored in his personal life. The meeting of Frederic and his future wife, Isabel Carnes (1836–1899; fig. 11)—the Paris-born daughter of an American businessman[13]—was wonderfully recounted by the artist's colleague Worthington Whittredge (1820–1910). According to Whittredge, while at a showing of *The Heart of the Andes*, Frederic "saw in the distance

Fig. 9. Frederic Edwin Church, *Niagara*, 1857, oil on canvas, 42½ × 90½ in., Corcoran Gallery of Art, Washington, D.C., Museum Purchase, Gallery Fund, 76.15

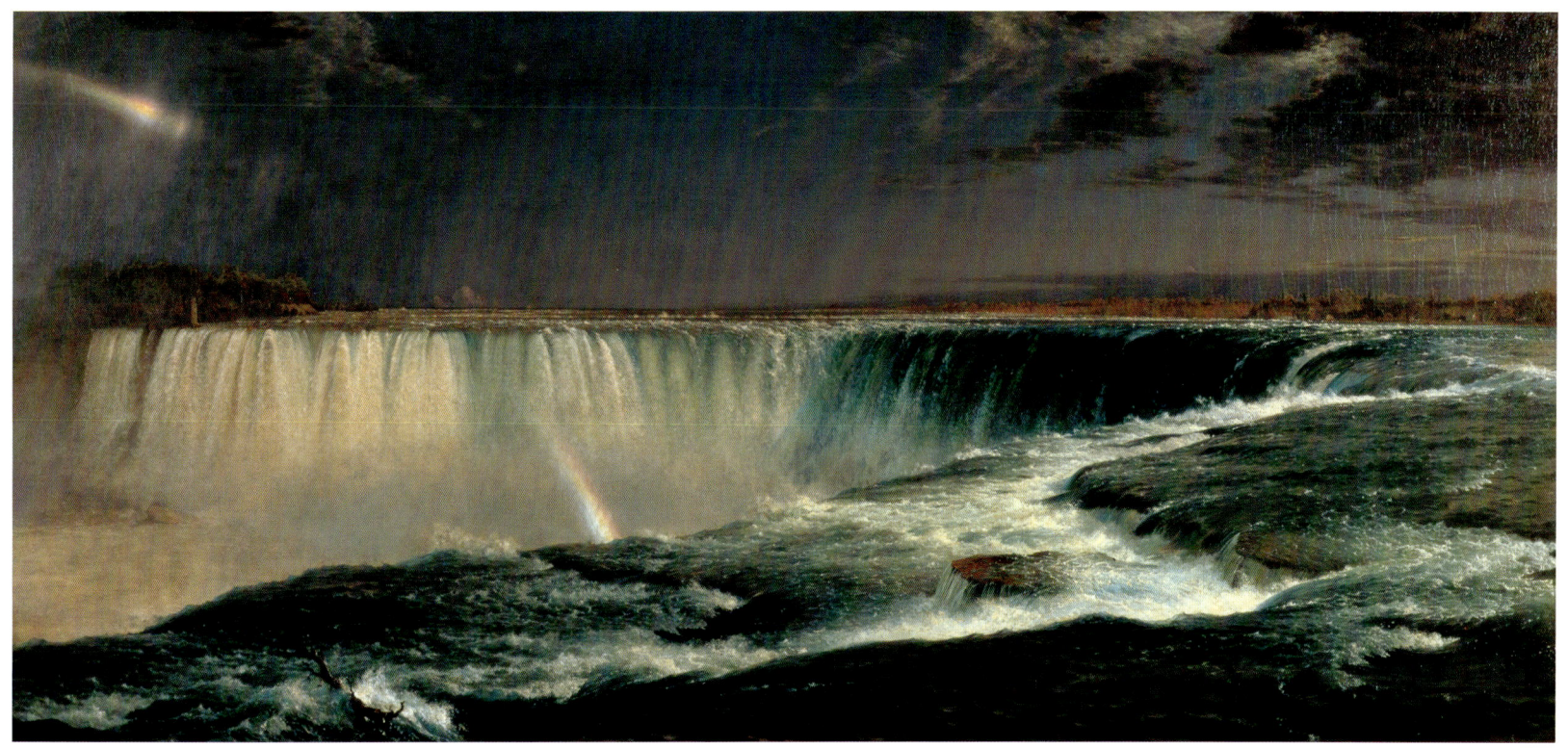

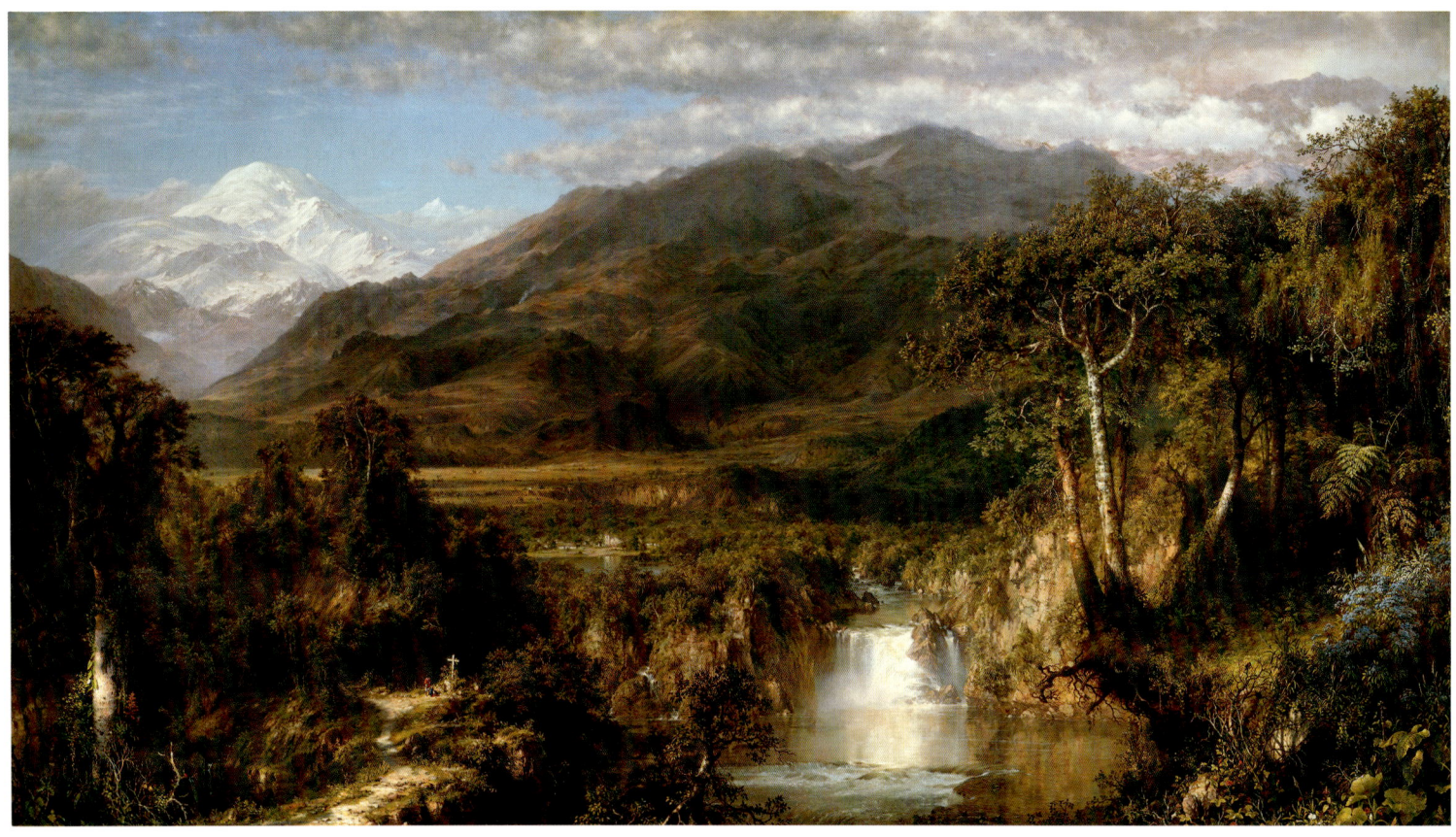

Fig. 10. Frederic Edwin Church, *The Heart of the Andes*, 1859, oil on canvas, 66⅛ × 119¼ in., The Metropolitan Museum of Art, Bequest of Margaret E. Dows, 1909, 09.95, Image © The Metropolitan Museum of Art

a ravishing vision" and pursued an introduction, "determined that he would know more about this vision and arrest it if it attempted to escape."[14] Indulging the double entendre, the *Boston Evening Transcript* reported, "Church has been successfully occupied with another Heart than that of the Andes."[15] The artist's friends were pleased for him; one commented that Isabel "is just what you would imagine an artist's wife, with soft curling golden hair, and a sweet face where the colour comes and goes every moment."[16] They were married on June 14, 1860, in Dayton, Ohio, the town where Isabel had spent most of her life, by Rev. Louis Le Grand Noble, Church's good friend and traveling companion to Newfoundland and Labrador.

The bachelor artist, when not on a sketching expedition, had lived in various rented rooms in New York City, though he spent most of his time in his studios, first at the American Art-Union, and then at the Tenth Street Studio Building. Requiring accommodations more suitable to married life, Church returned to the upper Hudson Valley in search of a permanent home. For some time, the successful artist had been thinking of purchasing a house or land in the area where his artistic career began, but it was not until he met Isabel that it became a priority.[17] The Hudson Valley was a logical location for the landscape artist. In his 1836 *Essay on American Scenery,* Cole proclaimed the virtues of the Hudson as a subject for art: "The Rhine has its castled crags, its vine-clad hills, and ancient villages; the Hudson has its wooded mountains, its rugged precipices, its green undulating shores—a natural majesty, and an unbounded capacity for improvement by art."[18] Cole expressed his own enchantment with the Hudson not only in paint and prose but also in poetry, referring to it as "a mirror'd heaven."[19]

Since Cole's untimely death in 1848, the areas in and around the Catskill Mountains had become places associated with Cole and the landscape movement he engendered. As T. Addison Richards related in *American Scenery Illustrated,* a book on the subject of "the Romance and Reality of American Landscape," the Catskill Mountains represented an escape from the "coy patrons and snarling critics" and had been a "cherished haunt of our great Cole. . . ."[20] In fact, Cole's own home had become a place of pilgrimage, cited as a destination in numerous travel and guidebooks.[21] Property with easy proximity to Cedar Grove, Kaaterskill Clove, and the Mountain House would have held a special appeal for Church. As Washington Irving maintained, the combination of the Catskill Mountains and their "detached position, overlooking a wide lowland region, with the majestic Hudson rolling through it, has given them a distinct character, and rendered them at all times a rallying point for romance and fable . . . owing to their being peculiarly subject to those beautiful atmospherical effects which constitute one of the great charms of Hudson River scenery."[22]

Just prior to his wedding, Church decided on the 126-acre parcel known locally as the Wynsant Brezie farmstead, in part because of the unique attributes of the section of the river it overlooked. On the east shore, the hilly terrain comes close to the banks of the river, providing raised viewing platforms. By contrast, the west bank contains a broad floodplain with the backdrop of the most dramatic views of the Catskills from Overlook Mountain to Windham High Peak, including Kaaterskill Clove. Here, the river itself is distinctive, narrow just to the north, but then immediately widening almost to a lakelike proportion to form the signature element known as Inbocht Bay, or the "bend in the river."[23]

Church's acquisition, situated a few miles south of the city of Hudson, included an old farmhouse, outbuildings to house livestock and store grain, plowed fields, orchards, pasture, a woodlot, and an area of swampy ground. Fortuitously, the parcel also included Red Hill, from which Church had sketched fifteen years earlier.

The farm was located almost directly across the river from the home of Church's late mentor. Church had maintained his friendship with Cole's widow and children in the years following his student days. He was particularly close to Cole's oldest son, Theodore, whom he hired to assist him in the long-term design and development of the land.[24] Together they planned what livestock to purchase and crops to put in,

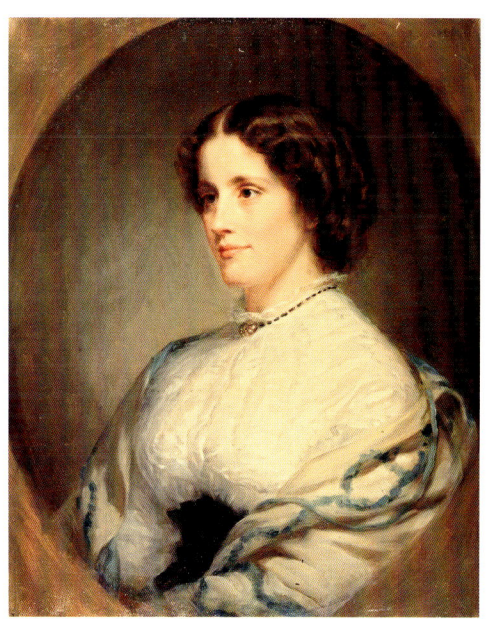

Fig. 11. George Baker, *Isabel Carnes Church,* c. 1860, oil on canvas, 27 × 22⅛ in., OL.1981.3

extensive tree plantings, and the excavation for a man-made lake. Under Church's direction, Theodore supervised all other property staff, including the farmer, and managed the property in general, fulfilling a vital role. The relationship was one of personal respect and attachment, as expressed by Theodore himself: "I always feel almost as if I was doing something for my own Brother when I am doing anything for you."[25]

During the summer of 1860, Frederic and Isabel stayed with the Cole family at Cedar Grove, a perfect place from which to visit their new property and oversee the building of their first home. The newlyweds hired the architect Richard Morris Hunt (1827–1895) to plan a small wood-frame house for them. In the spring of 1861, they took up residence in the home they named Cosy Cottage. Church depicted it in early autumn covered with Virginia creeper, as the vine was beginning to change to its glorious bright red fall foliage (fig. 12).[26] The cottage was situated in the midst of the farm, with a kitchen garden, a floral cutting garden, and rows of fruit trees just beyond its doorways. While the bulk of the hard labor was handled by the hired farmhands, Church thoroughly embraced gentleman farming, joking to a patron that at times it took precedence over his paintings: "In fact my hand is out in consequence of my attention being absorbed at the present with my farm. . . ."[27]

While excited about his new enterprise, Church balanced country life with his continued production and exhibition of significant canvases: *The Icebergs* (1861, Dallas Museum of Art), *Cotopaxi* (1862, the Detroit Institute of Arts), and *Coast Scene, Mt. Desert* (1863, Wadsworth Atheneum Museum of Art, Hartford). Less than two weeks before Church planned to publicly debut *The Icebergs*, Fort Sumter fell, marking the outbreak of the Civil War. In support of the Union, the artist renamed his painting *The North* and allocated all proceeds of the exhibition entrance fees to the Patriotic Fund to aid the families of Union soldiers. As the war accelerated, in a show of patriotism, Church, along with fellow artists, participated in New York City's Metropolitan Fair to raise funds to provide medical care for injured Union combatants.

Summers in the Hudson Valley offered a respite from the demands of Church's artistic career and the turmoil associated with the war. The Coles crossed the river often to spend the day with the young family. From farther afield, Frederic's and Isabel's relatives and their good

Fig. 12. Frederic Edwin Church, *Cosy Cottage*, c. 1870–72, oil on heavy academy board, 11⁹⁄₁₆ × 17⅜ in., OL.1977.315

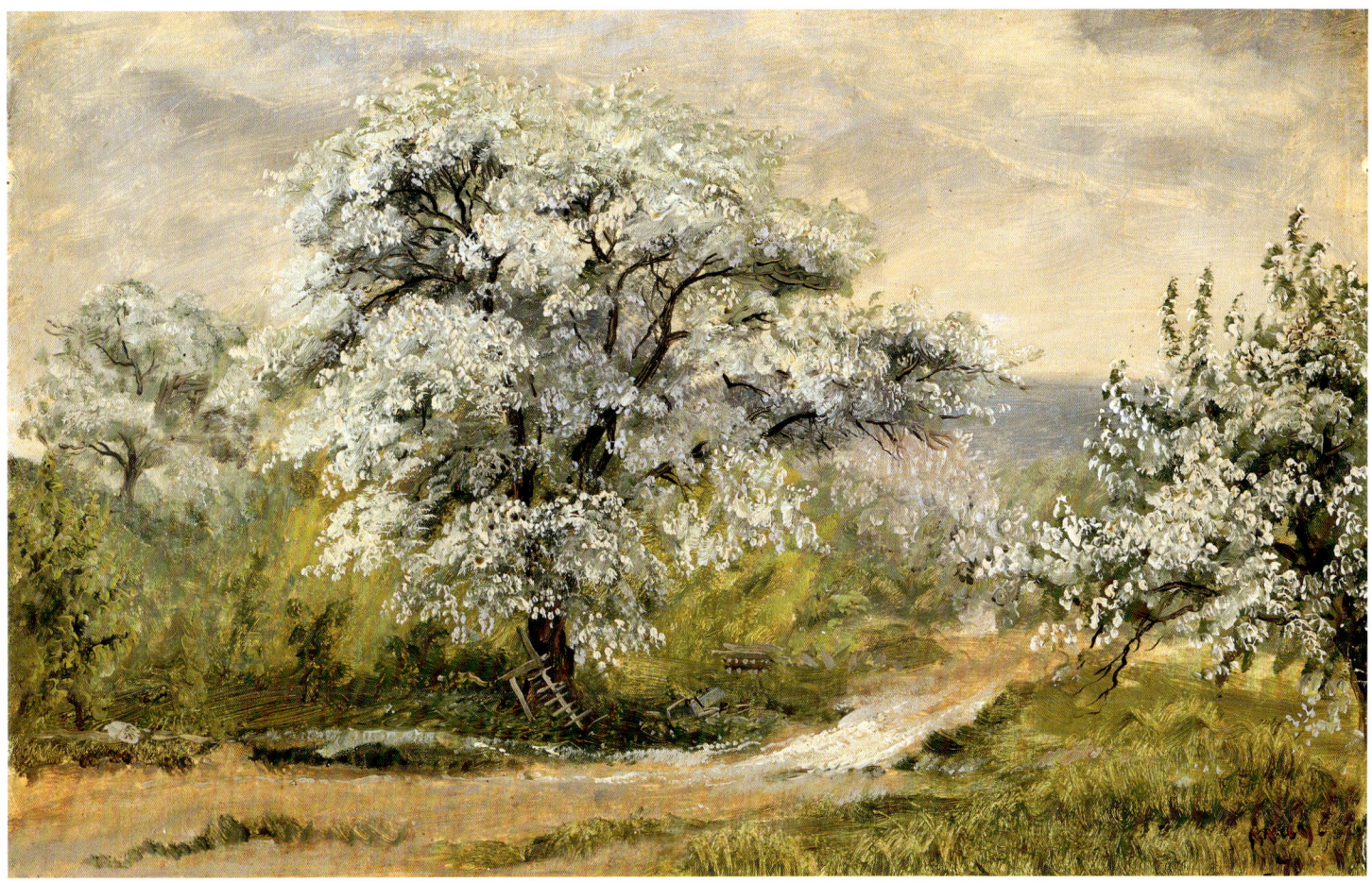

Fig. 13. Frederic Edwin Church, *Apple Blossoms at Olana*, May 1870, oil on canvas, 11⅝ × 18¼ in., OL.1981.23

friends the Albany sculptor Erastus Dow Palmer (1817–1904) and his wife came for extended visits. The birth of their son Herbert gave new life to the farm:

> Herbert enjoys the Farm as much as anybody—We have a coop of 15 chickens by the house and he feeds them out of his hand—He is fascinated by the horses—I have a pair of pigeons—one of them today marched into the parlor to the great delight of Herbert—Mother will be shocked to see how brown her grandson is—[28]

Church's remarks on Herbert's pleasure reflected his own passion for his home and involvement with farm life. "The country is very lovely now and the grand scenes which encircle my farm are getting their summer drapery—I should be happy to have the opportunity some time to show you the beautiful views I look daily upon."[29]

Artistically, Church assayed a number of the scenes that encircled his farm. In *Apple Blossoms at Olana* (fig. 13), he captured the apple orchard behind Cosy Cottage in its full

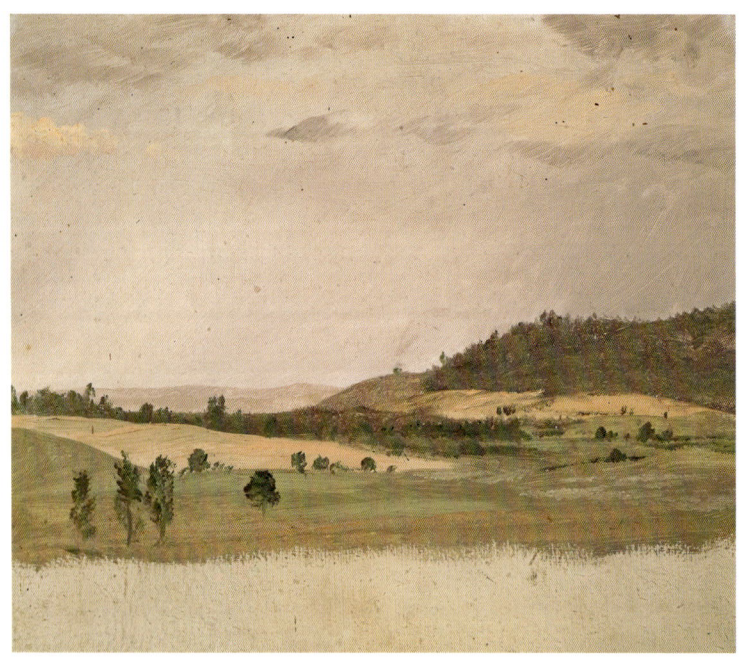

springtime glory. Church expressed both his own and Isabel's delight when he described the blooms in a letter: "She now sits under the apple trees in luxurious contemplation of the beautiful scenes. . . . These old patriarchs look like mountains of bridal bouquets."[30] Not purely ornamental, the orchard produced a bounty of apples, pears, peaches, and cherries, and Church proudly sent gifts of fruit to friends and family.

Turning his gaze southeast toward the distant Taconic Range, Church sketched *Blue Hill from Cosy Cottage* (fig. 14), one of five such prospects.[31] The Taconic hills are present in the far left, appearing almost as an outline or footnote, while on the far right, slightly truncated, Blue Hill is clothed in lush green; here Church realized his own descriptions of the "fresh verdure" of the season.[32] In a pencil sketch Church carefully portrayed *Bee Craft Mountain* (fig. 15), essentially a mapping of the view northeast from Cosy Cottage, which together with *Blue Hill from Cosy Cottage* composes

Fig. 14. Frederic Edwin Church, *Blue Hill from Cosy Cottage*, c. 1869–72, oil on brown cardboard, 9 × 10¾ in., OL.1977.237

Fig. 15. Frederic Edwin Church, *Bee Craft Mountain from Church's Farm*, August 1863, graphite and gouache on light green paper, 11¹⁄₁₆ × 16³⁄₁₆ in., OL.1977.183

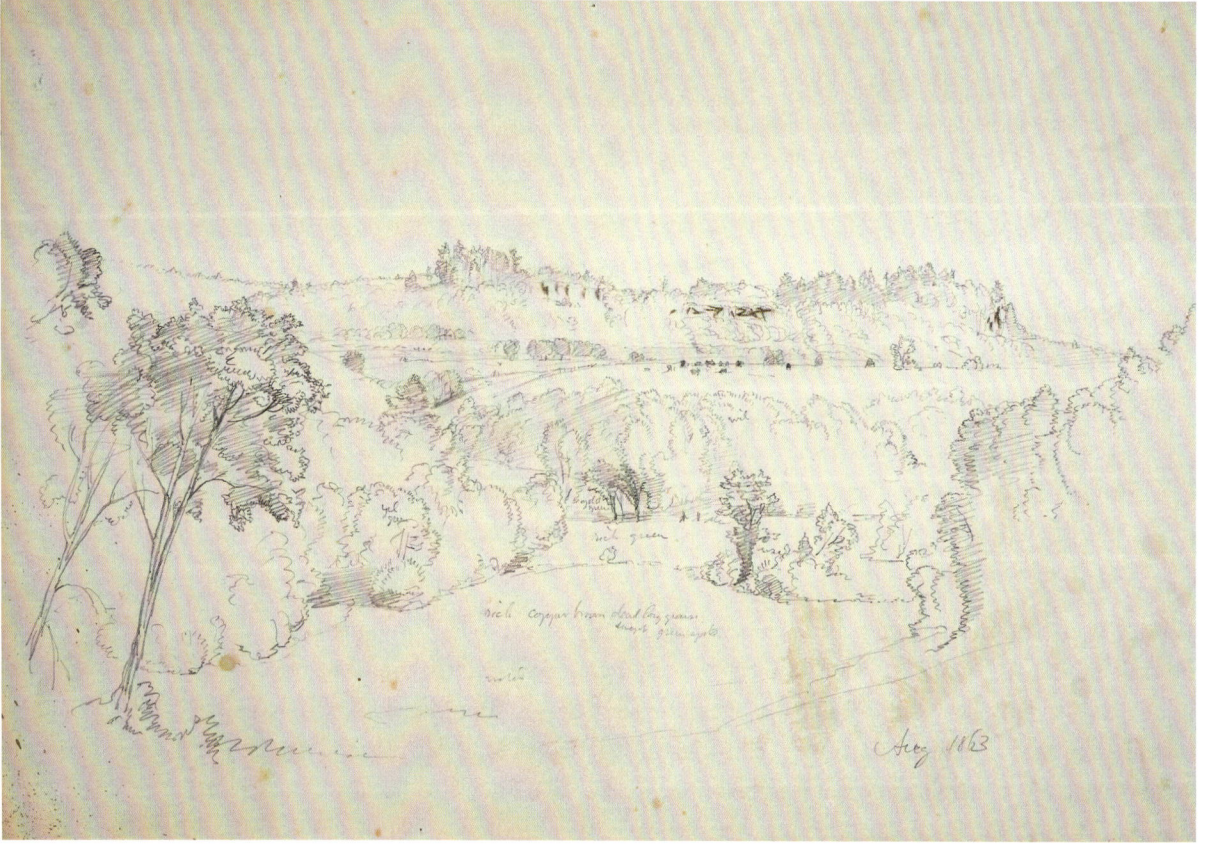

the entire eastern side of Church's early property holdings. Even had Church not dated the drawing "August 1863," the end of the season would be disclosed in his annotations: "rich copper brown dead long grass." With *Apple Blossoms at Olana*, these works suggest the nestled placement of the Churches' home within the farm environs.

Other areas of the property provided more panoramic vistas. In 1864, Church commissioned Arthur Parton (1842–1914), a local artist and student of William Trost Richards (1833–1905), to paint *Looking Southwest over Church's Farm from the Sienghenbergh* (fig. 16).[33] Parton, working from one of the higher points on the property, the upper slope of the Sienghenbergh—Dutch for "long hill"—detailed part of the grounds and the view south. He included the southern tips of the Catskills in the distance on the right side of the canvas and Inbocht Bay (the "bend" in the Hudson) in the middle background. Between the ends of the Catskills and Inbocht Bay is Quarry Hill, crowned with a clump of large evergreens. The other prominent hill in the middle ground on the left side of the canvas is Red Hill, from which Church had drawn *Scene from Red Hill* in 1845. To the left of Red Hill and extending beyond the edge of the painting rises the eastern slope of Crown Hill. Eventually Church dredged the area that is here depicted with neatly planted crops, and he removed the trees at the base of Crown Hill to create a lake. In the foreground Parton articulated mature corn stalks and some goldenrod in bloom to identify the scene as late summer, and the red plowed earth and recently felled

Fig. 16. Arthur Parton, *Looking Southwest over Church's Farm from the Sienghenbergh*, 1864, oil on canvas, 19¾ × 31 in., OL.1981.20

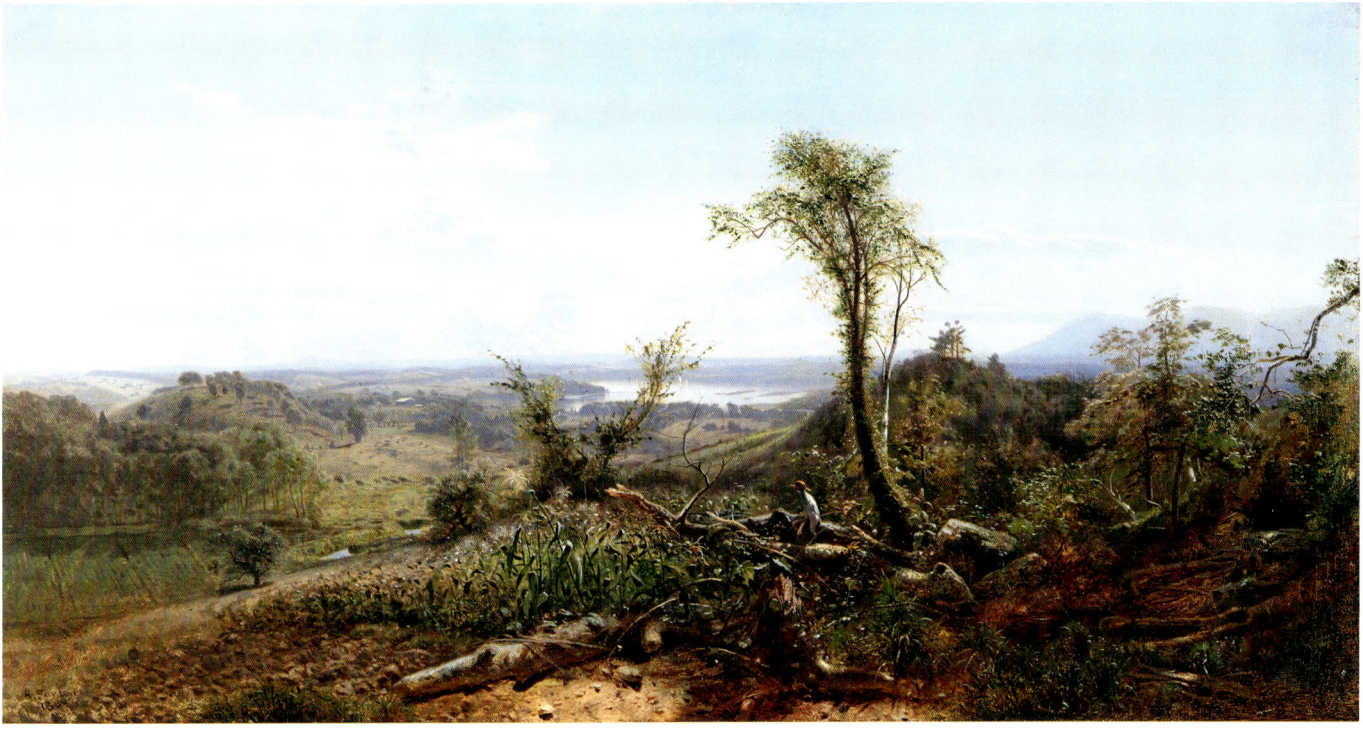

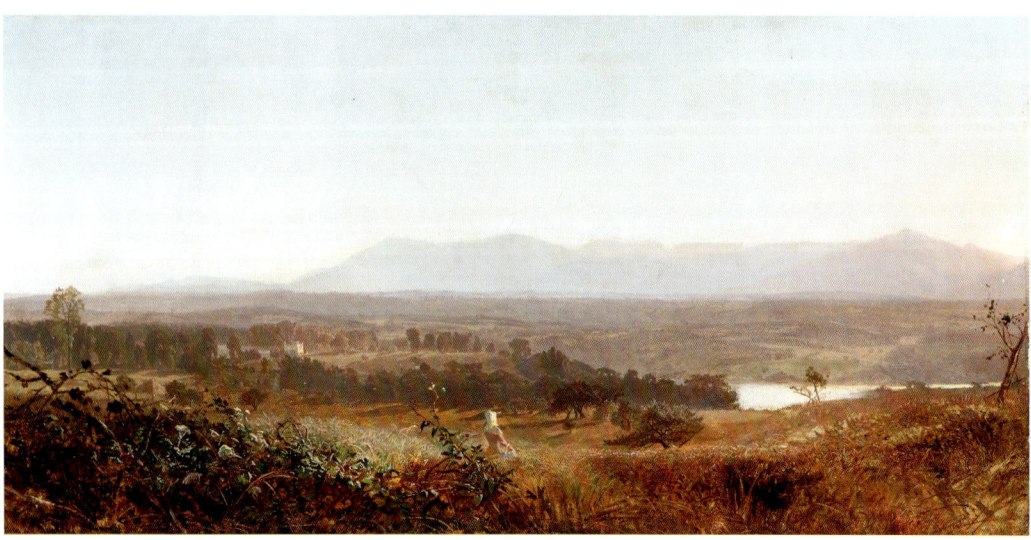

Fig. 17. Arthur Parton, *The Catskill Mountains from South of Church's Farm*, 1863, oil on canvas, 10¼ × 20¼ in., OL.1981.21

trees reference Church's first efforts to transform a hardscrabble countryside into an ornamental farm, a combination working farm and scenic parkland. On one of the felled trees, in the shade of the big American elm, Parton placed a farmer admiring the view.

Prior to the commission, Parton had painted the scene looking west over the late summer fields, river, and mountains in *The Catskill Mountains from South of Church's Farm*, 1863 (fig. 17).[34] The artist draws attention to the view, with the bonneted woman, gathering basket in hand, who, standing amid a field of grasses and Queen Anne's lace, shields her eyes from the late-day sun, pausing to admire the vista of the pink-purple range. These expansive views to the south and west became Church's focus as he enlarged his property over the ensuing years, through numerous land acquisitions, toward an elevated prospect.

Envisioning his home as more than a simple farmstead, in 1864 Church increased his holdings, purchasing a lot he had long admired, formerly owned by his late friend Rev. Dr. Bethune. Called by Church "the Bethune lot," the steep hillside bordered the original farm on the west and, like his own entrance, yielded access to the Oak Hill–Hudson Road, which led north to the city of Hudson and south to the Greendale Landing and railroad station. Church bought the Bethune lot expressly to build a new approach to the farm that afforded selected outlooks to the Hudson below as the road wound its way up the sharp ascent through picturesque woods and past rock outcrops. The artist revealed his intentions to his father, in May 1864, of "securing fine openings for the view," probably in reference to his plans for the new entrance drive.[35]

Contemporary taste and writings would have encouraged Church to make the most of his views of the Hudson. N. Parker Willis's "The Highland Terrace above West Point," in *The Home Book of the Picturesque*, described how the Hudson was revealed from

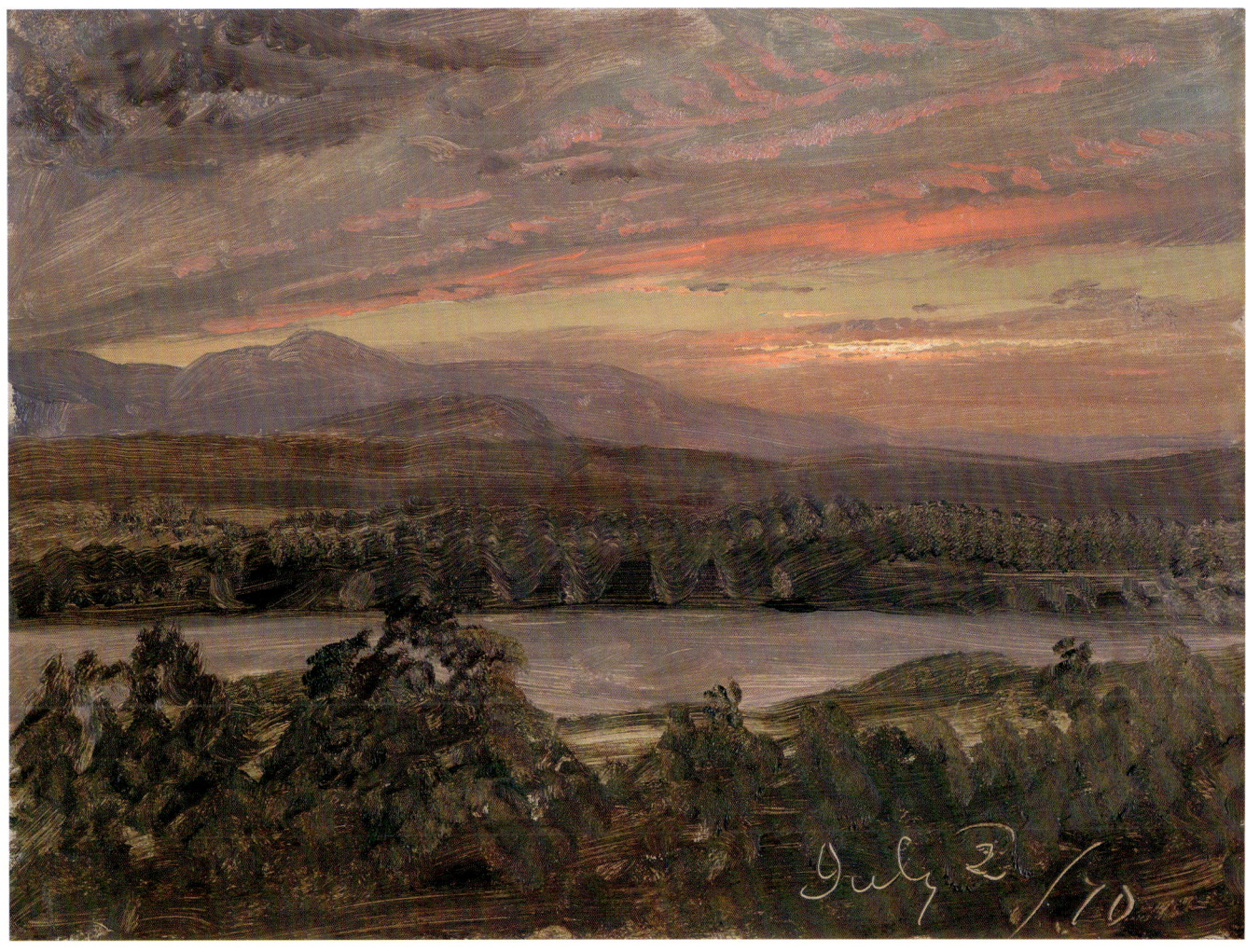

Fig. 18. Frederic Edwin Church, *Sunset from Olana*, July 2, 1870, oil on off-white academy board, 11 1/16 × 15 1/8 in., OL.1976.8

the winding roads of the Highland Terrace, an area one hundred feet above the Hudson River. "From every little rise in the road, it must be remembered, the broad bosom of the Hudson is visible, with foreground variously combined and broken; and the lofty mountains, (encircling just about as much scenery as the eye can compass for enjoyment), form an *ascending background and a near horizon* which are hardly surpassed in the world for boldness and beauty."[36]

In constructing Bethune Road, Church offered visitors to the farm similar views. Traveling up Bethune Road, a friend remarked on its successful layout in relation to the river: "The Drive went round and round the hill—Mr. Church has taken advantage of [every acre] of ground. . . . Every time we came to the Hudson, it was a new revelation, a complete surprise."[37] In the oil sketch *Sunset from Olana* (fig. 18), dated "July 2 / 70," Church captured a dazzling summer sunset, yellow and pinky red over the northern

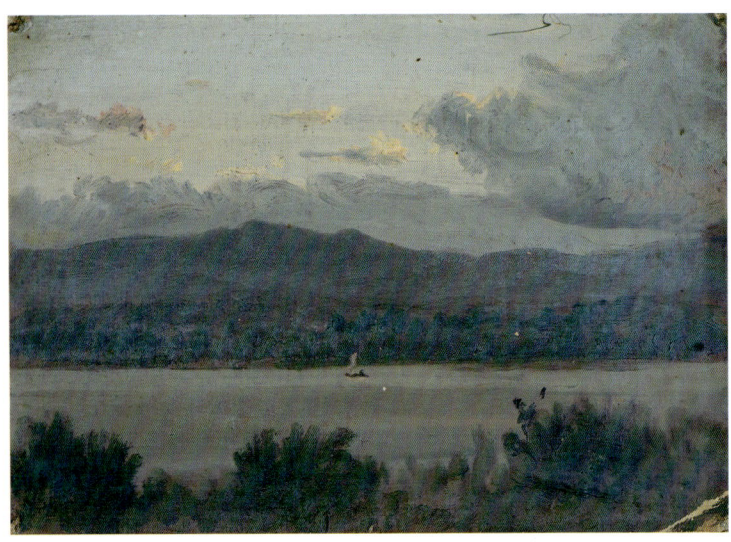

Fig. 19. Benjamin Bellows Grant Stone, *Catskill Mountains and Hudson River*, c. 1870, oil on canvas, 9½ × 13½ in., Greene County Historical Society, Vedder Research Library, Coxsackie, N.Y., 72.44.555, Photograph courtesy Ray Beecher

Fig. 20. Unknown photographer, *View of Olana Grounds in Winter, Showing Church's Studio and Main House*, c. 1880, photographic print within an album, 3¾ × 4¾ in., OL.1986.378.18.C

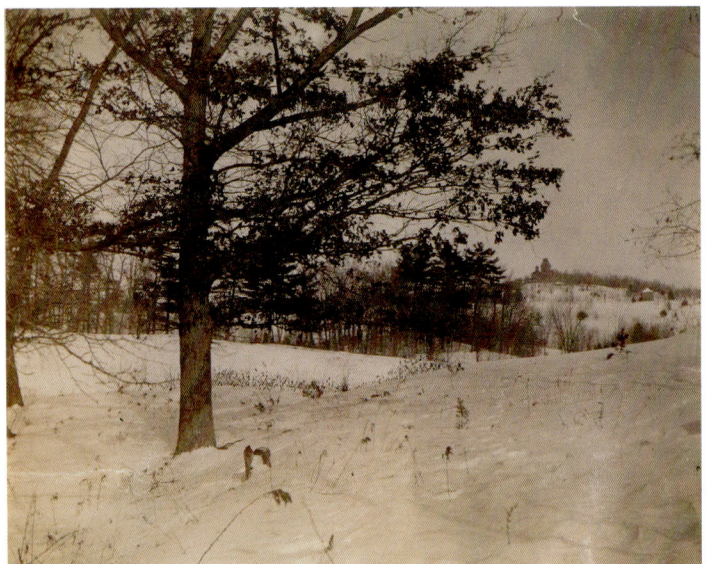

Catskills, with the softer colors of the upper sky reflected in the Hudson below. The foreground of treetops and the relation of the mountains and river indicate an upper loop of Bethune Road as Church's sketching spot.

Proud of the prospects from his new road, Church must have invited his friend the local artist Benjamin Bellows Grant Stone (1829–1906) to try his hand at the view from Bethune Road (fig. 19). Stone's sketch, on a piece of unstretched canvas, shows the same foreground of treetops obscuring the near shore and the same perspective of the Catskills as *Sunset from Olana* (fig. 18). In this peaceful late afternoon scene, the bright sail of a craft on the silvery river stands out against the trees on the far shore, with the Catskills beyond under low-lying clouds and a few white wisps higher in the sky. This quiet study in blue, green, and gray forms a stark contrast to Church's dramatic sky. Stone and Church became friendly in the mid-1850s; Stone's diary records visits between the two artists, both social calls that included their respective wives and meetings for art advice and assistance.[38]

Having built a road to take advantage of the views of the Hudson, Church turned his attention to designing a freestanding studio up the hill above the farm complex, from which he could admire the river. Up to this point, the artist had no designated building as a studio on the farm. The artist informed his father that he planned "to make a road to the place where I intend to build this summer." Church constructed the studio between 1864 and 1865 on what was his highest point of land.[39] The structure is barely visible on the right side of a later historic photograph (fig. 20). The location offered spectacular views down the pastoral slope of the Sienghenbergh to the farm, Red Hill, and Quarry Hill, and, farther in the distance, the wide bend in the river and the southern edge of the Catskills. Church had undoubtedly directed Parton to paint from this vantage point for the commission in 1864 (fig. 16). Church's mother-in-law, Emma Carnes, found this an attractive resting spot, noting in her diary that on a "fine, cool" day, she "went to my seat back of Studio."[40]

Tragically, in March 1865, Herbert and his newborn sister Emma died in a diphtheria epidemic. As a distraction from their grief, Frederic and Isabel traveled to Jamaica: "I am about taking Mrs. Church to the mountains of Jamaica for the summer for the change of scene, air and life—believing that we both will be much benefitted by the journey—"[41] Excited by the scenery, magnificent

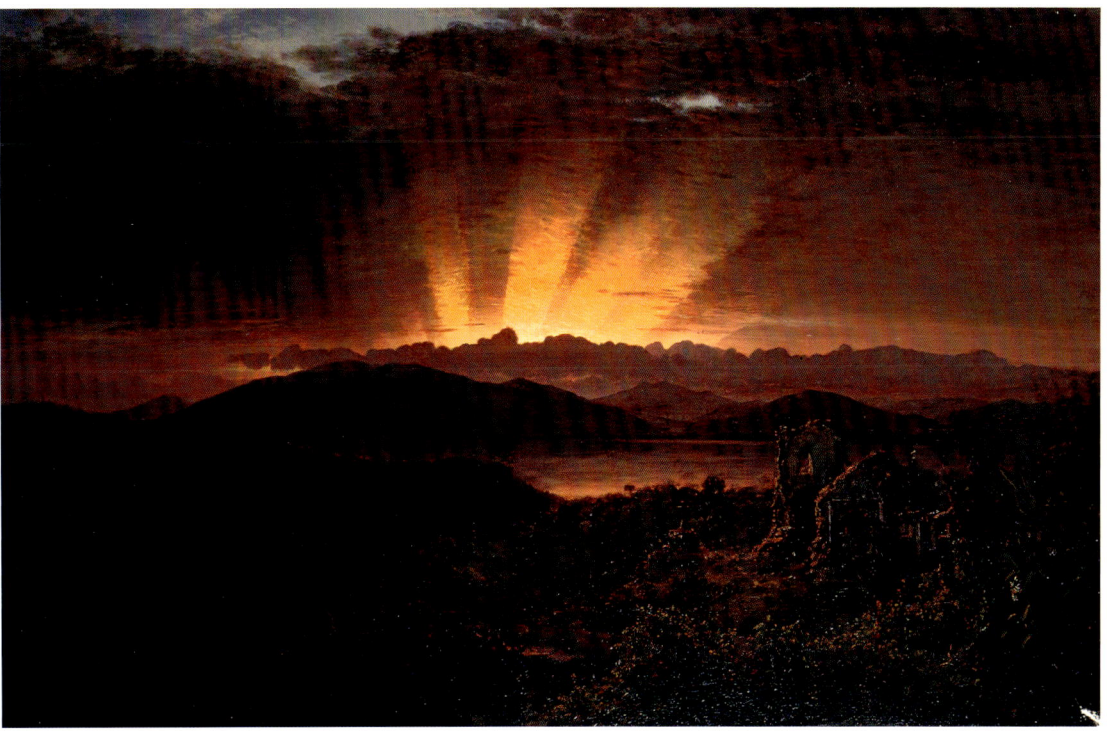

sunsets, and tropical foliage, the artist produced myriad oil and pencil sketches that inspired two major canvases: *The After Glow* (fig. 21) and *The Vale of St. Thomas* (1867, Wadsworth Atheneum). Returning from Jamaica refreshed, Frederic spent the fall sketching in Vermont, and then he and Isabel settled into Cosy Cottage for their first winter in the Hudson Valley.

Once home, Church had the opportunity to paint in his newly completed studio. He characterized the simple wood structure, twenty-four feet square with a porch of six by eight feet on the west side, near the northwest corner, as "a plain but ample studio on my farm...."[42] Church's studio was most likely inspired by the Italianate-style studio Thomas Cole had conceived and built at Cedar Grove in 1846. No longer extant, Cole's studio is known through photographic images and a pencil drawing by Church dated October 1848 (fig. 22). In the rendering, Cole's studio is depicted at right, with its large windows, northern porch or entrance, and ornate trim. The color note describes the building as "warm neutral," the roof "ornaments" as "orange brown," and the blinds as "light green."[43] Church's studio included a large window on the north side and a smaller window on the west side.[44] The artist observed: "The big window never fails to shed abundance of light no matter how dull the day may be."[45] The interior was a deep red, and for comfort it was heated by a coal-fired stove, enabling Church to paint year-round in his new building.

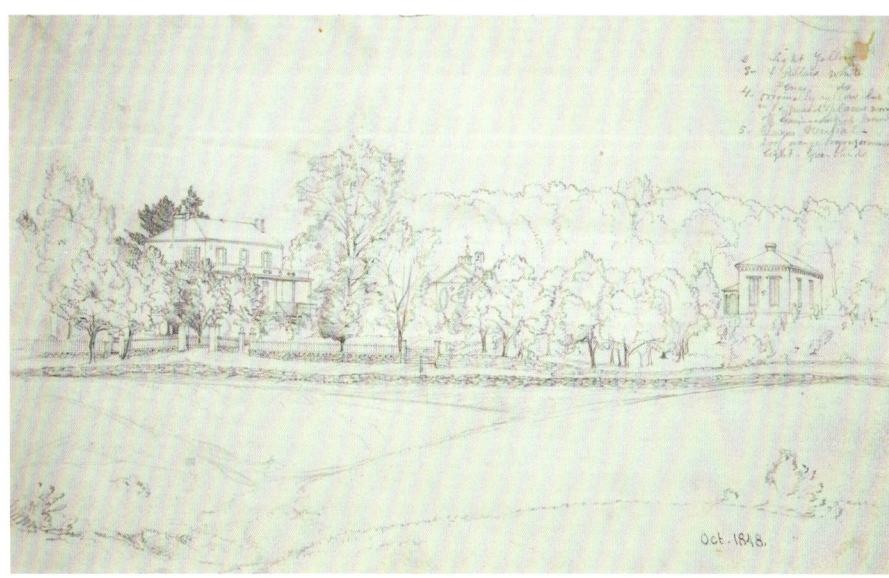

Church established a comfortable routine: "I am not much interrupted in my studio. I go up to it in the morning at nine or ten and stay until four our present dining hour—and I am accomplishing more than I ever did in my life before."[46] This communication is amusingly headed "Siberia Jany 1st, 1866," followed by the remark, "we have been snow bound. . . ."[47] Could this snowy January have inspired the artist to paint *The Hudson Valley in Winter from Olana* (fig. 23)? In this undated work, Church depicted the frozen Hudson Valley looking southwest from his studio, with Quarry Hill in the right foreground and the "bend in the river" under a late winter sky. Here Church worked in almost a monochromatic palette to express the chill of the nearly sunless winter sky—an apt depiction of a climate evocative of Siberia. Church eventually mounted this oil sketch on paper to canvas and framed it for display in his home, a personal memento of the view he enjoyed daily from his studio.

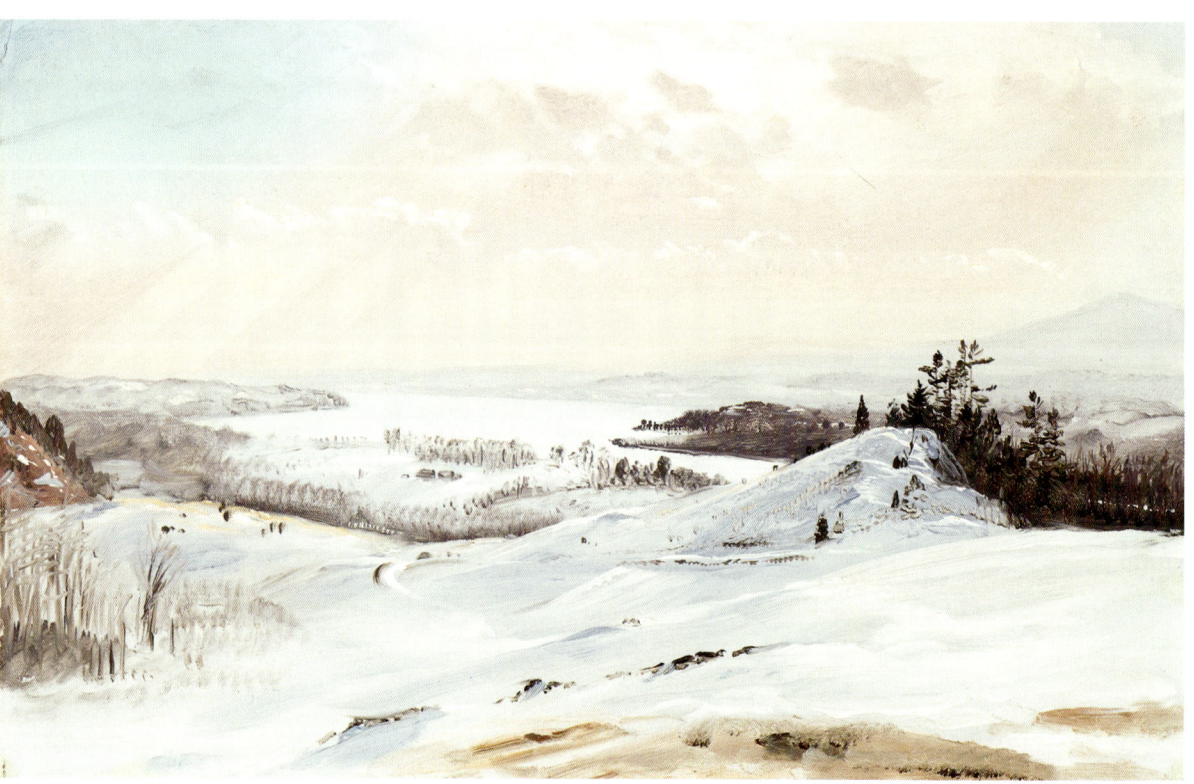

The same vantage point from the new studio provided the vista for one of the artist's few finished paintings inspired by the property, *View of the Hudson River Valley from Olana* (1867; fig. 24). Typical of Church's studio works, it combines elements from different locations. He probably borrowed from studies made in Maine or the Adirondack Mountains to add picturesque drama to the composition. The foreground, except for Quarry Hill with its dark evergreens, is augmented with exposed rock not found on the gently rolling slope of the Sienghenbergh, and the steep forested slope in the middle ground serves as a substitute for Crown Hill and Red Hill. The background depicts the wide expanse of the Hudson and the southern end of the Catskills.

A pencil and gouache sketch dated "Nov 1866" (fig. 25)[48] might have served as the template for the atmospheric effects in *View of the Hudson River Valley from Olana* (fig. 24). The color notes register the sky between the Shawangunks and Overlook Mountain as "orangeish," the sky to the right of Overlook as "more yellow brilliant," and the distant shore as "purple," skillfully capturing in words what Church translated

Fig. 24. Frederic Edwin Church, *View of the Hudson River Valley from Olana*, 1867, oil on canvas, 12¼ × 20⅜ in., Brigham Young University Museum of Art, Provo, Utah

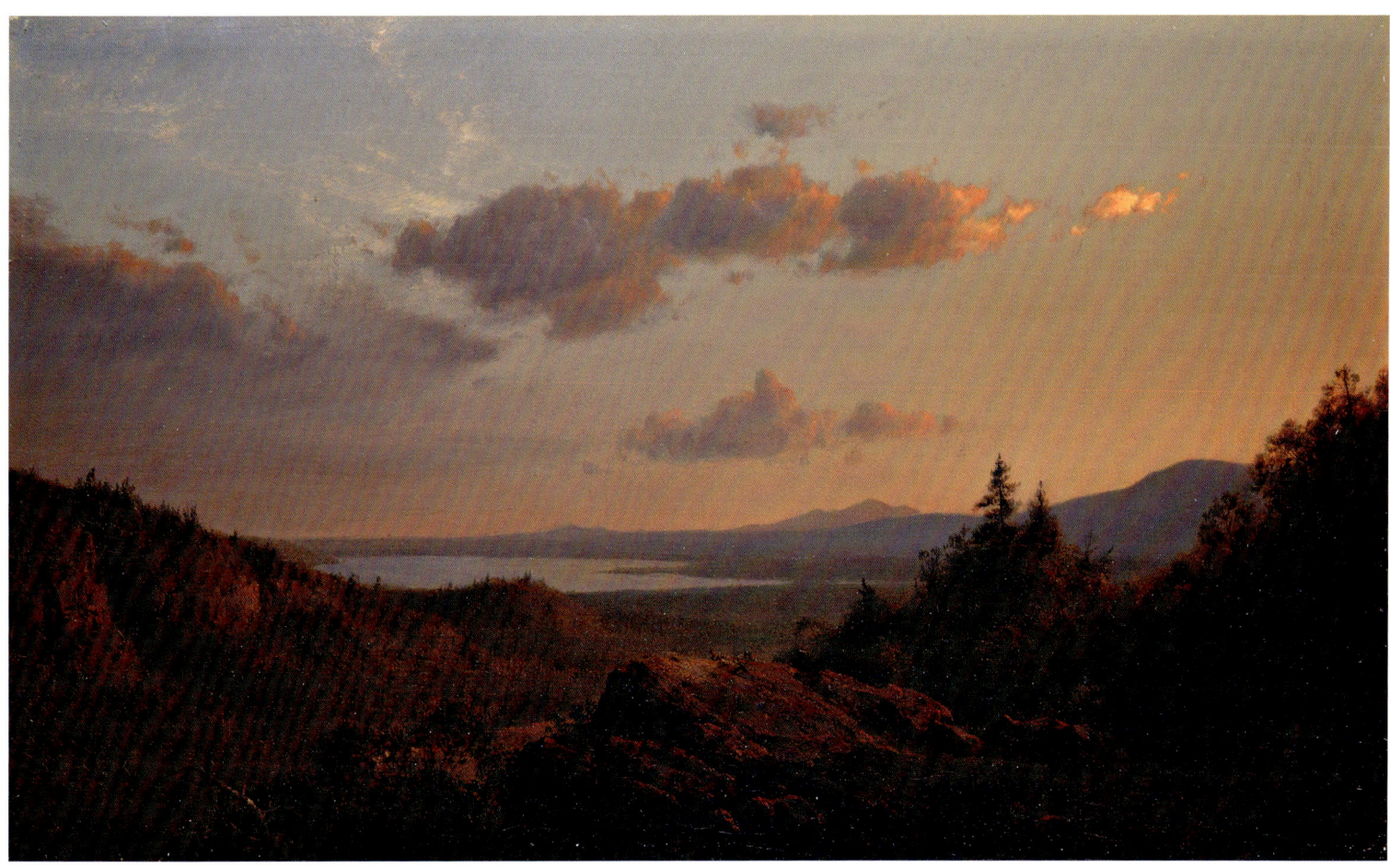

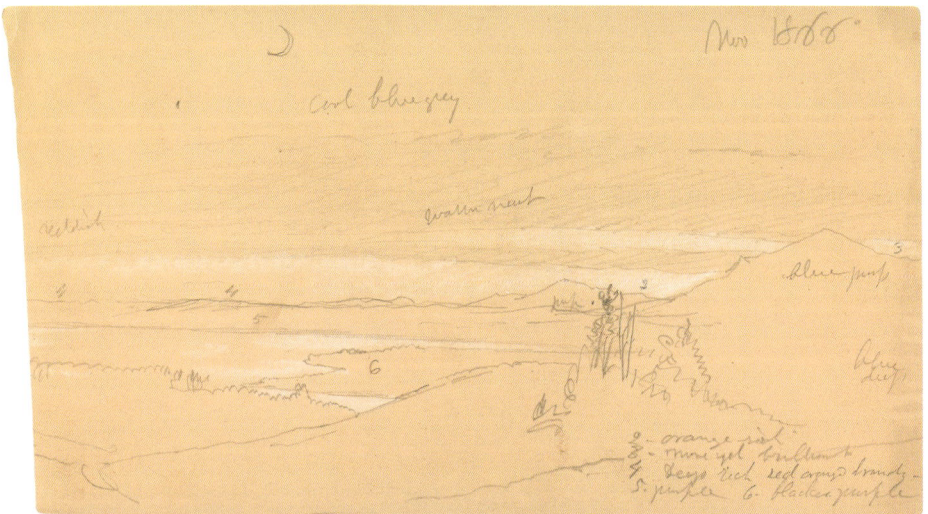

Fig. 25. Frederic Edwin Church, *River through Mountain Valley with Sky and Crescent Moon*, November 1866, graphite and white gouache on cream wove paper, 4¹³⁄₁₆ × 8¹⁵⁄₁₆ in., Cooper-Hewitt, National Design Museum, Smithsonian Institution, Gift of Louis P. Church, 1917-4-1092, Photograph: Matt Flynn

Fig. 26. Frederic Edwin Church, *Winter Sunset from Olana*, c. 1871–72, oil on buff academy board, 8½ × 13 in., OL.1976.13

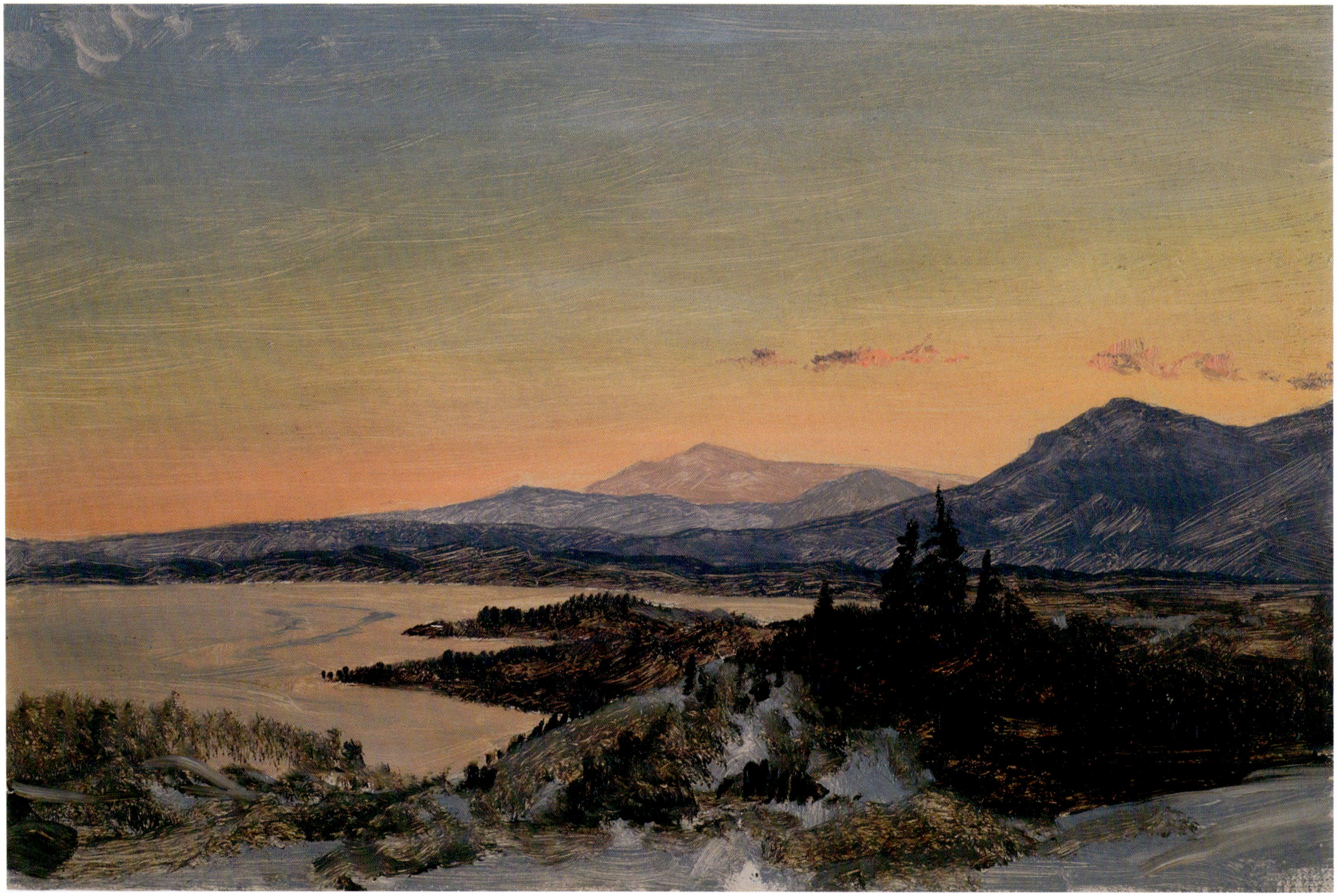

so subtly into oil in the finished painting and in the related sketch *Winter Sunset from Olana* (fig. 26).

Many visitors to the property penned descriptions that resembled the perceptions Church set down in his richly colored renderings of breathtaking skies. A guest "sitting spell-bound at the window" witnessed and carefully recorded a phenomenon similar to the one Church had articulated in *Winter Sunset from Olana* (fig. 26): "the sunset was marvelous. After it, while the sky was full of calm color, scarlet, orange, yellow, primrose, pale green, pale blue—up into deep blue—the sharp young moon came out, and the Hudson reflected it & the pale green and blue of the sky. . . ."[49]

Church, like many of his contemporaries, had a sketching vernacular: adjectives such as "brilliant" and "luminous" often appear in his letters as in his pencil drawings. Color notations such as "red orange" and "orange red" and "red" distinguish the subtle variations in the fall foliage, while "dazzling" is reserved for sunsets. "Intense dark blue" and "very luminous" specify the interplay of light and reflection in the sky and in the water. "Delicious" was a favored word, used frequently, to characterize both colors and effects.

Church at times used a numbered key with corresponding entries noted in the margins of his drawings (fig. 25). At other times, and in numerous instances when sketching from his own property, Church scribbled notes directly into the composition, portraying with immediacy his excitement at the fleeting effects. Recording a fading July sunset, the graphite drawing *Sunset from Olana* (fig. 27) is annotated with words such as "rich," "delicious," "smoky," and "dull," as well as color notations like "purple" and "greenish."

In the fall of 1867, Church expressed his desire to obtain new parcels of land so that he might execute his grander vision for the property: "Come and see my two new pictures which I am finishing—see my new buildings and other improvements. . . . I want to secure if possible . . . every rood of ground that I shall ever require to make my farm perfect—"[50] Church's artistic success and popularity made all of his activities newsworthy. A published account of that same year outlined Church's scheme to increase his acreage and build a new home:

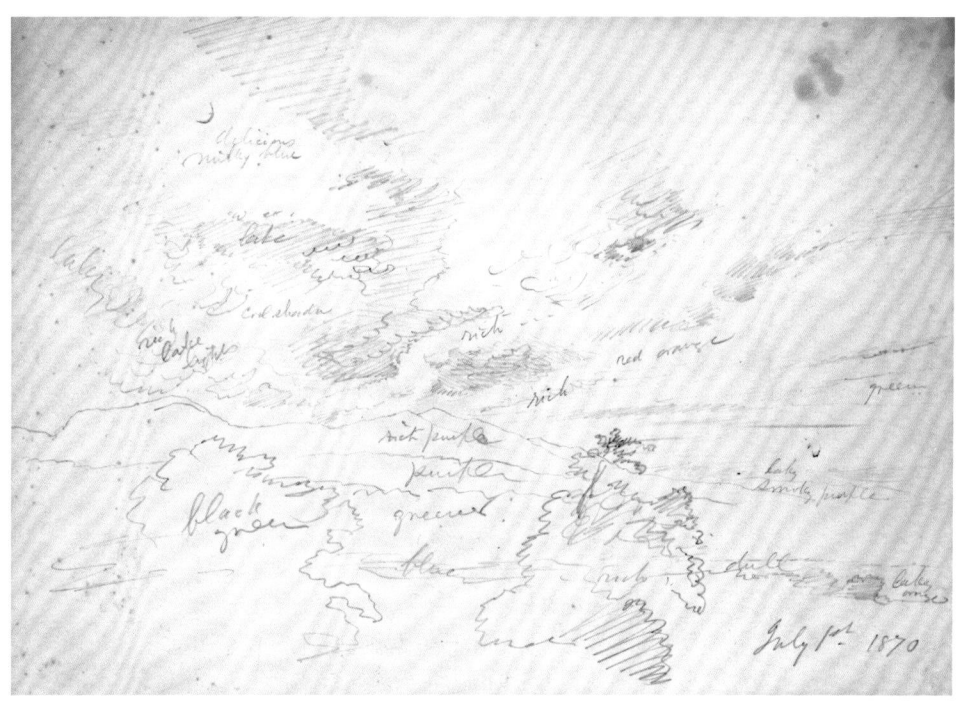

Fig. 27. Frederic Edwin Church, *Sunset from Olana*, July 1, 1870, graphite on heavy white wove paper, 9⅛ × 12⅝ in., Cooper-Hewitt, National Design Museum, Smithsonian Institution, Gift of Louis P. Church, 1917-4-282, Photograph: Ken Pelka

Mr. C . . . is now employed in laying out roads, planting trees, and, in various ways, rendering the place attractive. His cottage, of the Gothic style, is nestled in a vale, where the stretch of interior landscape reminds one of Devonshire, England. But this residence is only temporary. He proposes to build on the hill overlooking the river and, and taking in the sun-set view on the river and the grand outline of the Catskills. On this elevation now stands his studio, to which he introduced us.[51]

To help fulfill his plan for a new house overlooking the river, Church bought an additional eighteen acres later that same month, at last acquiring the hilltop, with its precipice facing the river. To his friend and patron William Henry Osborn, Church wrote:

I only wish and wait for an opportunity to take you and Mrs. Osborn there of a summer evening, when the sun's rays slant across the hills and if you don't both pronounce the views the most beautiful and wonderful—then deprive me of palette and brushes and set me at the desk of some confiding merchant to embarrass his affairs for him.[52]

The land secure, Church embarked on an eighteen-month-long trip to Europe and the Middle East, during which he produced hundreds of wonderful drawings and oil studies. These travels also directly influenced his concept for his future house and the extended grounds.

In November 1867 the Churches, their son Frederic Joseph, who had been born the previous fall, and Isabel's mother, Mrs. Carnes, began their journey. After brief stops in Paris and London, they sailed for Egypt, where they spent only a few nights before continuing on to Beirut. His thoughts never far from home, in another letter to Osborn, Church compared the pleasantness of their Mediterranean voyage to traveling on the Hudson: "The trip from Alexandria to Beyrout was really lovely, the sea being as smooth as the Hudson River."[53]

Isabel, "Freddie," and Mrs. Carnes remained safely in Beirut while Church undertook an expedition to Petra, Jordan, memorialized in the 1874 *El Khasné, Petra* (fig. 28), the only finished studio painting Church kept for himself and his family. In a departure from his sweeping panoramic landscapes, Church used the rock *siq* to focus and frame the distinctive bright pinky orange facade of the Khasné—once thought to be a treasure-house, now known to be a tomb.[54]

The Khasné was only one of many architectural marvels that fascinated the artist throughout the trip. Church had prepared himself for the experience months earlier by executing renderings of iconic old-world buildings under the tutelage of an architect in New York City.[55] While in the Middle East, Church visited monumental sites such as Hagia Sophia, Istanbul; the ruins at Baalbek, Lebanon; the Church of the Holy

Fig. 28. Frederic Edwin Church, *El Khasné, Petra*, by April 1874, oil on canvas, 60½ × 50¼ in., OL.1981.10

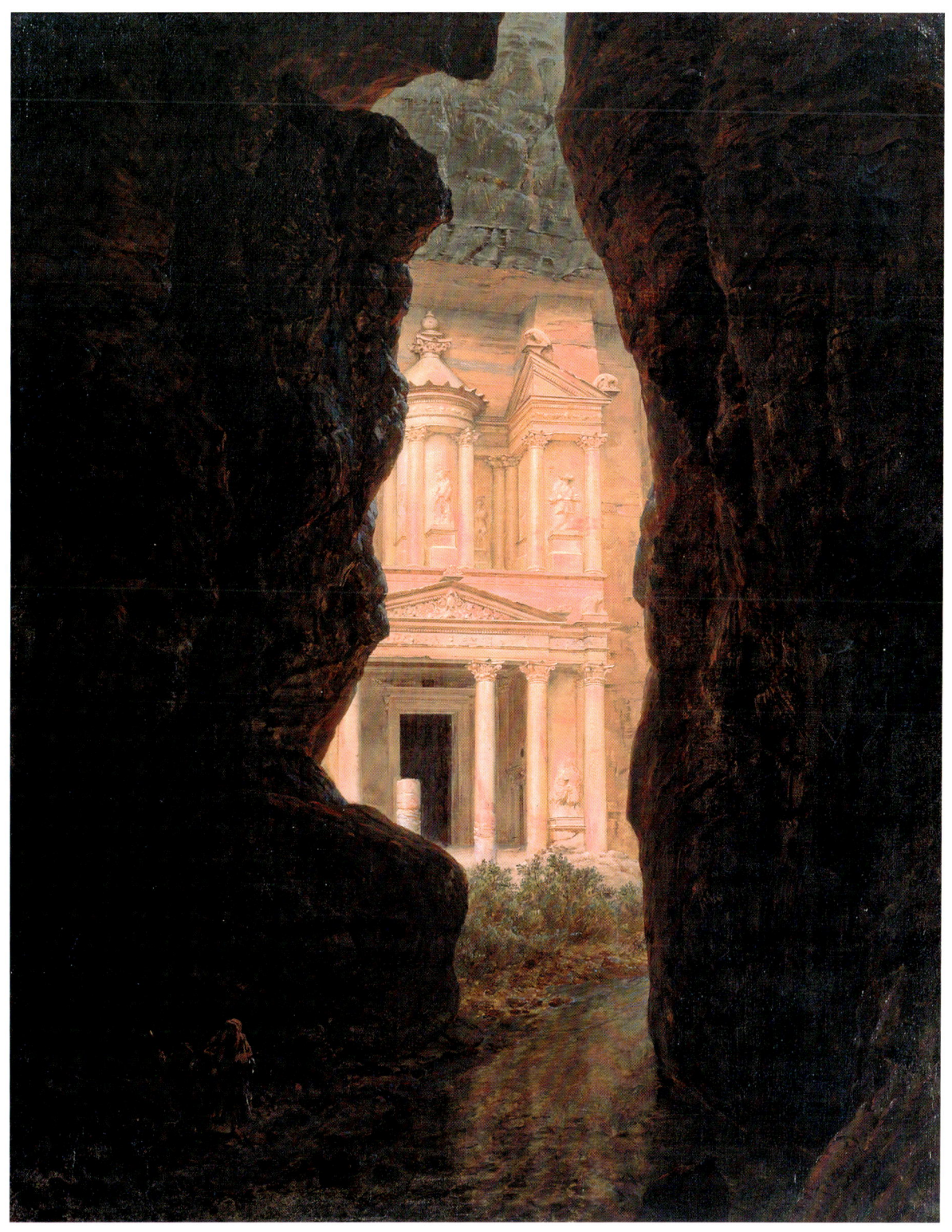

Sepulchre and the Tower of David, both in Jerusalem; as well as private homes. These experiences fueled his desire to build:

> These oriental Cities are strange to our eyes the houses are usually of stone with stone vaulted roofs. . . . The Dwellings are often quite grand They have a large room called the court in the center often 30 × 50 feet or larger—and perhaps 30 feet high and smaller rooms on each side these rooms are all paved with marble in patterns. . . . —I have got new and excellent ideas about building since I came abroad.[56]

Beyond admiring the structures, Church also appreciated how architecture could function in its surrounding topography:

> Beyrout is beautifully situated at the foot of a high range of mountains which are now snow clad, and the mountain sides are dotted all over with villages, convents, &c. From the houses on the summit of the hill on which the city is built, the views are charming. The house tops are flat and generally have a room or two built upon them with stairs leading to the roof, so that it is convenient as well as agreeable to enjoy frequently the fine panorama.[57]

Here, and elsewhere throughout the trip, Church admired hilltop homes with their impressive views, and he could not help but think of the similar advantages of his newly acquired property. As he wrote to a friend, "I have got a perfect situation and a perfect site on it."[58]

From the Middle East, the family traveled to Austria, Bavaria, and Switzerland. By October they were in Rome, staying among friends and the American artistic community. That winter, their son Theodore Winthrop was born. Church reported home, "We are almost as comfortable around our table—illuminated by a carcel lamp and warmed by an oak fire—as if we were lighted by petroleum and basked by hickory coals in our own cottage— But—the Tiber is not the Hudson."[59] These nostalgic and nationalistic sentiments reflected both Church's personal musings and the prevailing patriotic attitudes of Americans toward their native scenery in the mid-nineteenth century. These same feelings were conveyed by a contemporary writer, George William Curtis, in *Lotus-Eating*: "A few evenings afterward I was standing with a fellow-countryman upon the terrace of the castle of Heidelberg, looking out toward the glorious opening of the Neckar Valley upon the plain of the Rhine, and was severely taken to task by him for my indiscreet Rhenish raptures and absolute light-speaking of the Hudson."[60] Church, while in Rome, made the short walk from his studio near the Piazza del Popolo to the bank of the Tiber and captured the river and view across in a pencil sketch flowing over two joined sheets of paper, dated March 18, 1869.[61]

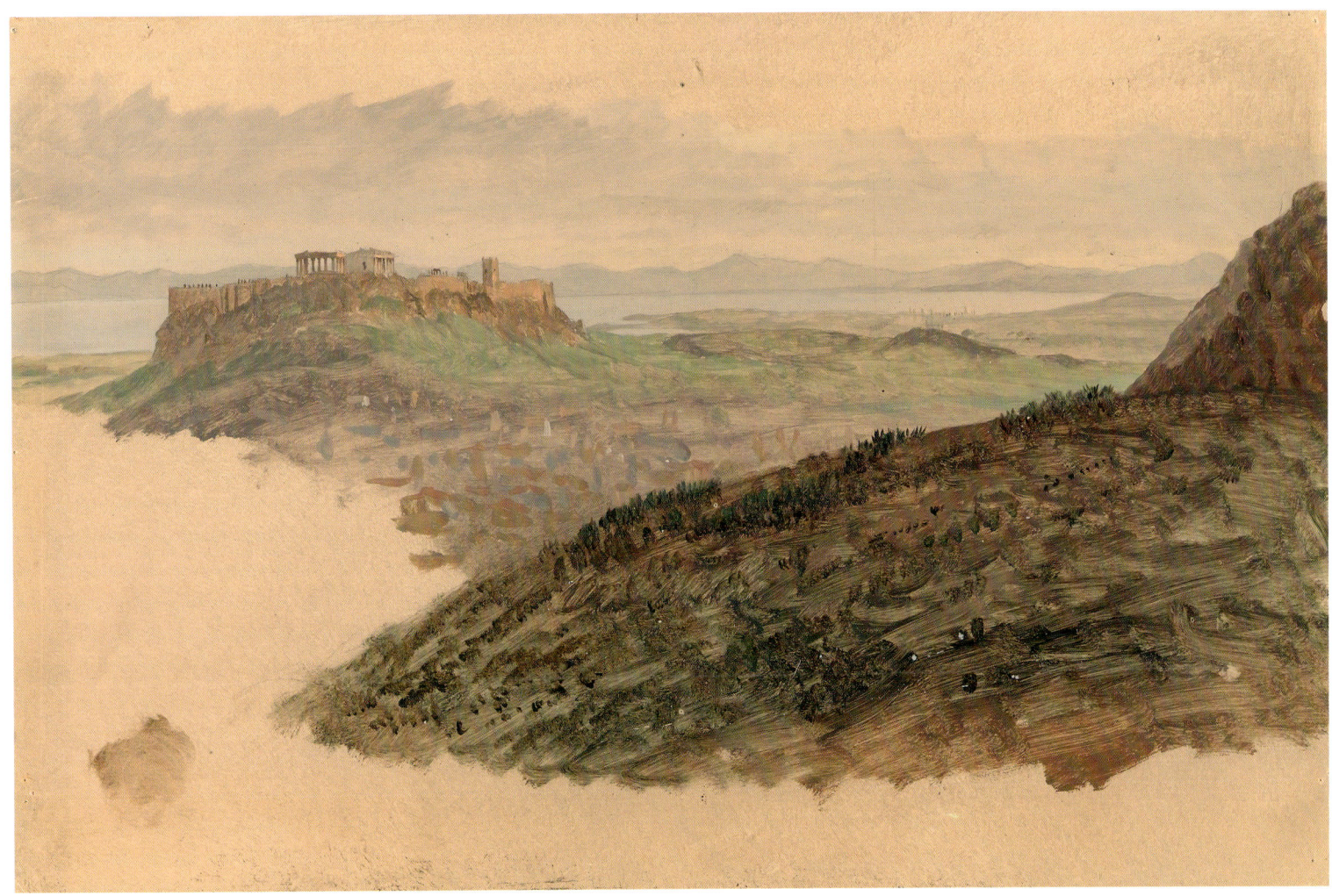

Leaving Isabel, Freddie, Mrs. Carnes, and the new baby in Rome, Church traveled to Greece in April. More than any other building, Church was enraptured by the Parthenon, "working from morning to night," as copious studies in oil and pencil of "the splendid ruins" attest (fig. 29).[62] He expressed his reaction in several extensive letters:

> The Parthenon is certainly the culmination of the genius of man in architecture. Every column, every ornament, every moulding, asserts the superiority which is claimed for even the shattered remains of the once proud temple over all other buildings erected by man. I have made architectural drawings of the Parthenon and fancied before I came to Athens that I had a good idea of its merits. But in reality I knew it not. Daily I study its stones and feel its inexpressible charm of beauty growing upon my senses. I am glad I came here. . . .[63]

Fig. 29. Frederic Edwin Church, *Athens with a View of the Acropolis*, April 1869, oil and graphite on paperboard, 13 × 20⅛ in., Cooper-Hewitt, National Design Museum, Smithsonian Institution, Gift of Louis P. Church, 1917-4-360-a, Photograph: Matt Flynn

Augmenting his depictions and accounts are ninety photographs Church purchased abroad and in New York City. In addition, he brought home an artifact from this sacred locale, as recorded by the *Boston Evening Transcript*: "Church the artist, has brought home many trophies of travel, such as a Bedouin Arab's spear, a suit of Damascus armor, a huge bit of the Parthenon. . . ."[64]

Church was particularly awestruck by this hilltop temple and the commanding view out to the Adriatic Sea and the Hymettus mountains. For Church the Parthenon was the "culmination of the genius of man in architecture." Knowing that he would soon be building, he hoped to take a bit of the "genius" home with him and incorporate it into his site on the Hudson.

During his travels in the Middle East and Europe, Church took advantage of the wide variety of goods available and began the process of acquiring furnishings for his future home. Oriental rugs, ceramics, textiles, and weapons were accumulated and sent back to New York. "I think it would amuse you and Mrs. Osborn to see the medley in the box—for there are rugs—armour—stuffs—curiosities . . . crowded in together, and some of the other boxes have old clothes (Turkish), stones from a house in Damascus, Arab spears—beads from Jerusalem—stones from Petra and 10,000 other things."[65] In Rome, Church purchased close to sixty old master paintings for a room already conceived specifically for their display, a room harkening back to the medieval and Renaissance halls of Europe (fig. 30).[66]

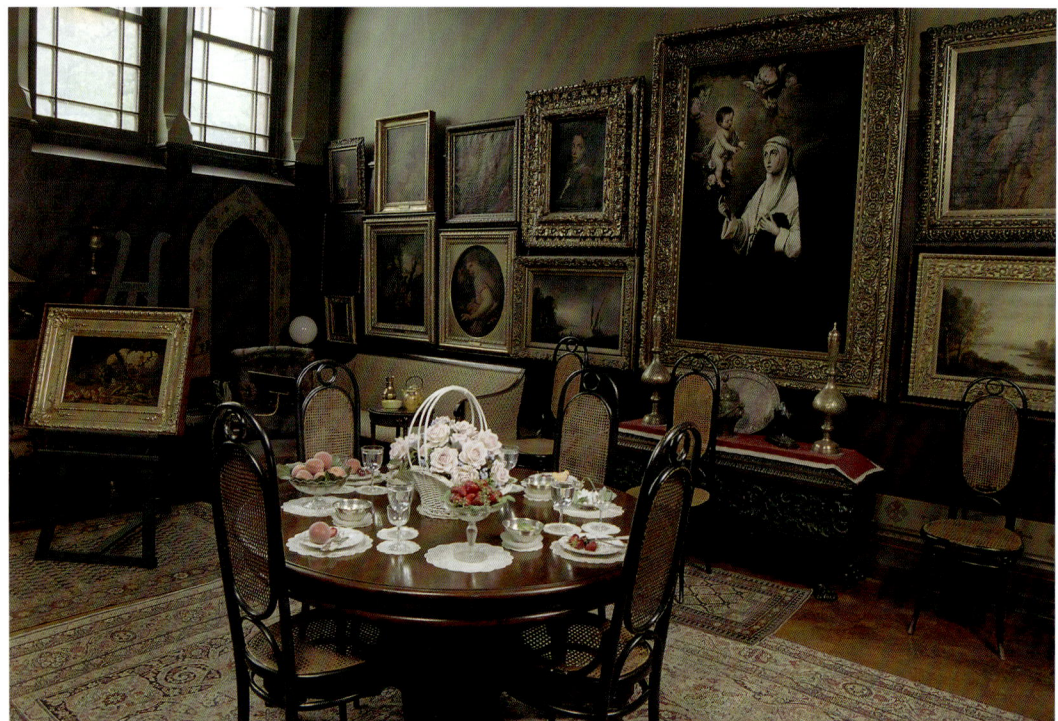

Fig. 30. Nicholas Whitman, *Dining Room at Olana with Old Master Paintings*, photograph, 2003

In the early summer of 1869 the Churches returned to the United States, and Frederic focused on designing and building their new home. The 1870s stretched Church's talents in new directions. Civic duties involved him in committees related to the improvement of Central Park and the development of the Metropolitan Museum of Art in New York City, of which he was a founding trustee. He also nurtured the budding careers of two young men, both sons of family friends: Walter Launt Palmer (1854–1932) and Lockwood de Forest (1850–1932). The Churches celebrated the births of two more children: Louis

Palmer, born April 30, 1870, and a daughter, Isabel Charlotte, affectionately called Downie, on July 17, 1871. Throughout, Church avidly sketched for his own enjoyment and painted exhibition pieces inspired by his trip to Europe and the Middle East, including *Jerusalem from the Mount of Olives* (1870; the Nelson-Atkins Museum of Art, Kansas City, Missouri), *The Parthenon* (1871; the Metropolitan Museum of Art), and *El Khasné, Petra* (1874; fig. 28).

While abroad, ever mindful of the dramatic scenery embracing his new plot of land, Church often remarked on the relation of buildings to their surroundings, from homes in Beirut, castles in Europe, to, ultimately, the Parthenon. Informed by the architecture of Beirut and Damascus, Church endeavored to meld attributes of the homes he had admired in the Middle East—open homes that interacted with their environment—with his own magnificent grounds. He sought a very different result from the wood-framed Cosy Cottage, which sat nestled within the farm. The new house would be of stone, and it would command the Sienghenbergh slope, constituting a crowning feature both within the park and from the river below.

Once home, armed with the ideas, sketches, and photographs he had amassed during his trip to the Middle East, Church hired Calvert Vaux as the architect to help him realize his vision.[67] In 1857, Vaux had published *Villas and Cottages*, a book that laid out his philosophies, with engravings of completed buildings as reference. Vaux asserted that "in country houses the design has to be adapted to the location, and not the location to the design," a principle that could be applied to great advantage when orienting and drafting a showplace for Church's property.[68] Vaux also freely borrowed from all traditions, including non-Western motifs, and therefore was receptive to the ideas with which Church had returned from his trip to Europe and the Middle East.

As co-creator of Central Park, with Frederick Law Olmsted, Vaux was well known; he was also the brother-in-law of Church's friend and fellow painter Jervis McEntee (1828–1891). While Vaux and Church worked on the latter's house, they served together on committees for the Metropolitan Museum of Art. Church also acted as a commissioner for Central Park during this time, being nominated by both Vaux and Olmsted, who noted: "Church's name was first suggested by Vaux, and we both did what we could to secure his appointment. . . ."[69]

The evolution of the building from conception to realization is well documented in both the progressing plans and elevations by Vaux and the hundreds of sketches by Church (fig. 31).[70] Church's

Fig. 31. Office of Vaux, Withers & Co., Architects, *Architectural Drawing, Plan of Principal Floor, Olana*, June 23, 1870, ink and watercolor on off-white paper, 18³⁄₁₆ × 18½ in., OL.1980.1621

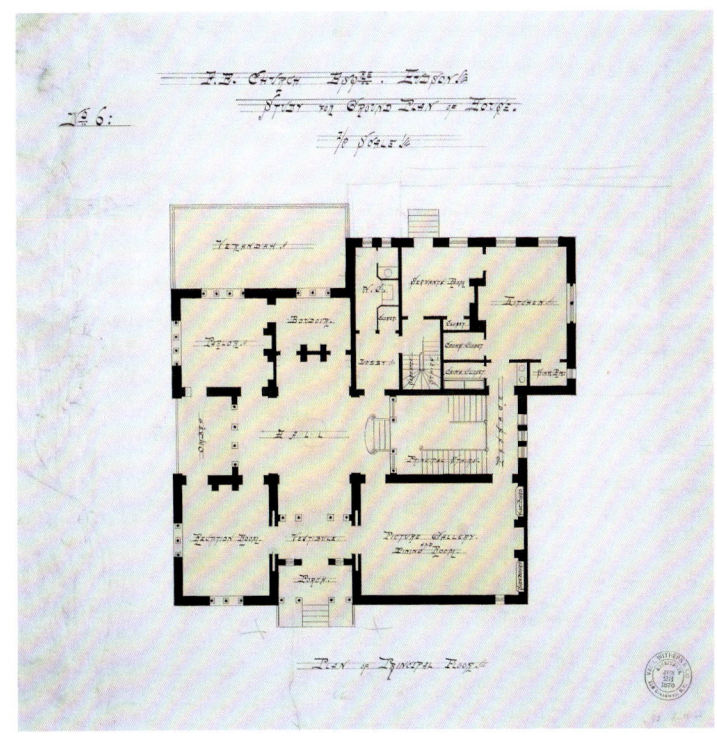

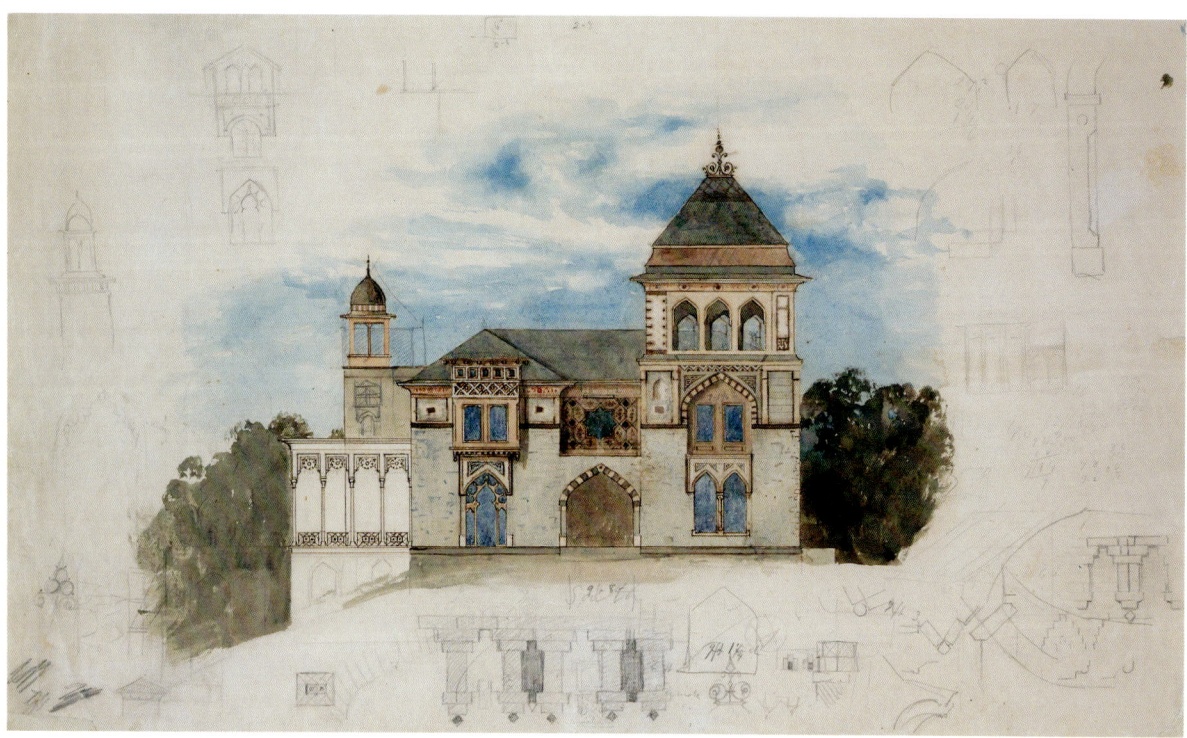

Fig. 32. Frederic Edwin Church, *Southwest Facade,
Olana,* c. 1870, watercolor, ink, and graphite on
paper, 13 × 21¹⁵⁄₁₆ in., OL.1980.40

are of dizzying variety, ranging from multiple stair railing options doodled on a scrap of
paper to interior stencil motifs drawn from his numerous books on Persian architecture
to very finished watercolor studies of individual facades illustrating ornamental tile and
brickwork (fig. 32). Beyond the schemes for clearly decorative work are other ideas
about window placement and the interrelation of rooms. Certainly, Church was also
interested in orienting the house and its flow around the outstanding features of his
property. As the views made up one of the most significant attributes, questions of window placement, orientation, and shape were paramount (fig. 33). Essentially, from the
house one would look out at a "living landscape painting," with the river and mountains as background and a middle ground and foreground landscaped by Church himself.

Numerous published sources inspired Church and served as reference material.
Vaux's *Villas and Cottages* (1857) probably influenced Church's choice of architect. For the
landscape and the location of the house, Church surely consulted Charles H. J. Smith's
Landscape Gardening (1853), which recommended that instead of providing "a *continuous*
view of the mansion," the approach road allow "a striking glimpse from a turn or two
in the roadway"; that "the view from the house should. . . . surpass all others. . . ."; and
that "of all the varied materials in the composition of natural scenery, there is none that
produces more beauty, variety and interest than water. . . ."[71] For the decorative details
Church found inspiration in the plates of Jules Bourgoin's *Les Arts arabes* (1868) and

Pascal Coste's *Monuments modernes de la Perse* (1867), as recounted by Lockwood de Forest: "I was a great deal with Mr. Church for nearly 10 years. I staid [sic] with him painting in his studio and going over his plans for the house he was building, and studying all the books on Persian and Oriental architecture in the evenings."[72] Church had ready and continual access to all of these volumes, which belonged to his personal library.[73]

Vaux and Church ultimately executed a building that aimed for a gracious transition between the natural surroundings and the living spaces, allowing family and guests to move easily from the exotically furnished interior onto the grounds beyond. The central Court Hall opened onto the park through the Ombra, serving as an informal entrance with large stone steps to the south lawn (fig. 34). This space provided "a contrast of light and shade" and "shelter from the weather"; it was mostly contained within

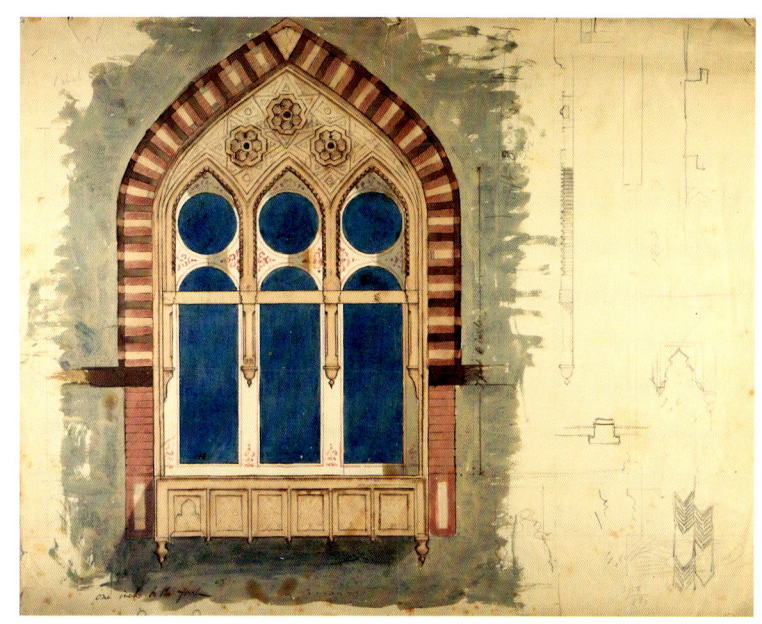

Fig. 33. Frederic Edwin Church, *Architectural Sketch for Window, East Facade, Olana*, c. 1870, watercolor on paper, 14⅞ × 18½ in., OL.1982.666-recto

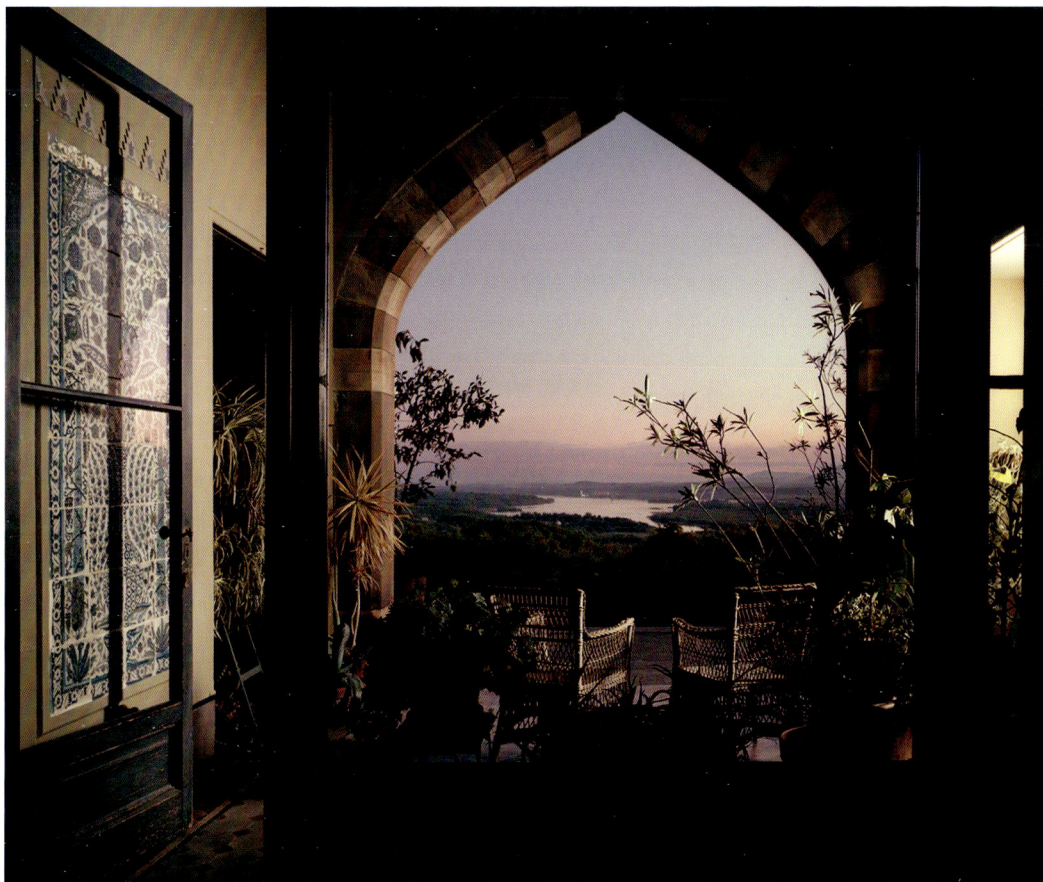

Fig. 34. Len Jenshel, *View South through the Ombra at Olana*, photograph, 1988

57

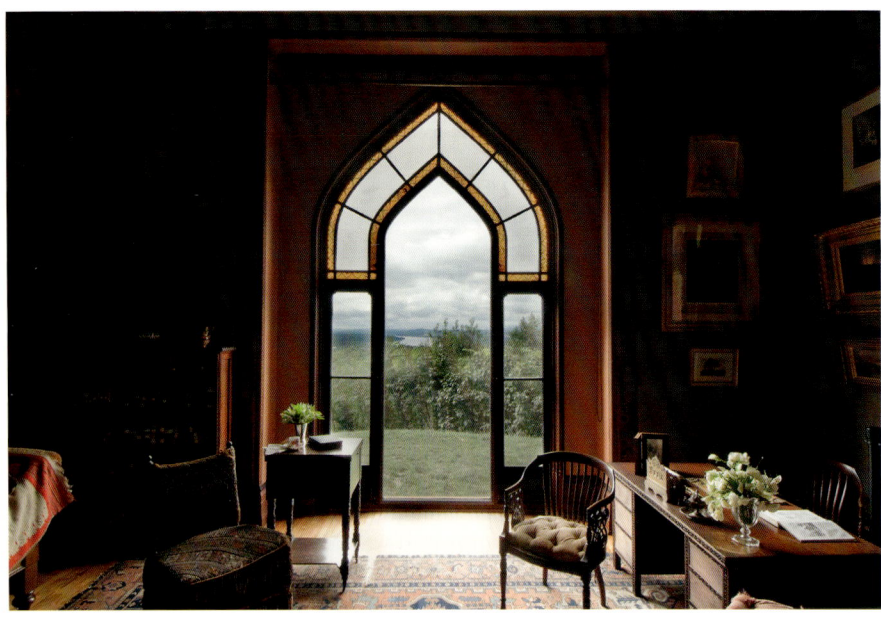

Fig. 35. Nicholas Whitman, *Sitting Room at Olana with View of the Hudson*, photograph, 2008

the building, its southern side an open arch to a large porchlike stone slab.[74] The Ombra was also a place of repose, serving as an open-air conservatory during the summer and in the colder months protected by a storm window. A guest observed that "in the winter the open porch in front of Mr. Church's house is enclosed & filled with plants, so as you come down the great staircase you feel as if you were in a sunny bower. . . ."[75]

On the west side of the house, a covered porch, sometimes called by the Churches and their friends the veranda, at other times the piazza, was accessed by double doors from the sitting room and library. From this veranda one achieved a panoramic view, described by a journalist: "From the room on the West you step out upon a large portico, overhanging the precipitous descent towards the Hudson, and overlooking the mountain and river scenery,—"[76] A visitor had a similar reaction: "I wandered around & got into a kind of verandah, which commanded another beautiful view. I propped my self on the banister and looked until it disappeared in darkness."[77]

The layout of the house and its high position on the Sienghenbergh encouraged the cooling summer breezes to flow through the house from the Ombra and veranda. The interplay of the building and nature was further enhanced by planting vines on the house, similar to the plantings at Cosy Cottage. The use of "enclosing verdure" was considered "appropriate decoration" at the time: "by vine and herbage, flower and fruit, the dwelling is made to seem a growth rather than a construction . . . and a true picturesque effect obtained."[78]

From inside the house, large arched windows—each a unique shape and size—provided "frames" for views of the river, the parkland, and the lake Church had created. To enhance these "pictures," Church designed elaborate decorative surrounds for some of the windows that mimicked the idea of a frame around a painting. This "framing" was especially dramatic in the Court Hall and Sitting Room (fig. 35). A journalist described the effect looking out from the Churches' bedroom: "A window of a single pane of plate glass is surrounded by a frame, in such a manner as to give one the impression of gazing at a beautiful picture of river and mountains instead of looking through a window."[79] Church himself noted with satisfaction: "The house will be a curiosity in Architecture but it will be convenient and the picture from each window will be really marvelous."[80]

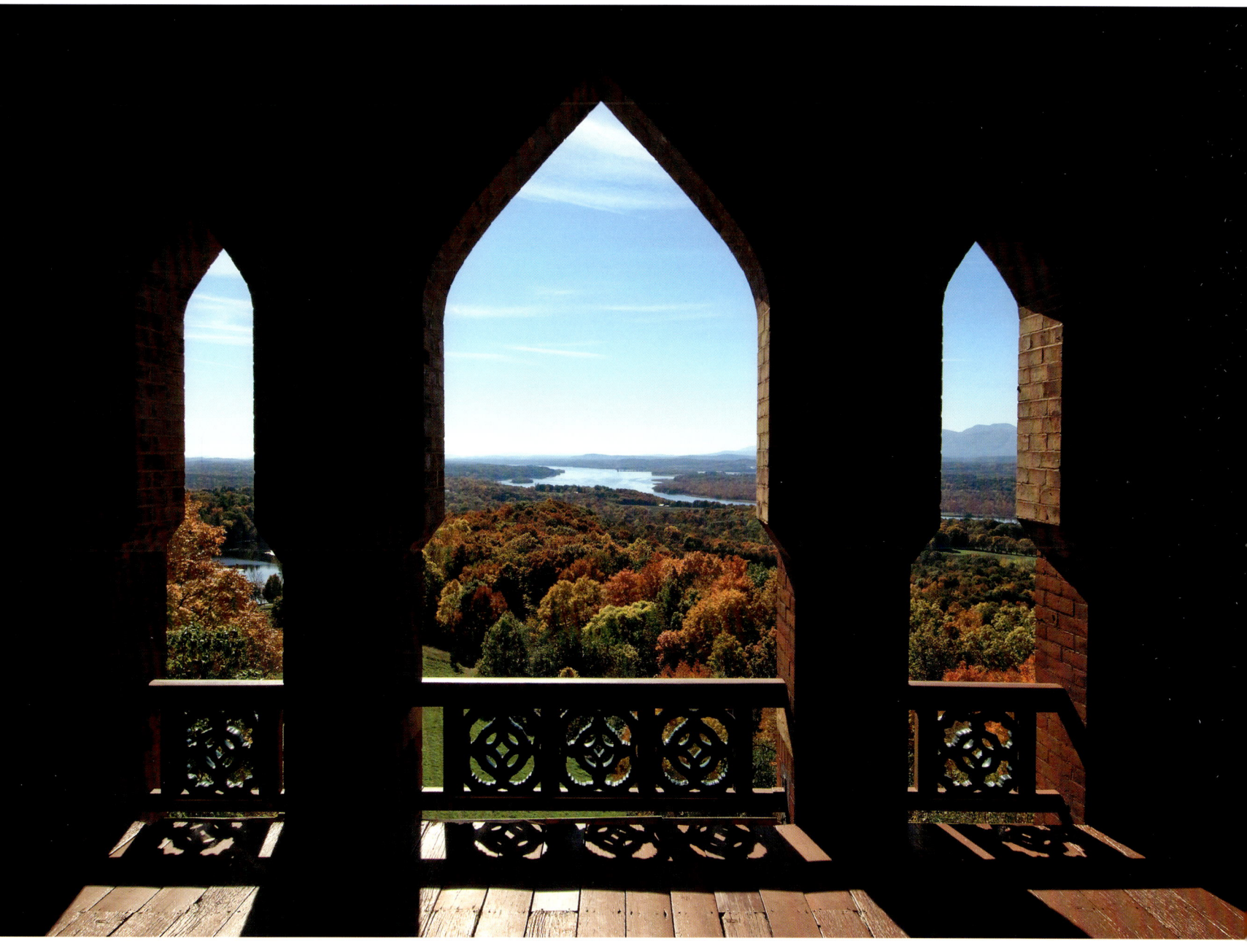

The Bell Tower on the southeastern corner of the building made the ultimate viewing platform, framing the view in a trio of pointed arches: "Mrs. Church took us up into the tower to see the sunset—a regular tower—with arched openings painted & decorated with Mexican tiles—Of course I am not going to describe the sunset to you—but I felt all through it that we ought to be looking at it on our knees" (fig. 36).[81]

Fig. 36. Nicholas Whitman, *View South through the Bell Tower at Olana*, photograph, 2008

An article written early in the building process gave a clear account of the attributes of the building site's primary river orientation and Church's efforts to best situate the new house in relation to his views:

The artist who, of all our artists, has the quickest eye for beauty has set his seal of choice on this part of the Hudson. . . . Directly across the river and on the grandest of hill-tops, a shiny platform shows the basements of a country house which Mr. Church is building at the summit of extensive lands, and near the rustic lodge and studio he had many Summers rested, and where in secluded leisure several of his masterpieces have been finished. . . . What a marvelous thirty-mile view extended as a back-view beyond it! Its front view westward is indescribably superb, uniting river and mountains.[82]

Fig. 37. Nicholas Whitman, *East Facade of Olana*, photograph, 2008

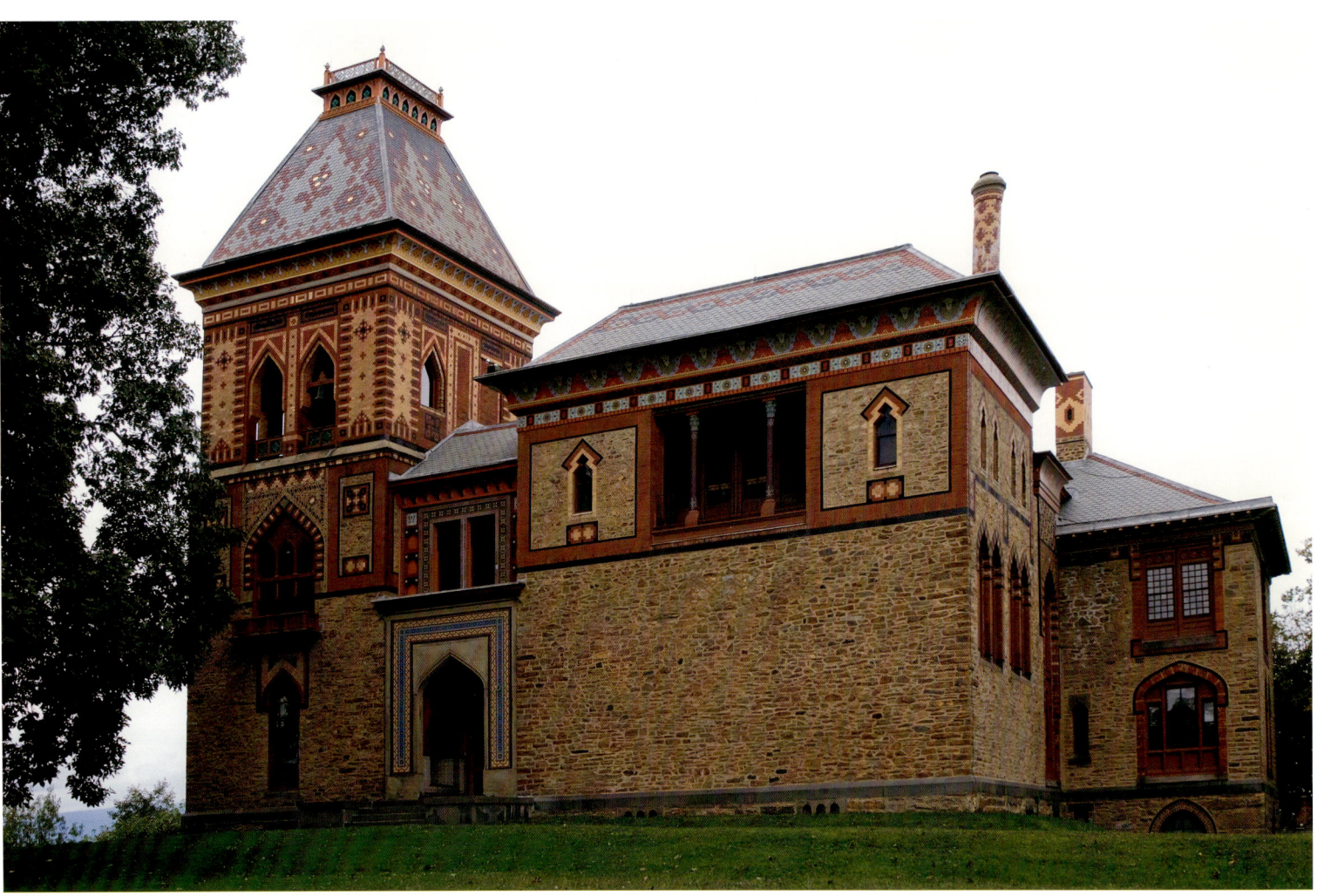

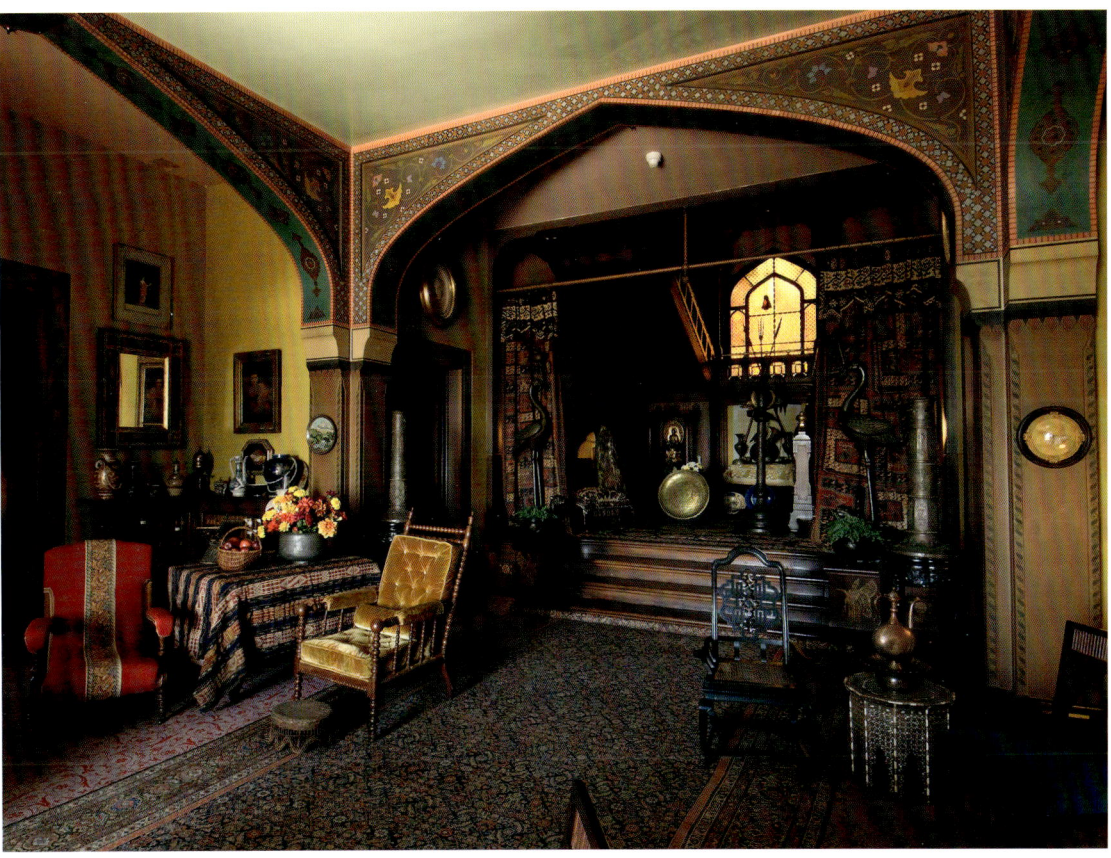

Fig. 38. Nicholas Whitman, *The Court Hall*, photograph, 2008

Yet the house served as more than a viewing lens; it was also a blank "three-dimensional canvas" on which Church could "paint." His exterior scheme included tiles from China, England, and Spain, elaborately painted cornices, ornamental brickwork, and Japanese teapots as finials (fig. 37). Inside, the same interest in objects from diverse ages and cultures formed a unique ensemble portrayed as a "museum of fine arts, rich in bronzes, paintings, sculptures, and antique and artistic specimens from all over the world" (fig. 38).[83] As completed, the new home reflected the era, as well as the exceptional exuberance and imagination of its creator. There is no aspect of the decoration of the building that does not bear his artistic imprint.

The lure of his paintbrush and pencil constantly pulled Church away from construction. Sketches from this period convey the virtuosity of the artist—his ability to capture exquisite color and to quickly fix on paper fleeting and temporal effects. All the works reveal a man who had become so completely familiar with his environment that their rendering had become second nature, allowing him to focus on the ever-changing weather conditions, times of day, seasons, and qualities of light.

"The winter scenery here is marvelous," Church wrote to a friend, trying to entice him up for a visit. "The weather is splendid, mild, clear and quiet. Gorgeous sunset and brilliant nights." He reported that the young Churches, who thrived on skating and sleighing, "are preposterously well—cheeks, chins, noses, all rosy—and their spirits are unquenchable." As for himself, "I am painting small pictures—one nearly done—a view from near the house site. . . ."[84] Numerous dated and undated sketches in oils and pencil, as well as more finished depictions of winter, were the fruit of the artist's enthusiasm and a recess from building endeavors.

Snow Scene, Olana, inscribed "Feb 71," was painted from the studio. It shows Quarry Hill to Red Hill and the beginnings of the lake, a major feature of the property produced by dredging the "muck" from swampy ground and selling it to a local farmer (fig. 39).[85] In *View from Olana in the Snow*, Church ascended for a loftier view, extending his breadth of vision to include Overlook Mountain and the Shawangunks (fig. 40). Perhaps the artist hints at approaching spring in the melting ice on the Hudson and the warm-colored earth and grass peeking through the snow-covered foreground. Detectable in the middle ground of both sketches are the graceful curves of the South Road winding

Fig. 39. Frederic Edwin Church, *Snow Scene, Olana*, February 1871, oil on paper, mounted on canvas, 12¼ × 19½ in., Private collection, Photograph courtesy Olana Research Collection

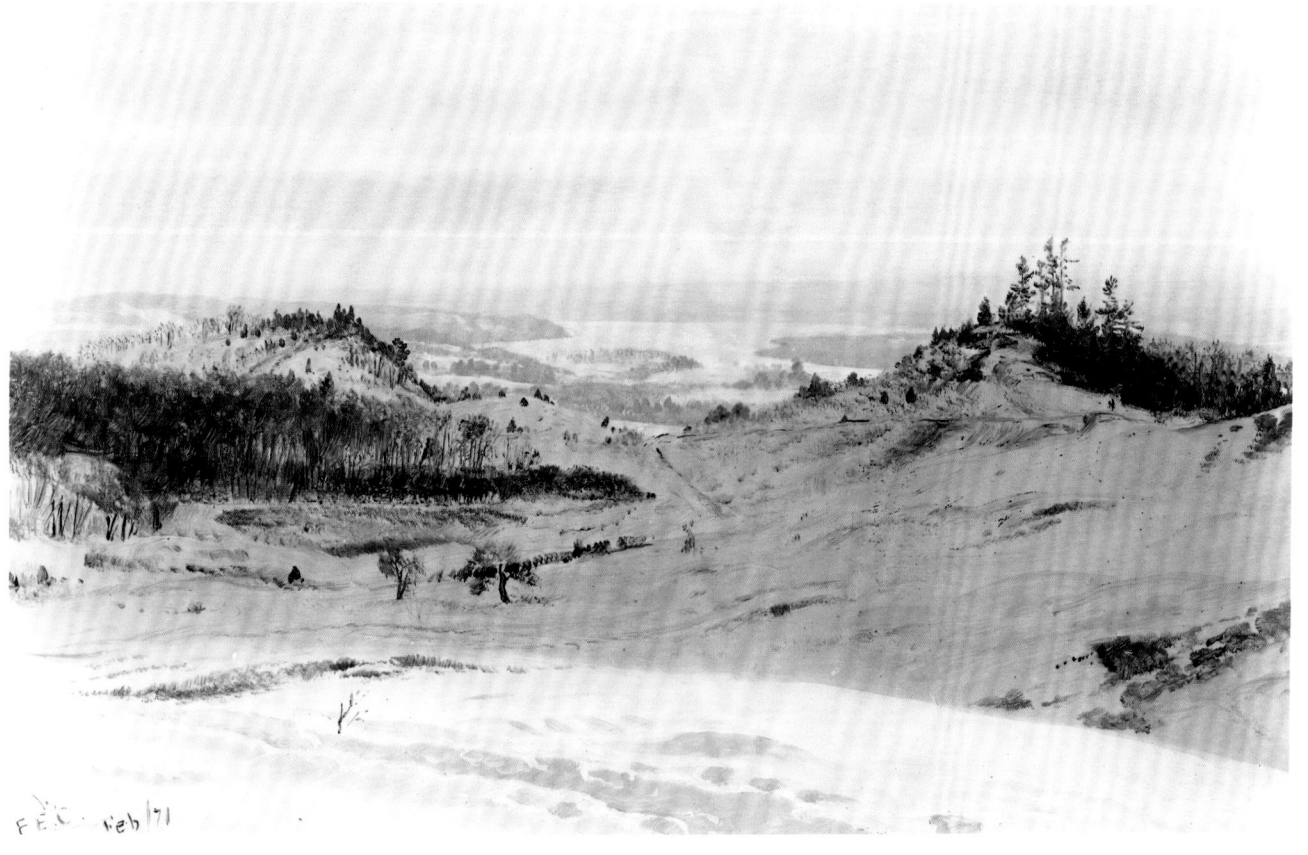

FE̲C̲ · Feb/71

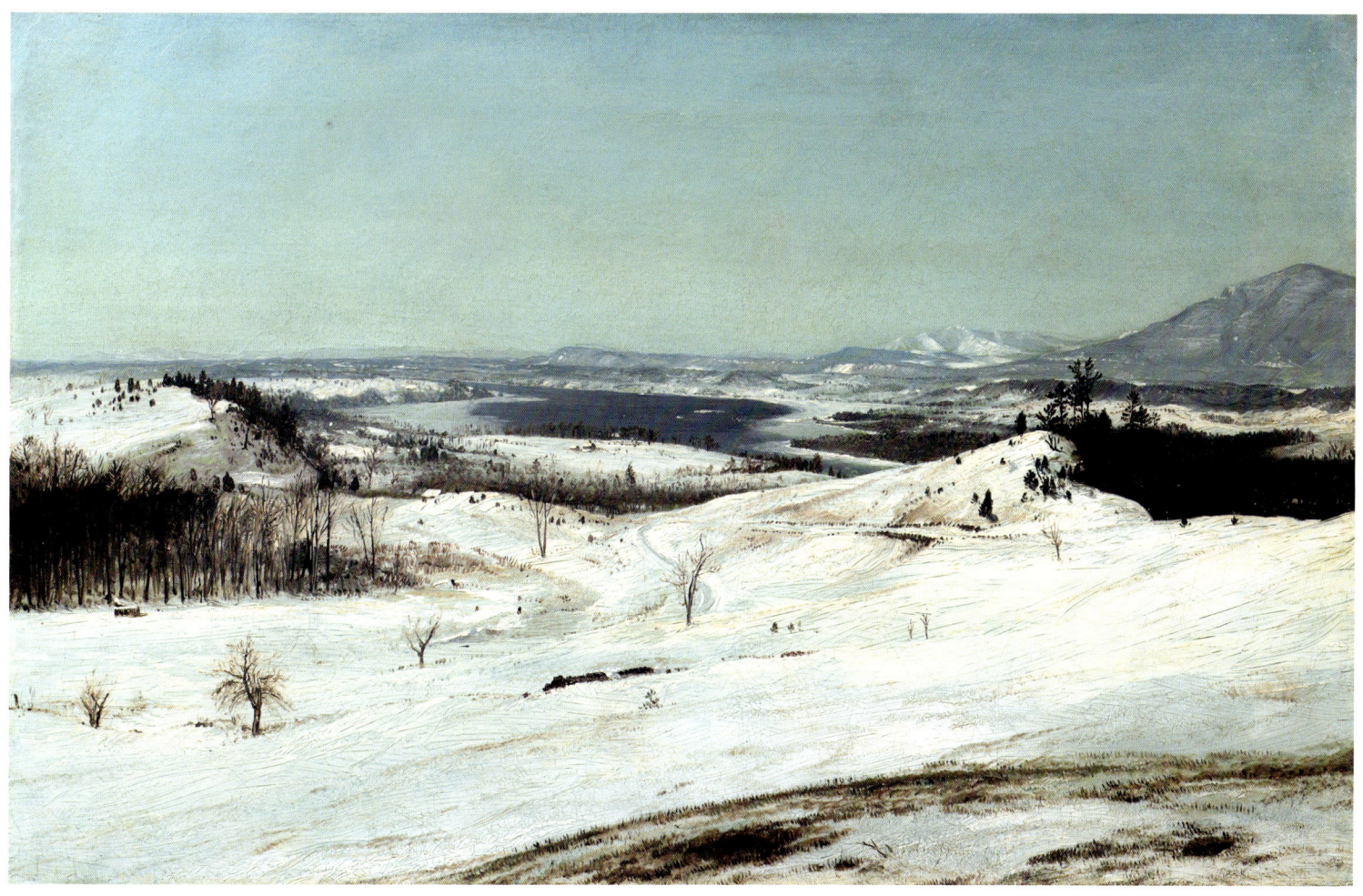

up the hillside past artfully placed trees toward the freestanding studio and eventually to the new building site.

Changing his format in *The Hudson Valley in Winter from Olana*, Church aimed for the effect of "The river a clear mirror of ice," the frozen water reflecting the pink tints in the sky (fig. 41).[86] The vertical canvas opens up to a bright blue sky, high fluffy clouds, and a wonderful recession into space not present in the other works. In their subdued palette and celestial restraint, all three of these very finished sketches—oils on paper that the artist mounted to canvas and framed for display in his home—contrast strikingly with Church's signature vivid skies.

With the pause in house building during the winter, and removed from the daily New York City art scene, Church had the time to make "a study from my studio window of a sunsets [*sic*] or twilight nearly every day...."[87] Even in cold weather, the artist ventured out to paint on the grounds. Working quickly, he captured a fleeting brilliant orange

Fig. 40. Frederic Edwin Church, *View from Olana in the Snow*, c. 1871, oil on paper on board, 13½ × 21¼ in., Colby College Museum of Art, The Lunder Collection

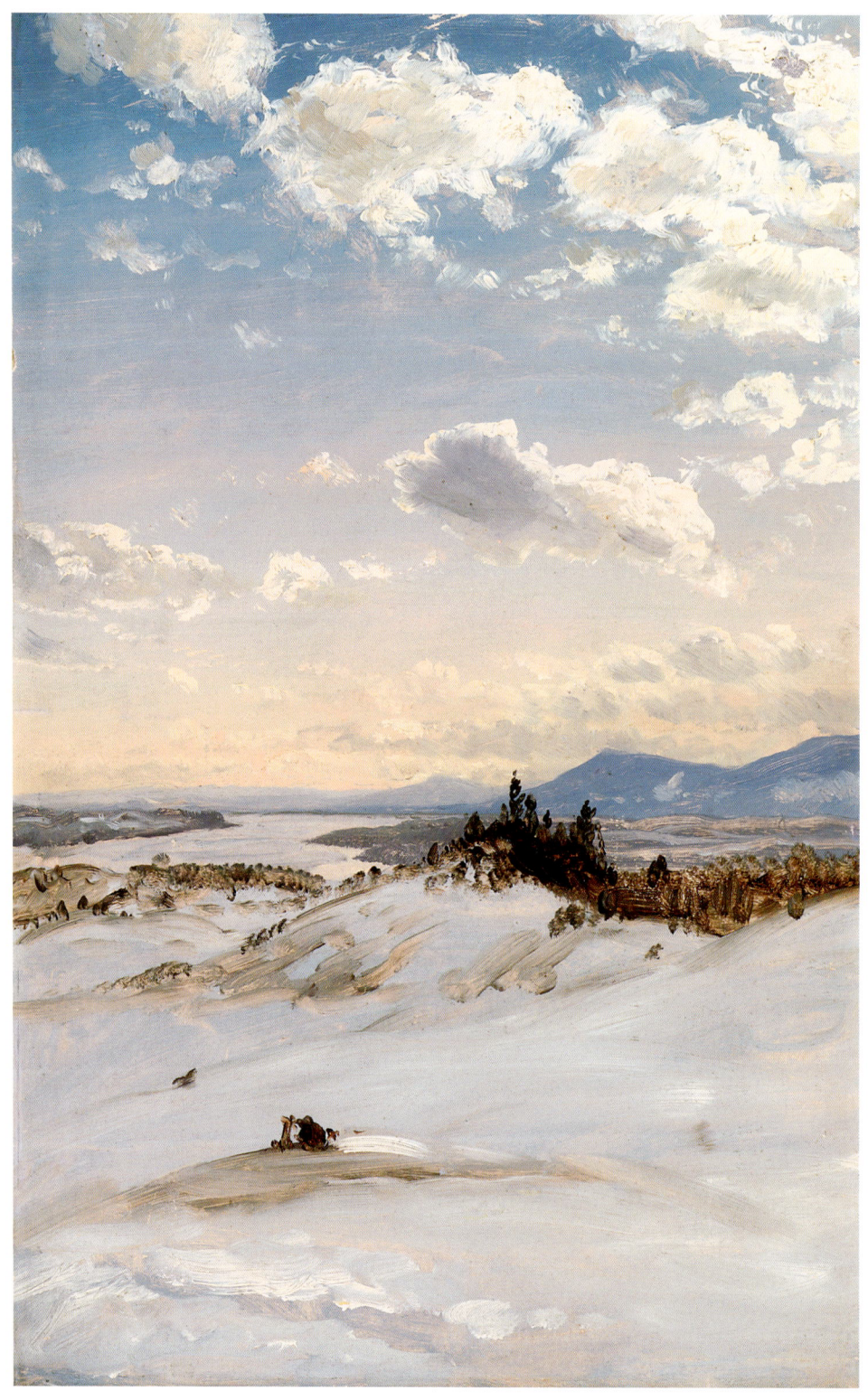

Fig. 41. Frederic Edwin Church, *The Hudson Valley in Winter from Olana*, c. 1871–72, oil on paper mounted on canvas, 20¼ × 13 in., OL.1981.14

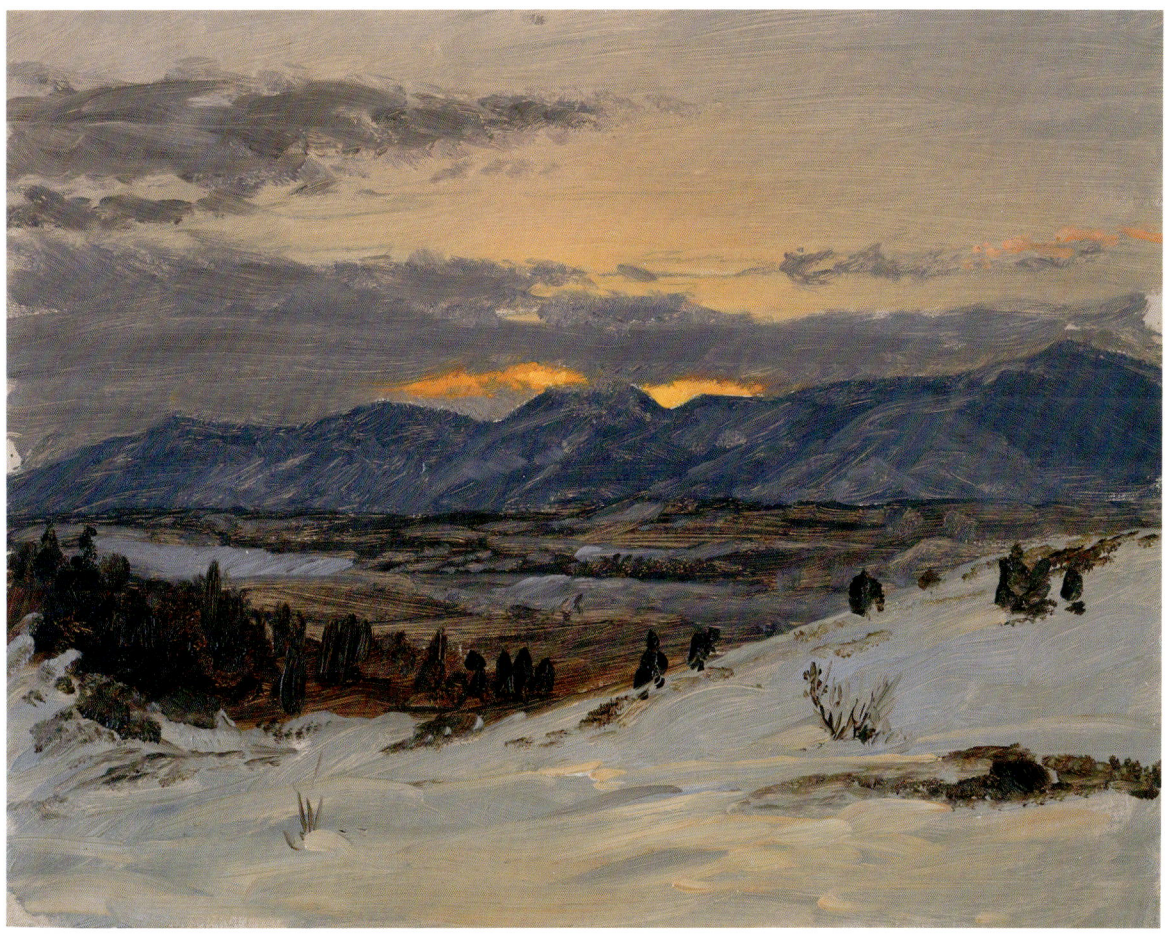

sunset glowing beyond Indian Head Mountain in *Winter Twilight from Olana* (fig. 42), which is intensified by the blue-gray mountains below and the paler blue-gray clouds above. The sketch was most likely executed from an upper bend in Bethune Road.

With the spring thaw, Church turned his attention again to construction, teasing his good friend Palmer to come down to the site and "dig, build and chisel."[88] He and Isabel had their hands full with their newborn daughter, Church writing, "I have been so occupied with our new baby that I haven't had time to write to you or anyone else unless the business was pressing."[89] The farm came alive again, delighting Church with its beauty and its bounty: "The farm is Magnificent— Such a show of bloom on the fruit trees the world never saw. The season is marked by the extraordinary display—"[90]

Summers brought new colors and unpredictable weather conditions. *Sunset across the Hudson Valley* (fig. 43), inscribed "June 70" with the butt end of the paintbrush, exhibits the rich green foliage and grass that led Church to boast, "see how beautiful we are— I mean the scenery of course. Plenty of rain has glorified the country. . . ."[91] The verdant

Fig. 42. Frederic Edwin Church, *Winter Twilight from Olana*, c. 1871–72, oil on off-white academy board, 10 1/16 × 13 in., OL.1976.4

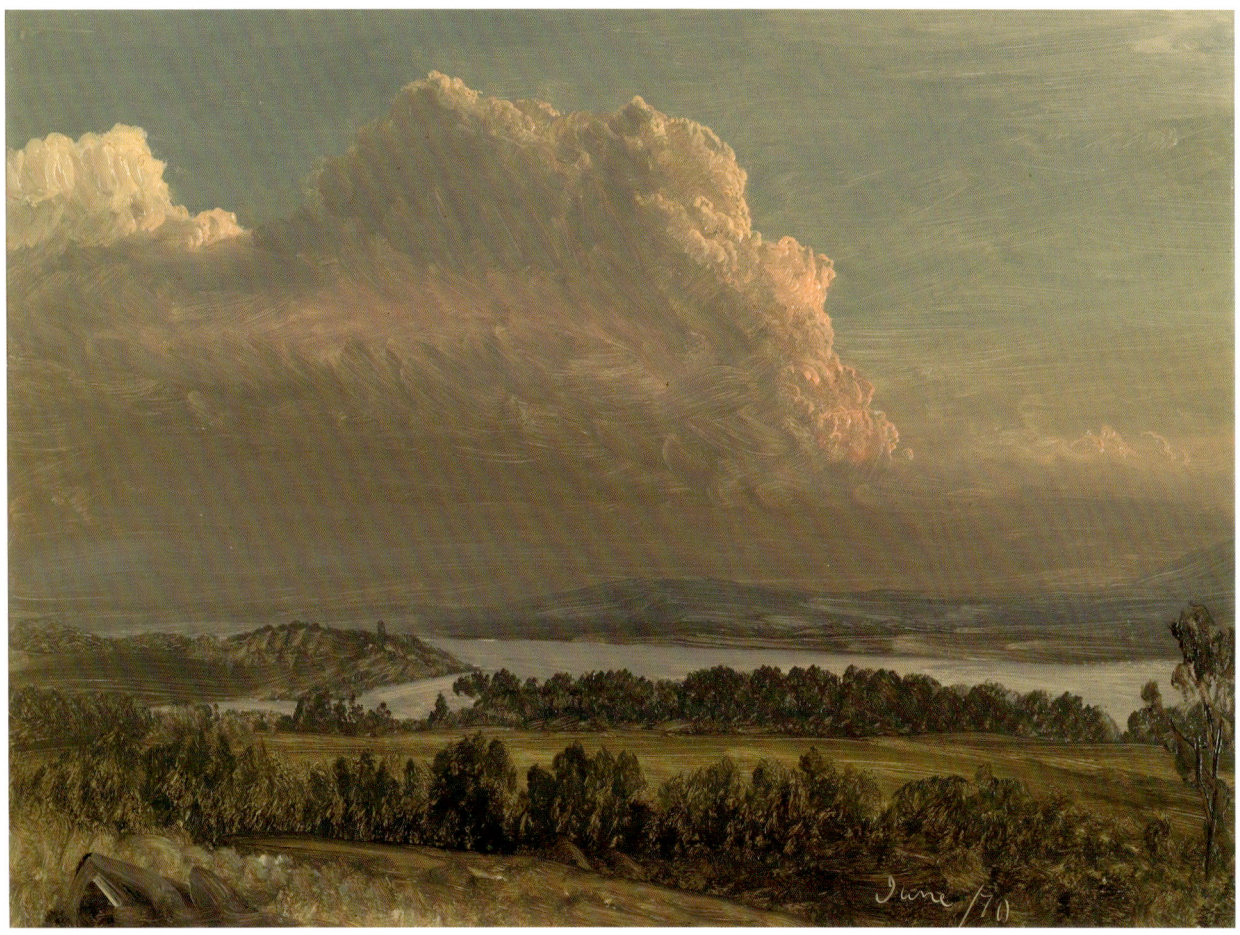

Fig. 43. Frederic Edwin Church, *Sunset across the Hudson Valley*, June 1870, oil and graphite on paperboard, 11⅛ × 15¼ in., Cooper-Hewitt, National Design Museum, Smithsonian Institution, Gift of Louis P. Church, 1917-4-582-a, Photograph: Matt Flynn

scene is dominated by the large pink-bottomed summer cumulus clouds, recalling the spirit of Church's earlier New York and New England paintings, as in *New England Scenery* (fig. 8). To his friend Palmer, anticipating the arrival of his son Walter to begin studying landscape painting, Church emphasized the clouds: "The country is so magnificent now there are so many cloud effects that I often wish he were here." He added, generously, "My studio—advice and materials—&c. are all at Wallies disposal. . . ."[92]

Summer Sunset from Olana (fig. 44), painted from Bethune Road in a cool blue-purple palette, depicts the wide expanse of river and the effect produced after the retreat of a typical late-day summer thunderstorm in the Hudson Valley. The coming and going of summer storms, which sent down torrents of rain for an interlude and then resolved into clear sunshine, always caught Church's attention: "We are having daily showers which clear up at evening with commendable regularity giving us gorgeous sunsets and twilights which are worth a pilgrimage to see."[93] By contrast, *Looking West from Olana* (fig. 45) embodies the warm glow of a hazy summer evening. Though inspired by the

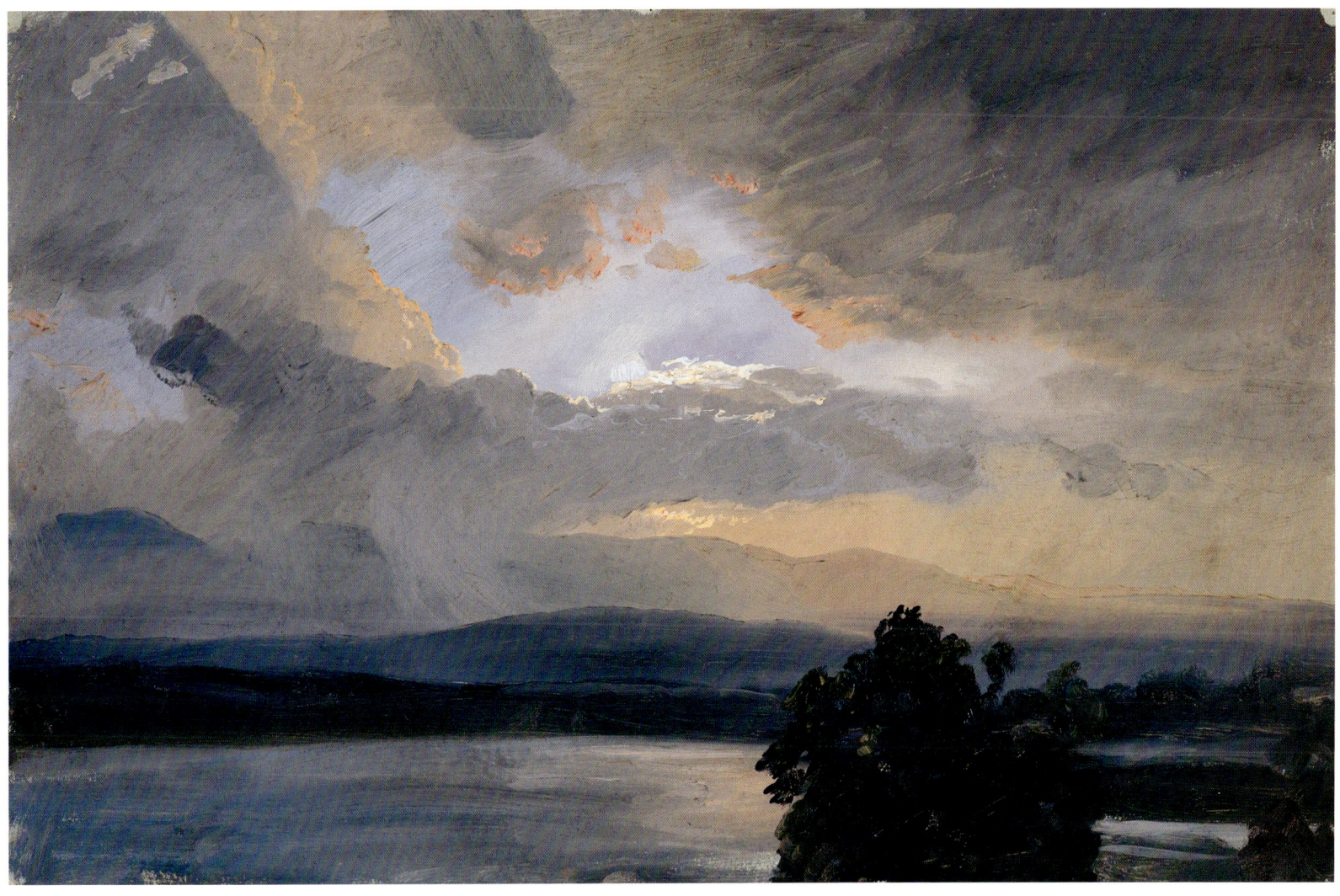

same location, *Looking West from Olana* is more finished; Church probably added the final touches in his studio.

Church also continued to execute his landscaping plans, planting trees, building carriage drives, improving the parkland. His appreciation of these efforts was enhanced by his family's enjoyment of the setting: "They [the children] have got a set of basket panniers (sent from England) which are strung one on each side of a donkey so with Winnie on one side and Louis on the other and Freddie in the middle guiding—they present a jolly appearance. . . . highly picturesque . . . and they go all about the farm and picnic in the woods."[94]

In October 1870, Church told the landscape painter Martin Johnson Heade (1819–1904), "We are having splendid Meteoric displays—Magnificent sunsets and

Fig. 44. Frederic Edwin Church, *Summer Sunset from Olana*, c. 1870–74, oil on off-white academy board, 11 9/16 × 18 1/16 in., OL.1977.207

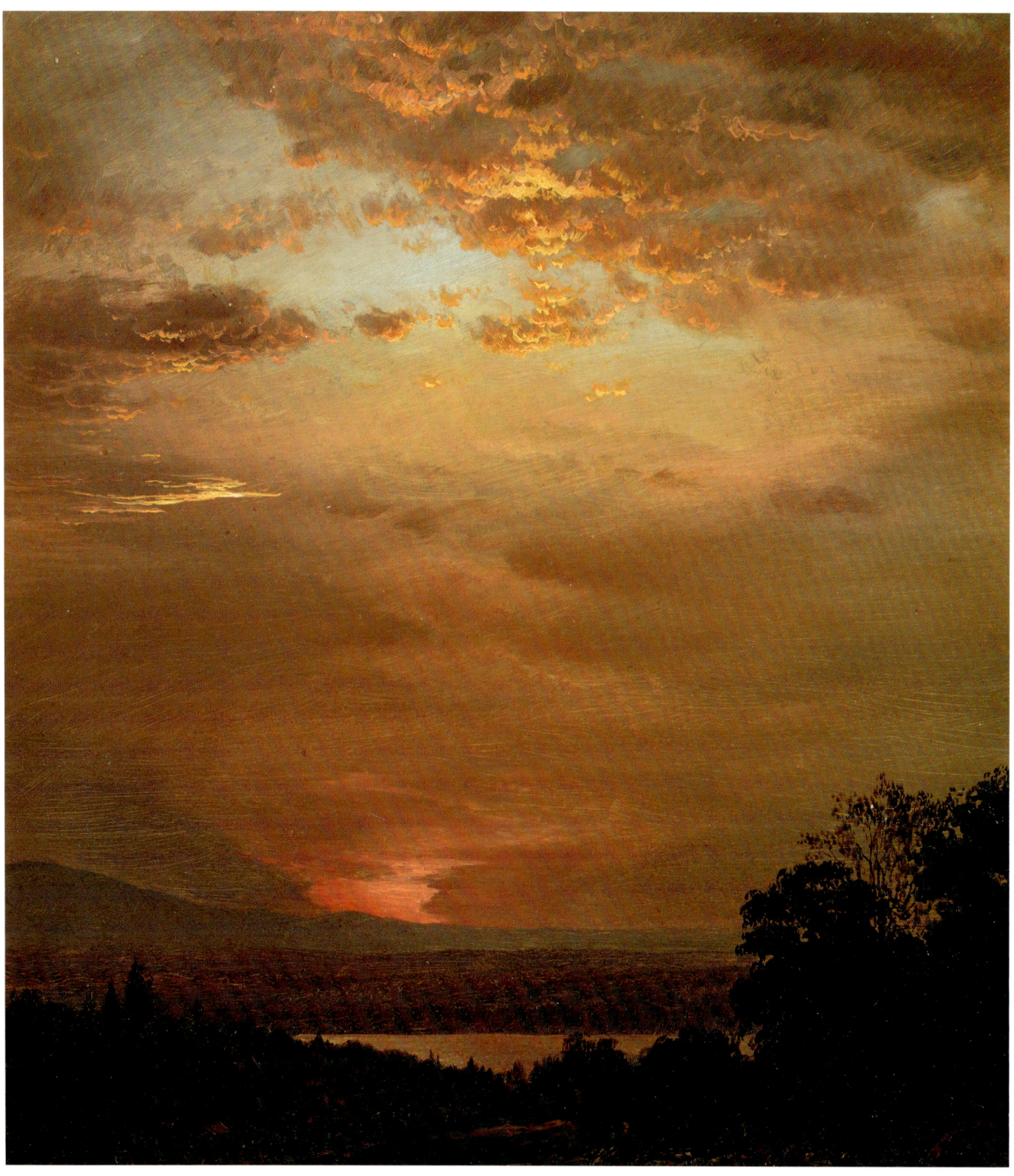

Auroras—red, green, yellow, and blue—and such—in profusion I have actually been drawn away from my usual steady devotion to the new house to sketch some of the fine things hung in the sky."[95] Looking across the river in early fall, Church was intrigued by the juxtaposition of electric orange and a slice of robin's-egg blue to the lugubrious rain cloud above and the mountains below, creating the dark drama of *Sunset across the Hudson Valley, New York*, dated "sep / 70" (fig. 46). A single small sailboat toward the far right shore emphasizes the vastness of the scene. In its somber theatricality, it evokes the work of his mentor, Thomas Cole.[96]

The increasingly vivid autumnal hues that transformed the Hudson Valley by early October were the subject of *Catskill Mountains from the Home of the Artist* (1871; fig. 47), a commission from his longtime friend and sometimes doctor, Fessenden Nott Otis (1825–1900). For the rock outcroppings and cows in the foreground, Church probably consulted his portfolios of drawings from other locales—since neither would have been found by a visitor to this part of the property.[97] This work is the largest and most finished depiction of the Hudson River and Catskill Mountains from the artist's land. Years later, at the auction of Dr. Otis's collection, Church purchased back the painting, remarking, "I was glad to get the picture because it is a view from my Place."[98] The two men also shared a love of travel in the Southern Hemisphere. At the same auction, for display in his house, Church purchased a number of pre-Columbian objects that Otis had unearthed at an archaeological dig at "Bugolitas Province Chiriqui—New Granada."[99]

In the late autumn of 1872, the construction of the main house had sufficiently advanced that the Church family could take up residence. A few months earlier a large party, including Calvert Vaux and the McEntees, came up for the day to visit. Jervis McEntee's diary records the day and Church's accomplishments:

> Vaux, Mary, Gertrude, Marian, Lorry Stoddard and I went up to Church's by the 10:40 train and returned in the evening. It was a magnificent day, the wind blowing freshly from the Northwest. After a nice dinner at his little cottage we went up to his new house which approaches completion. The upper story is plastered and I believe they intend to get into it this fall. It is certainly a beautiful house and commands one of the finest views

Fig. 45. Frederic Edwin Church, *Looking West from Olana*, 1864, oil on artist's board, 13 × 12 in., Jamee and Marshall Field Collection

Fig. 46. Frederic Edwin Church, *Sunset across the Hudson Valley, New York*, September 1870, oil and graphite on thin cream paperboard, 12 11/16 × 13 7/8 in., Cooper-Hewitt, National Design Museum, Smithsonian Institution, Gift of Louis P. Church, 1917-4-582-c, Photograph: Matt Flynn

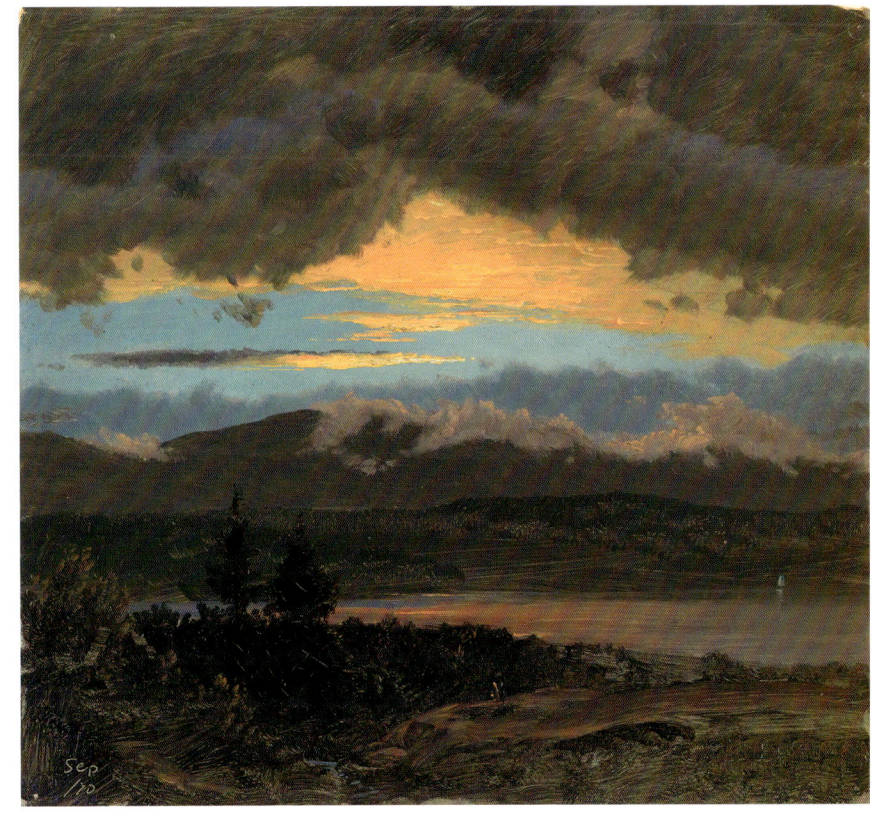

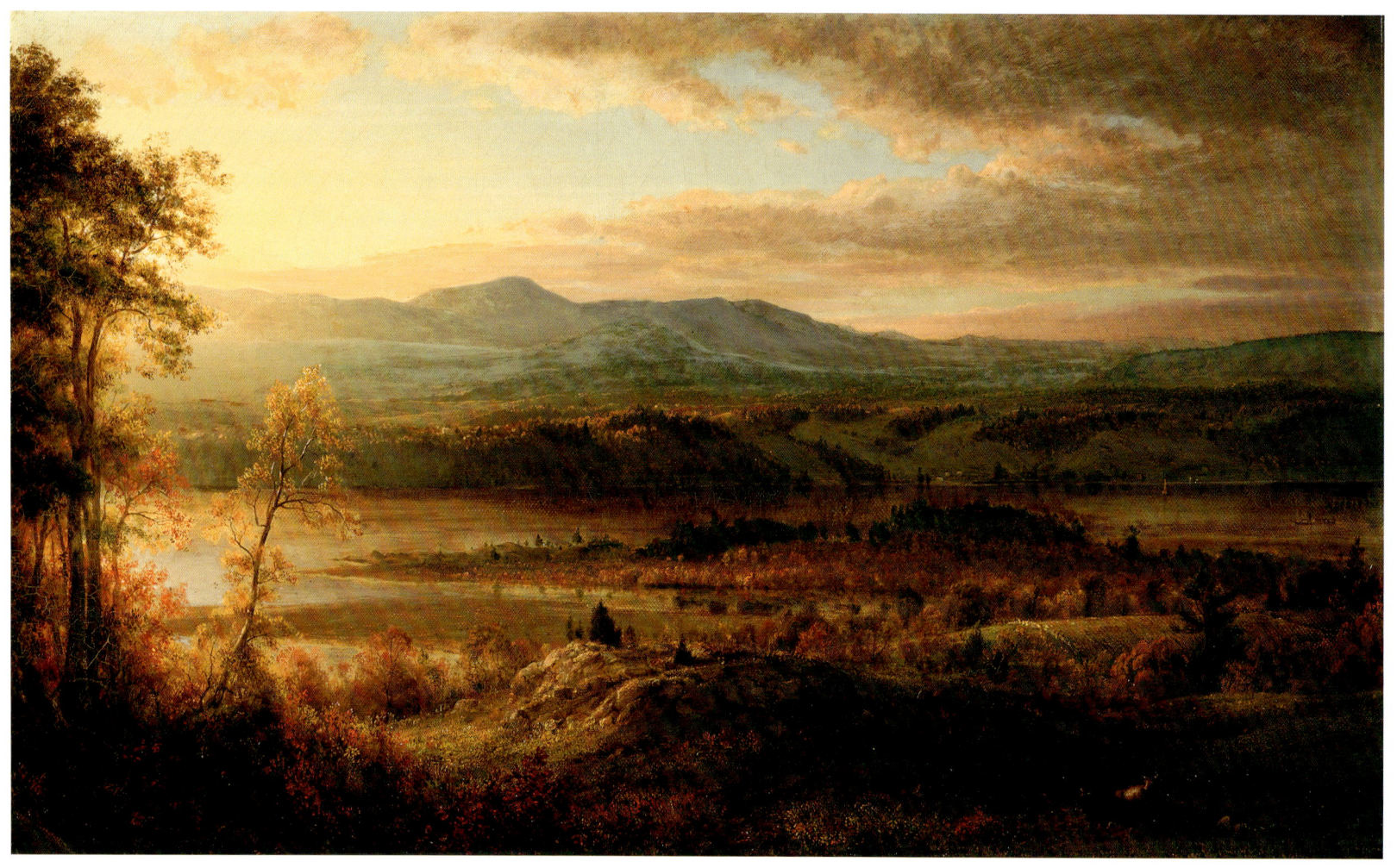

Fig. 47. Frederic Edwin Church, *Catskill Mountains from the Home of the Artist*, 1871, oil on canvas, 22⅛ × 36⅜ in., OL.1981.13

of river and mountain in the country. Church devotes nearly his whole time to building his house, and with his peculiar talent has produced a satisfactory result. The color of the house on the outside by the judicious use of colored bricks with the stone is very harmonious and agreeable. It looks like an artist's work.[100]

Clouds over Olana (fig. 48) is a celebration of the near completion of the new home. Dated August 1872, this cloud study is anchored by the lush green Sienghenbergh slope crowned by the house—easily identifiable by the distinctive Bell Tower.

When the Churches moved into their new home, the house and grounds had not yet acquired the name Olana. A variety of names were ventured in letters during the 1870s. "Olâna" first appeared as the heading of a letter from Isabel to Gertrude McEntee, the painter Jervis's wife and Calvert Vaux's sister, in 1878.[101] A contemporary account credited Isabel of thinking of the name, described as "the old Latin name for a place in Persia, to which the artist's home bears some resemblance in situation."[102] By the early 1880s the couple had settled on "Olana."

Scholars have connected the name to two books in Church's library. Isabel's 1879 Christmas gift to Frederic, Strabo's *Geographica*, discusses "Olane" as one of the "treasure-storehouses" on the Araxes River, and James Morier's *A Second Journey through Persia, Armenia, and Asia Minor, to Constantinople, between the Years 1810 and 1816*, also owned by the Churches, identifies Olana as a fortress on the Araxes River with a view of the fertile valley and of Mount Ararat, where Noah's ark was said to have come to a rest. Just as the name "Cosy Cottage" had evoked the small, simple dwelling it described, the Churches had chosen a name for the new home that embodied its character and location, drawing associations between their own Middle Eastern–inspired house with its view over the Hudson and an epic Persian stone fortress perched high above the Araxes River.[103]

Church's new abode and its parklike setting were discussed in an 1876 series in the *Art Journal*, "The Homes of America." The piece highlights the "residence of Mr. Church, the artist," and as with most contemporary accounts of the house, the article includes a discussion of the view:

> The site for the residence was selected by Mr. Church after a careful study of the river-shores, and commands so many views of varied character and beauty, that here may be almost said to culminate the glories of the Hudson. . . . In the deep valley flows the Hudson River between high and wooded banks. To the south it suddenly broadens to a width of two miles, forming a beautiful lake with picturesque shores.[104]

The article was illustrated by two engravings: a slightly inaccurate portrait of the house and a view south to the widening of the Hudson titled *View of the Grounds from Mr. Church's Residence* (fig. 49). A few evergreens in the foreground almost obscure Overlook Mountain

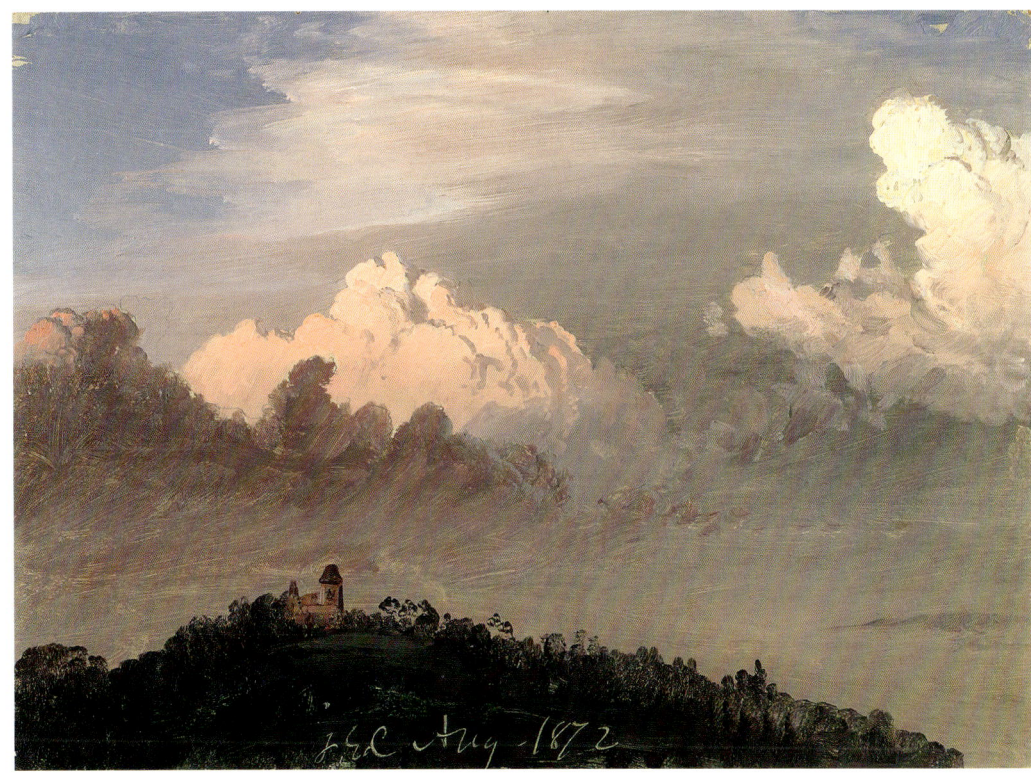

Fig. 48. Frederic Edwin Church, *Clouds over Olana*, August 1872, oil on off-white paper, 8 11/16 × 12 1/8 in., OL.1976.1

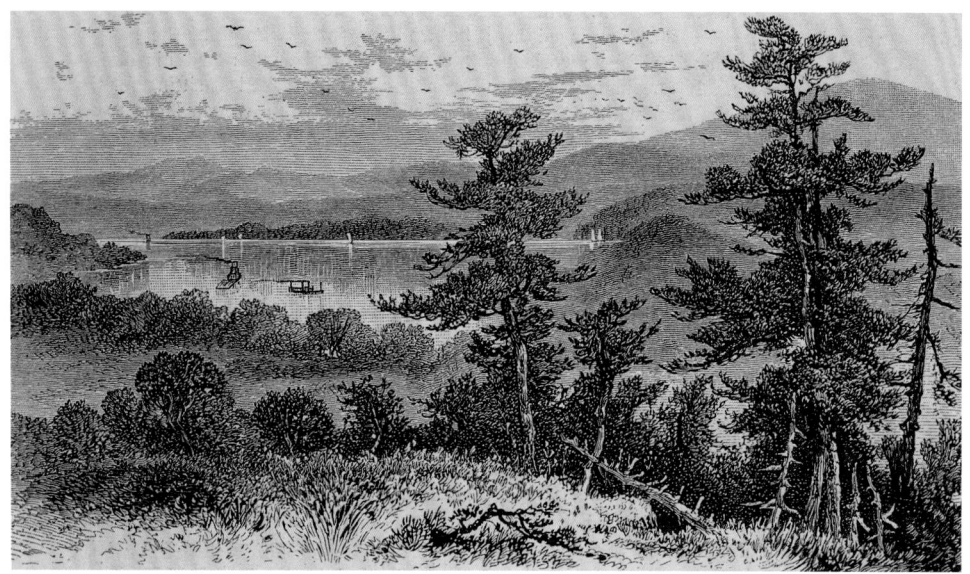

Fig. 49. Unidentified artist, *View from the Grounds of Mr. Church's Residence*, engraving, from Martha Lamb, "The Homes of America," pt. 5, *Art Journal* 20 (August 1876): p. 247, OL.2000.166

in the background, placing the focus on the opening of the river with numerous sailing ships and steamboats. Interestingly, in the reviews of other homes in the series, the view is often mentioned, but none besides Church's was deemed worthy of illustration.[105]

Church critiqued the article to his friend Amelia Edwards:

> I have cut out of an Art Journal a very imperfect wood engraving of the House which I enclosed although if I did not feel certain that you would some-time honor that home with your presence, I should hesitate about sending it, so little does it give of the spirit of the original— This sounds egotistical for I designed the house myself. It is Persian in style adapted to the climate and requirements of modern life— The interior decorations and fittings are all in harmony with the external architecture. It stands at an elevation of 600 feet above the Hudson River and commands wonderful views of the sky, Mountains, rolling and savannah country, villages, forest and clearings. The noble River expands to a width of over two miles forming a lake like a sheet of water which is always dotted with steamers and other craft.[106]

As the above makes clear, Church showed no hesitation in articulating his intense pride in his home and his desire for friends and colleagues to visit. Edwards, his correspondent above, was one of many who witnessed both the fantastic creation Church had designed and the spectacular views with their own eyes.

In the closing years of the 1870s Church painted his last large commission, an Alpine scene, *The Monastery of San Pedro* (1879; Cleveland Museum of Art). By then Americans had shifted their art interest to the new French trends—away from the realism of the Hudson River School toward the style of the Barbizon painters. Church suffered from increasingly debilitating arthritis in his hands, from which he sought relief, beginning in 1883, by wintering in Mexico. In the 1880s, despite waning artistic popularity and his ailment, the artist continued to sketch for his own enjoyment, inspired by Mexican scenery and favorite views from his own property. A small, quickly executed pencil drawing that delicately transcribed a rainstorm over the "dark slate blue water" of the Hudson inscribed "Home June 82" leaves no doubt as to the location (fig. 50).

Instead of painting large canvases, Church focused his artistic energies on further enhancing his property. The 1886 *Plan of Olana*, a surveying project made in college by Church's son Frederic Joseph, detailed the realized vision of the artist (fig. 51). In his own words Church conveyed the process of creating his three-dimensional masterpiece: "I have made about 1¾ miles of road this season, opening entirely new and beautiful views. I can make more and better landscapes in this way than by tampering with canvas and paint in the studio."[107] The artist's concept of his landscaping efforts as analogous to painted compositions was firmly rooted in the prevailing attitudes of the landscape writers and practitioners of the era. Olmsted described the views he orchestrated within New York City's Central Park as "pictures" through which visitors would wander.[108]

In the summer of 1884 Church began work on two new ornamental drives at Olana. Lake Road wound its way around the sensuous curves of the shoreline, connecting the farm buildings with South Road and providing peeks at the house from across the ten-acre man-made lake the artist excavated to

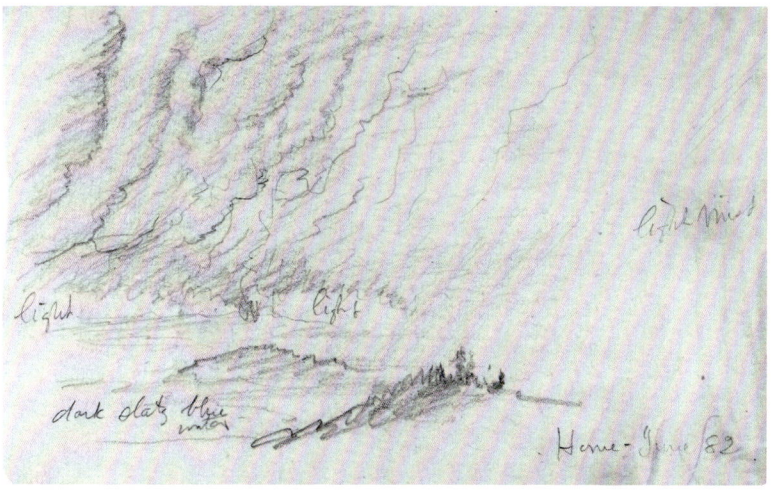

Fig. 50. Frederic Edwin Church, *Mist over River and Hills*, June 1882, graphite on cream wove paper, 3¹⁵⁄₁₆ × 6⁹⁄₁₆ in., Cooper-Hewitt, National Design Museum, Smithsonian Institution, Gift of Louis P. Church, 1917-4-1086, Photograph: Matt Flynn

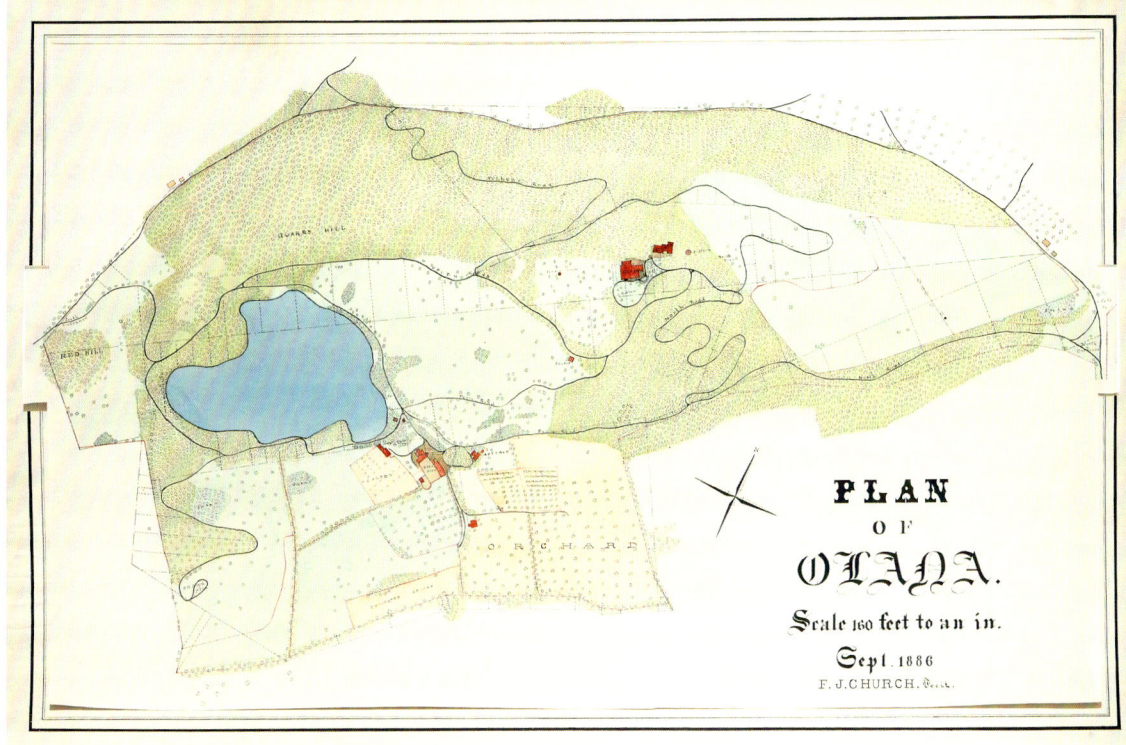

Fig. 51. Frederic Joseph Church, *Plan of Olana*, September 1886, ink and watercolor on paper, 22⅛ × 36¼ in., OL.1984.39

balance his distant river view (fig. 52). Ridge Road was constructed through the north meadow Church had purchased six years earlier, offering sweeping panoramas west across the river to the Catskills and north up the Hudson (fig. 53). While the earlier Bethune Road wound its way up the lower hillside, close to rocks and banks, contrasting the intimacy of a tree-enclosed drive with occasional glimpses of the river and distant mountains, the new road was laid out on the relatively flat plain of a ridge, making almost a circuit, just below the top of the Sienghenbergh. The fields surrounding the new road had previously been pastureland, used to graze livestock. Over the ensuing years, with the careful planting of trees and the selective allowance of secondary growth, Church further refined the views from Ridge Road by adding a picturesque foreground to the sweeping vista.[109]

Emma Carnes, while staying at Olana during the summer of 1884, recorded in her diary Church's involvement in the work of Ridge Road, starting in mid-August: "Mr. C out all a.m. at his new road, north end of place."[110] Mrs. Carnes made her own foray to the road site, noting, "I walked from North view seat to where new road will join Bethune Road." By early fall, the road was at least partly accessible by carriage, for the matriarch "Drove on new road as far as woods, very rough now, but will be beautiful in views."[111] One of these trips around the carriage roads was captured in a photograph of Mrs. Carnes and her granddaughter Downie in the donkey cart (fig. 54).

The mid-1880s were a very lively time at Olana, the heyday of the Churches' hospitality, entertaining their friends and colleagues. It was not unusual for them to have as

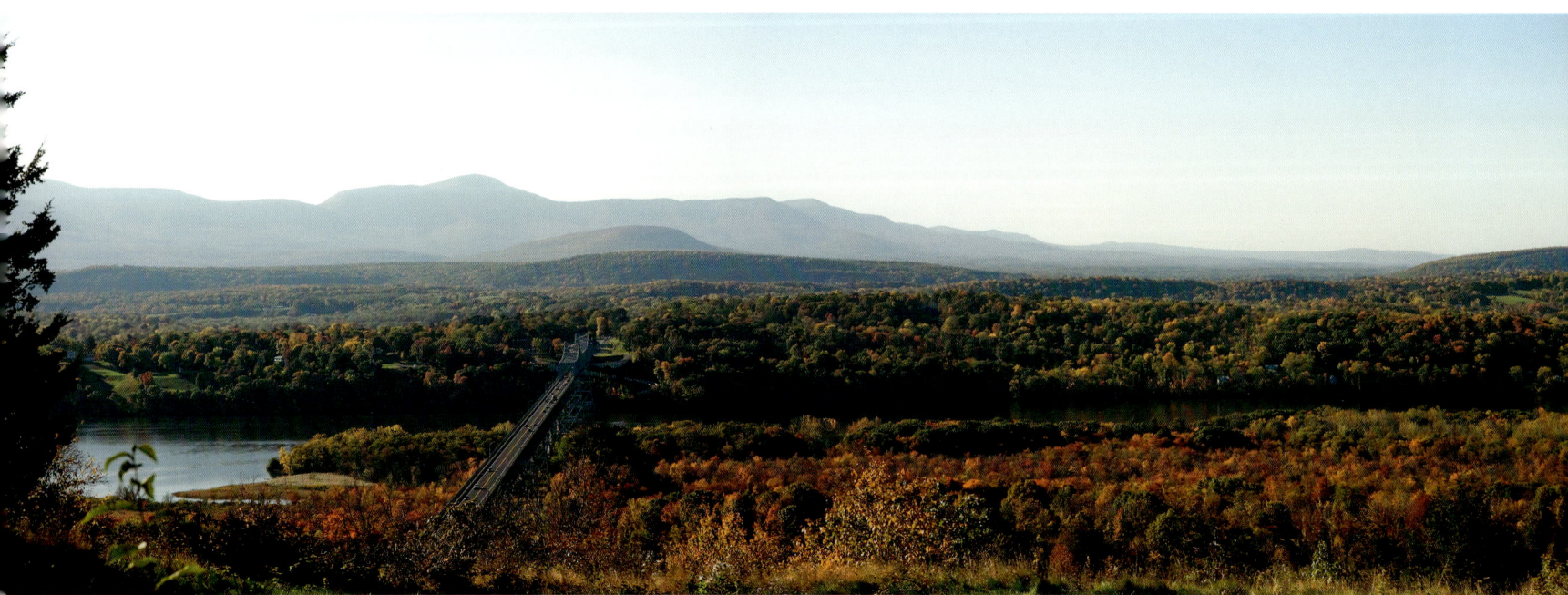

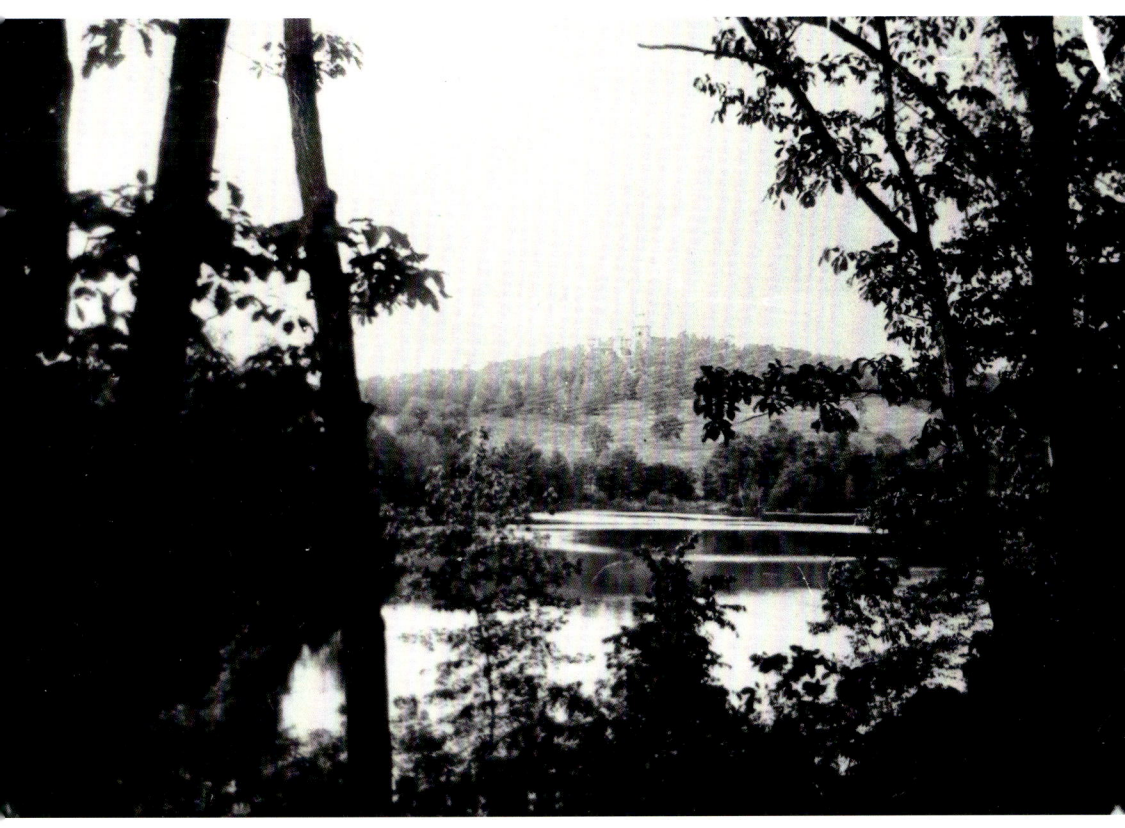

Fig. 52. Granville Hills, *House and Park from across the Lake*, Olana, albumen print, c. 1890–1903, 4¼ × 7¹⁄₁₆ in., OL.1986.378.11.D

Fig. 53. Nicholas Whitman, *View from Ridge Road*, photograph, 2008

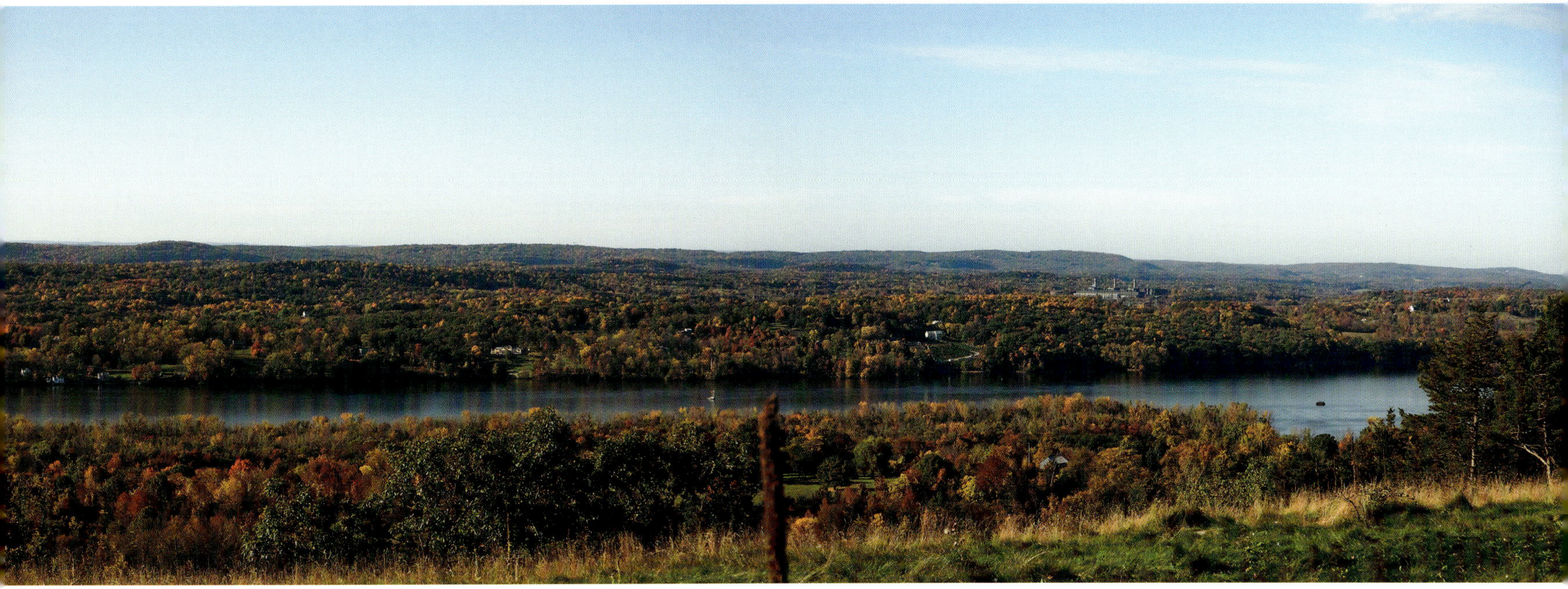

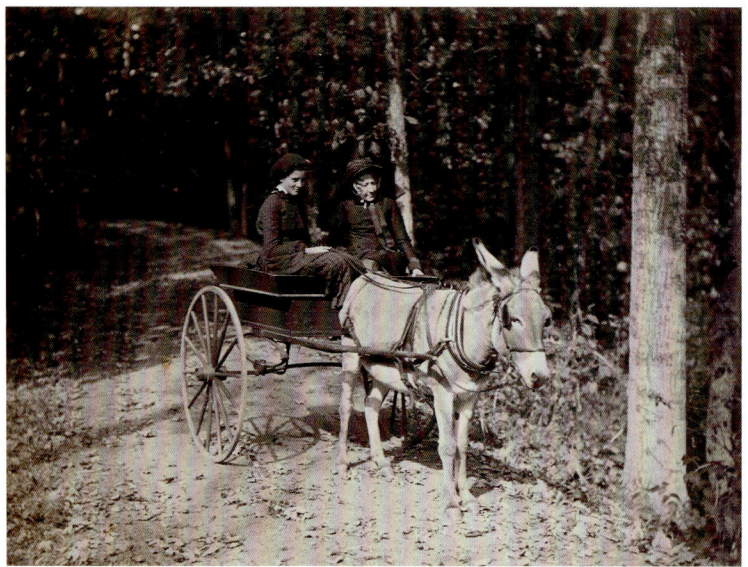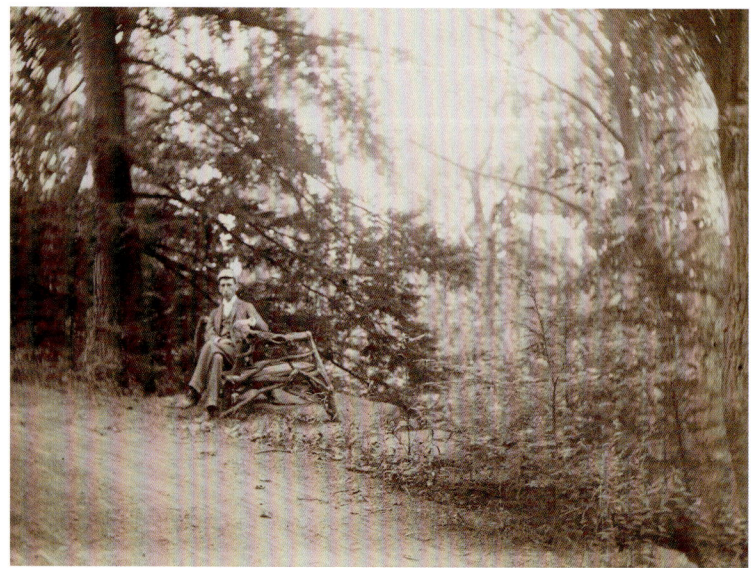

Fig. 54. Robert and Emily de Forest, *Downie Church and Emma Carnes in a Donkey Cart, on a Carriage Drive at Olana*, October 11, 1884, photograph, 9⅜ × 11 in., OL.1982.1520

Fig. 55. Unknown photographer, *Louis P. Church Seated on a Rustic Bench at Olana, Probably near Ridge Road*, c. 1890s, photograph, 3 × 5 in., OL.1986.425

many as fifteen guests in residence at one time. Visitors took full advantage of the property. The novelist Susan Hale, who became a friend to both Frederic and Isabel, as well as their children, made the first of her numerous visits to Olana in 1884. After arriving, she penned a letter to her sister emphasizing Church's artistic enhancement of his landscape and the consistent presence of the river from many vantage points: "The place is so large I can walk miles without going off of it. It is very pretty, great avenues of trees, a pond, nooks of shade and always the wide view of the river and mountains."[112] Church provided rustic benches to accommodate those who ventured out on foot. A photograph shows Louis Church resting in one, enjoying a view created by his father's selective removal of trees (fig. 55).

Residents, whether permanent or temporary, walked or drove around the property almost daily. From the carriage drives, family and guests experienced "passages of scenery": the intimate setting of the farm; the more dramatic vistas available throughout the grounds; and prospects of the house (fig. 56).[113] For the Fourth of July holiday in 1884, Olana guest Erastus Dow Palmer "drove us all in a big wagon around the place after dinner."[114] Various letters and diary entries attest to the popularity of this leisure pursuit, visitors often recounting their drives and walks to friends and family. Church echoed their sentiments, writing, "She [Isabel] drives out mornings and evenings and enjoys the shade of our woods. These woods by the way never looked so well thanks to the rains. Indeed our scenery has been simply marvelous this summer—We are having a great many friends visiting thus and their enthusiasm is very pleasant to hear."[115]

The Hudson not only provided magnificent views, it also brought visitors to Olana. Church's colleague Jervis McEntee, who typically arrived by train, recalled his voyage

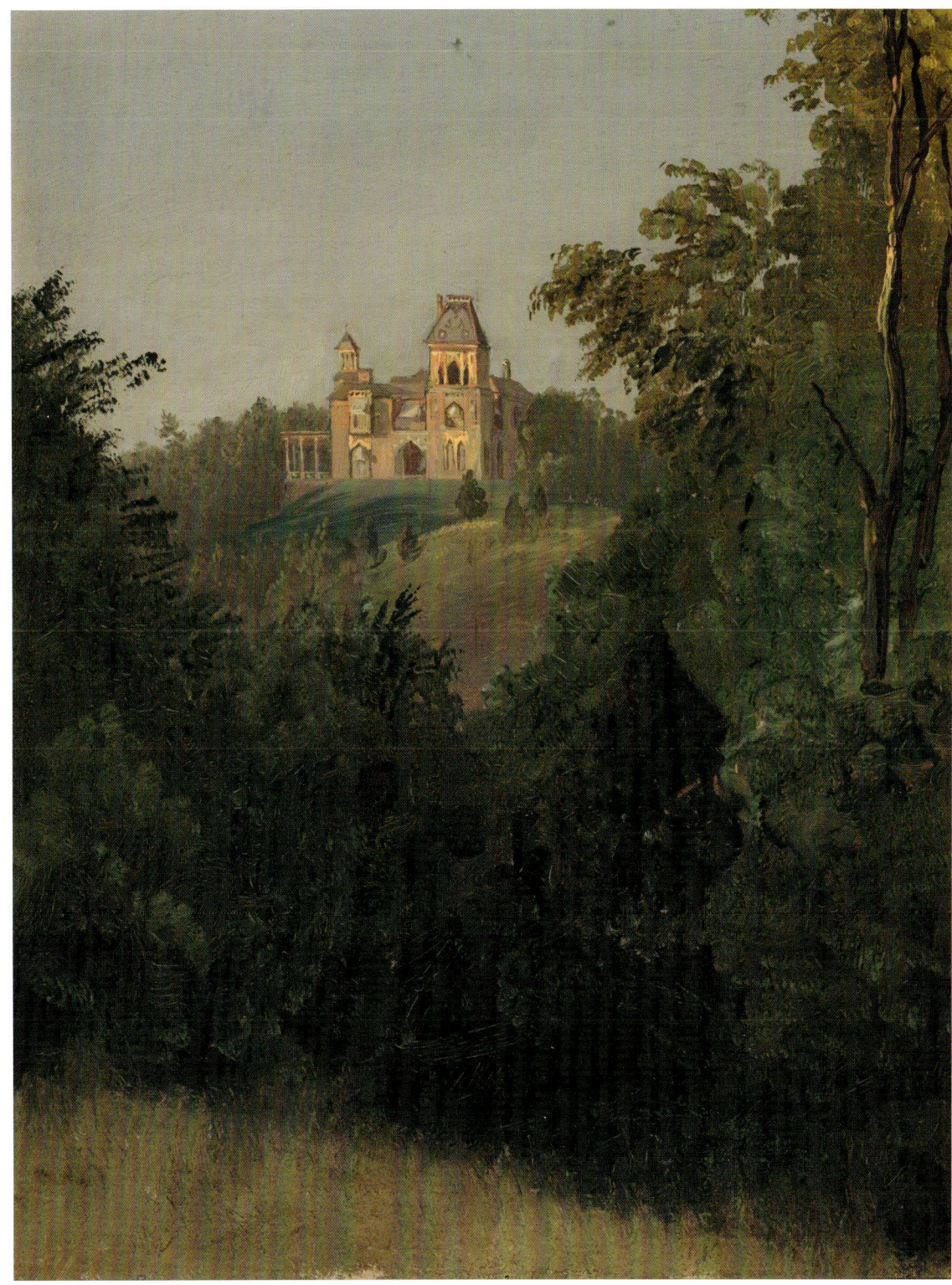

Fig. 56. Frederic Edwin Church, *Olana from the Southwest*, c. 1872, oil on thin paperboard, 12 1/16 × 9 9/16 in., Cooper-Hewitt, National Design Museum, Smithsonian Institution, Gift of Louis P. Church, 1917-4-666, Photograph: Matt Flynn

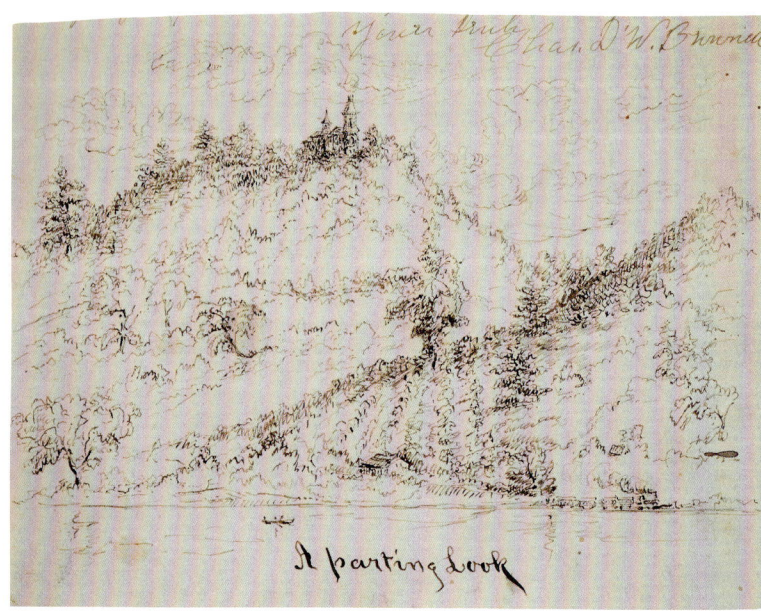

Fig. 57. Charles de Wolf Brownell, *A Parting Look*, 1888, brown ink on paper, 3¾ × 5 in., OL.1982.1137

up the Hudson in his diary: "I went up to Churches by invitation on Monday last by the day boat. I had a delightful sail and Winnie [Church's son] with Michael the coachman met me at the landing at Hudson and drove me to the house." There, McEntee was given "a beautiful room in the S.W. front of the house looking down the river...."[116] During these stays he employed himself in artistic endeavors: "Had a very pleasant visit at Church's and most delightful weather. I made a few sketches."[117]

The artist Charles de Wolf Brownell (1822–1909) and his wife were also guests at Olana. Brownell and Church shared Hartford as a hometown and both had been drawn to the tropics; Brownell spent a great deal of time painting in Cuba and, like Church, had traveled to Jamaica and Mexico. An ink sketch by Brownell documents the end of a stay. Sent to Church as a thank-you, it is inscribed "A Parting Look" and signed "Yours Truly Chas DW Brownell" (fig. 57). Drawn from the Hudson looking back up the river to Olana ornamenting the top of the Sienghenbergh, it features a boat on the river, the train puffing down the shore, and a field of cultivated land. Church was probably flattered to receive this delightful tribute to his hilltop creation. An almost identical image in Brownell's notebook captioned "1888 On the Hudson Olana: Residence of Frederic E. Church May 29" fixes the date of the sketch sent to Church.[118]

Church's students captured aspects of their teacher's landscaping efforts. Walter Launt Palmer, who had trained with Church before studying in Paris and even shared Church's space at the Tenth Street Studio Building, painted *Road to Olana* during the winter of 1887–88 (fig. 58) as a homage to his teacher and a nod to his student days, when Church had painted many snow scenes of his property. In an impressionistic style that makes a sharp contrast to Church's depictions of winter (figs. 23, 39, and 40), Palmer's watercolor shows a snow-covered, wooded hillside with a winding road—perhaps Bethune Road or North Road. Regardless of the exact location, the image evokes the winding, climbing aspect of the wooded carriage drives Church devised to bring guests and visitors into the natural beauty that surrounded his home.

The public was also made welcome. In 1883 Mrs. Carnes commented on the visiting public in her diary: "Lovely day.... Raft of strangers walked around."[119] A decade later, Louis Church wrote from Algiers on January 11, 1894, of meeting two families who had spent a summer in the Catskills five years previously, when they "drove through our place nearly every day."[120] The *Hudson Register* recommended the grounds to tourists:

The home of Frederick [*sic*] E. Church the artist, is one of the most conspicuous features on the right side of the upper Hudson. It is just opposite Catskill, situated on a high hill, most of which, if not all, is owned by Mr. Church. It can be seen from miles around. A drive to the grounds which Mr. Church is very kind about throwing open to visitors, is one of the pleasantest trips made by people spending the summer in the vicinity.[121]

Public access to private homes and parks was common in nineteenth-century Britain, and a few homes in the United States had adopted this custom. Estates with extensive grounds in Highland Falls and Fort Montgomery, near West Point, allowed local residents to

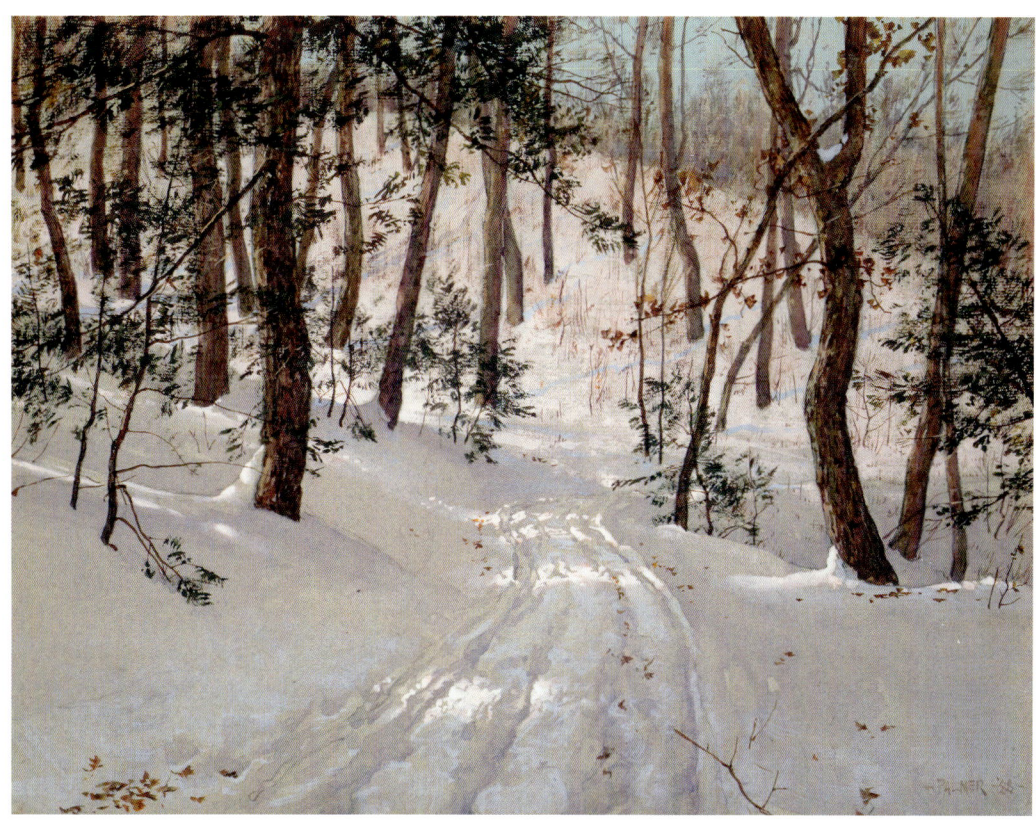

Fig. 58. Walter Launt Palmer, *Road to Olana*, 1888, watercolor and gouache on paper, 13¼ × 17¼ in., Albany Institute of History and Art, Gift of the estate of Miss Evelyn Newman, 1964.31.40

tour them on Sunday afternoons.[122] Church might have also been influenced by Daniel Wadsworth, who opened to the public the grounds and viewing tower of his home Mount Video near Church's hometown of Hartford.[123] Professionally, Church was certainly accustomed to sharing his artistic achievements with the public through his "Great Picture" exhibitions and reception day at the Tenth Street Studio Building.

In addition to his work on the landscape, Church was making small changes to the house—designing bookshelves for the Court Hall, adding a balcony on the second story, making repairs to the roof, and finishing a new room in the attic. These smaller projects culminated in a second building campaign: the addition of a new studio wing off the west side of the house. The wing included a downstairs apartment for guests and another tower. For this project Church did not employ an architect, taking on himself its design and execution. Church kept Brownell abreast of the project, writing a month after the latter's visit to Olana, "I am indeed busy night and day with my plans and as I am architect and make the drawings you can readily believe that I have little spare time. The walls are already two feet on an average above ground. I wonder if I shall work as hard in the new Studio as I do in erecting it." And a month later, "The Studio progresses well—the walls of the second story are going up—solid masonry. . . ."[124]

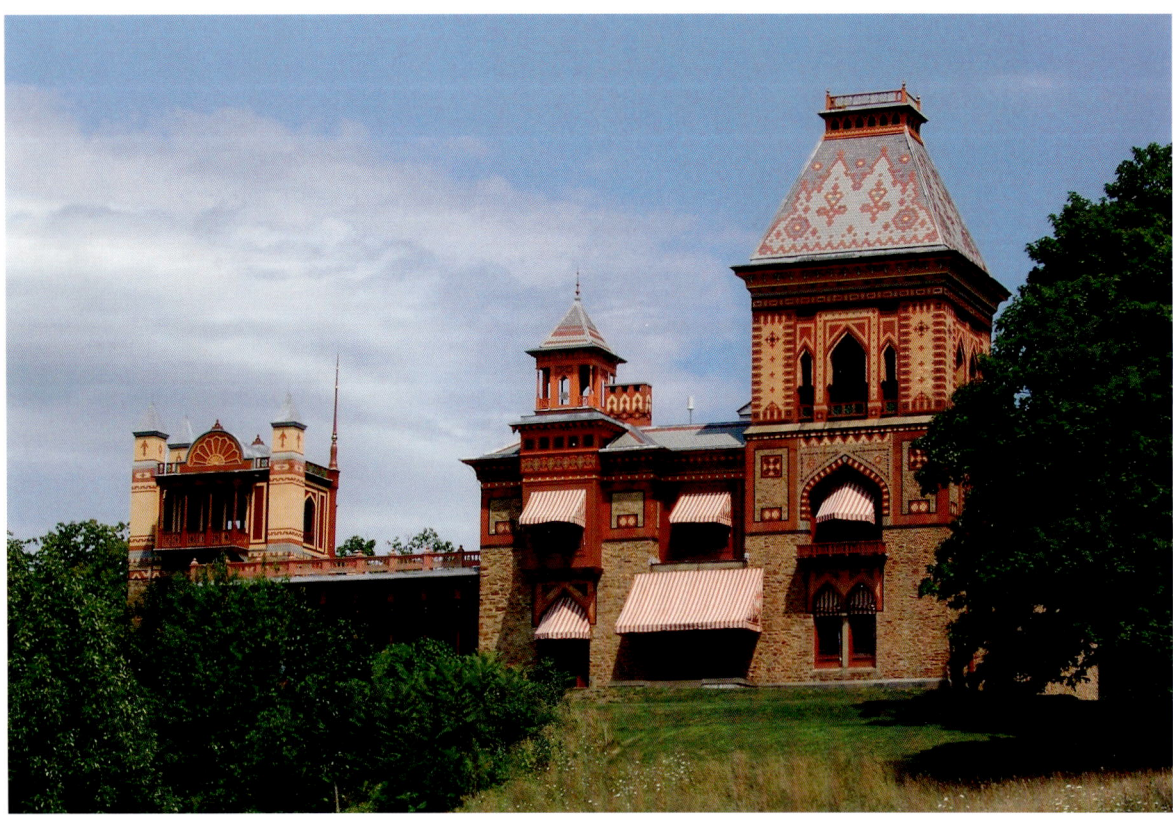

Fig. 59. Carri Manchester, *South Facade of Olana,*
with Studio Wing at Left, photograph, 2007

While genuinely excited about the project, Church was also clear about the implications of an older artist no longer at the height of his career building a new studio. He confided to his longtime friend Charles Dudley Warner:

> I can fancy the thought now passing your mind—"Building a Studio at his age and with his infirmities!"
>
> Well, we will call it a Mausoleum. It is solid enough to make a suitable shell for all the Pharaohs. It is very interesting work anyhow and our Verandah makes a capital stage for overlooking the work as it progresses. . . . Olana never looked as well as now. . . .[125]

Frustrated by his arthritis, Church enjoyed turning his energies and talents to building. With the completion of the studio wing in 1890, Church packed up the contents of his space in the Tenth Street Studio, and for the first time in close to fifty years no longer occupied studio space in New York City.

By 1890, Church had completed all major improvements to the house and to the grounds that now totaled 250 acres (fig. 59). A journalist summarized, "As I looked out from its broad veranda . . . the scene that spread before me filled me with regret that I had the soul of an artist without the power to wield the brush. It seemed the spot of all others to lend inspiration, and it is no wonder that the fame of Mr. Church is so great and lasting. . . ."[126] Everyone who visited was moved to describe and praise it in some way. Grace King called it "a perfect Eden of picturesque beauty," and Samuel Clemens, better known as Mark Twain, wrote with characteristic wit of his visit, "It was an ideal holiday, in a Garden of Eden without the Garden of Eden's unprotection from weather."[127]

In the ensuing years, the Churches entertained less and their grown children moved away, but the couple continued to enjoy their property. Church's artistic output was largely restricted to small sketches made while wintering annually in Mexico, traveling with friends and fellow artists. Walter Launt Palmer journeyed with Frederic in 1895, creating an album of photographs for his mentor as a remembrance of their adventure.[128] Church took advantage of the opportunity to add to the collections at Olana, purchasing hats, pottery, and paintings in Mexico to decorate the studio wing (fig. 60).

Fig. 60. Nicholas Whitman, *The Studio at Olana*, photograph, 2008

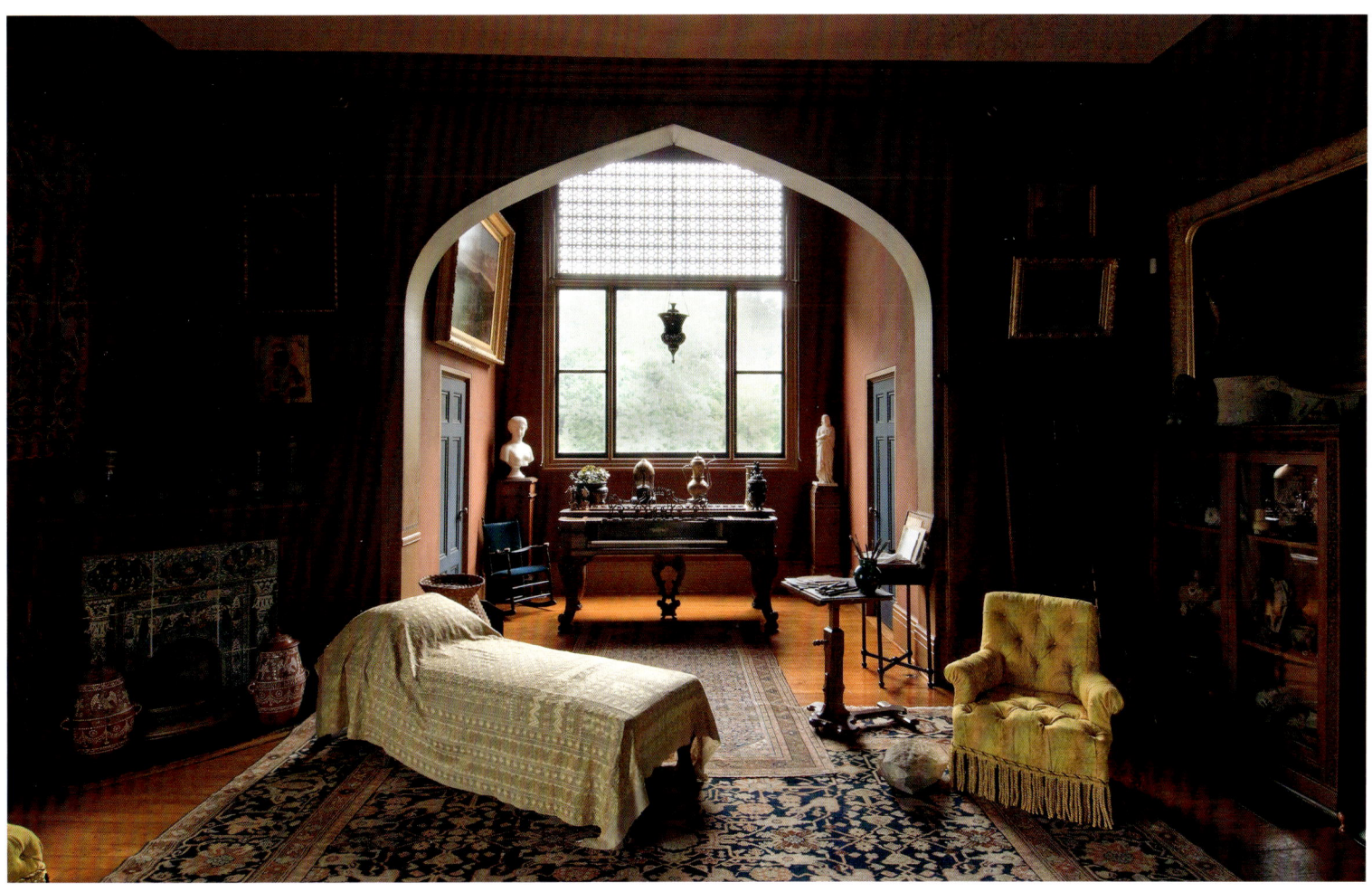

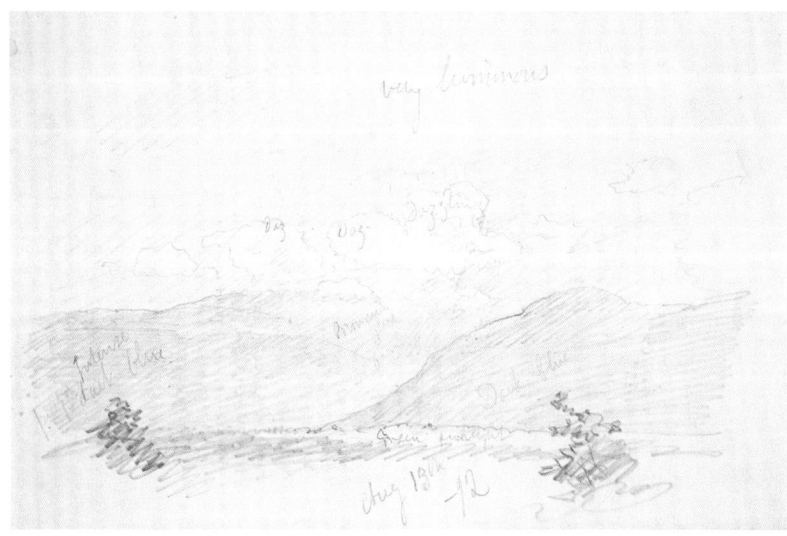

Fig. 61. Frederic Edwin Church, *Rain and Clouds over the Catskills*, August 13, 1892, graphite on white wove paper, 4⁹⁄₁₆ × 7 in., OL.1980.1511

Fig. 62. Attributed to Louis P. Church, *Sunset View from Olana*, March 1898, photograph, 4¼ × 6½ in., OL.1987.162

A series of letters from this period reveals that Church's keen powers of observation were still as acute as ever, even if age and arthritis hindered his hands. From Olana in the spring of 1891, Church mused, "You notice that I write in an absent minded sort of way, crossing out and inserting words; well it is owing to the magnificent effects this morning—beautiful clouds, an opalescent atmosphere, and lovely tints in the landscape distract me every minute...."[129] Later that fall, Church observed in a letter to fellow artist John Ferguson Weir, "It is [a] particularly lovely Autumn here rich coloring, no frost as yet and mainly still soft weather toned to suit an Artists eye...."[130]

On occasion, Church was still moved to draw from his property, as on August 13, 1892, when he quickly sketched a rain shower over the Catskills across the river. *Rain and Clouds over the Catskills* was composed with an economy of graphite strokes and gentle shading, providing only a suggestion or touchstone for elements now so familiar to Church that he could portray them in a cursory way (fig. 61).

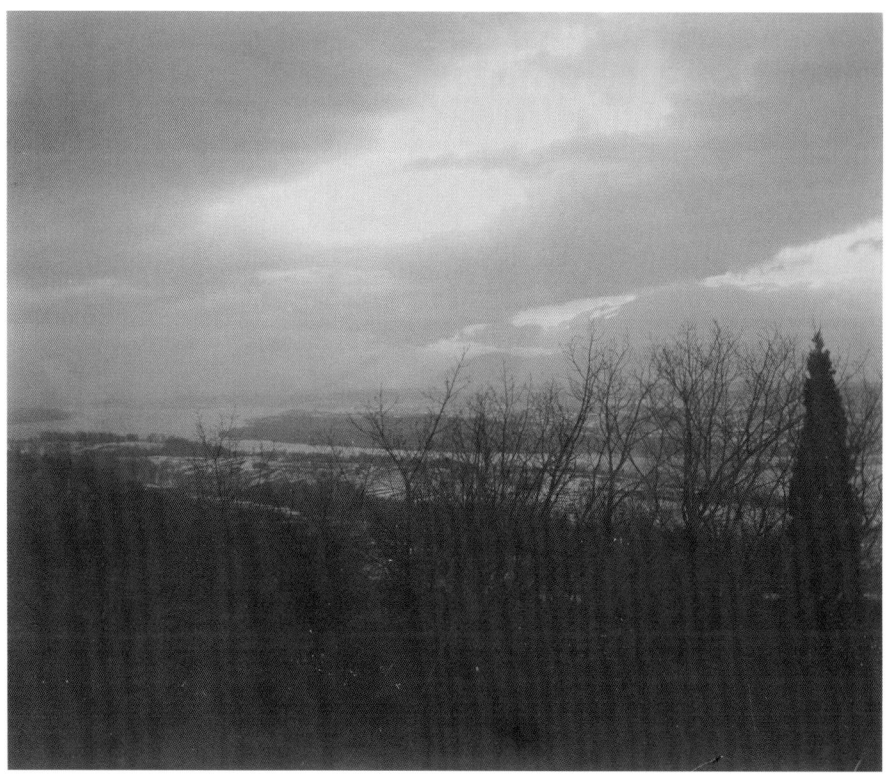

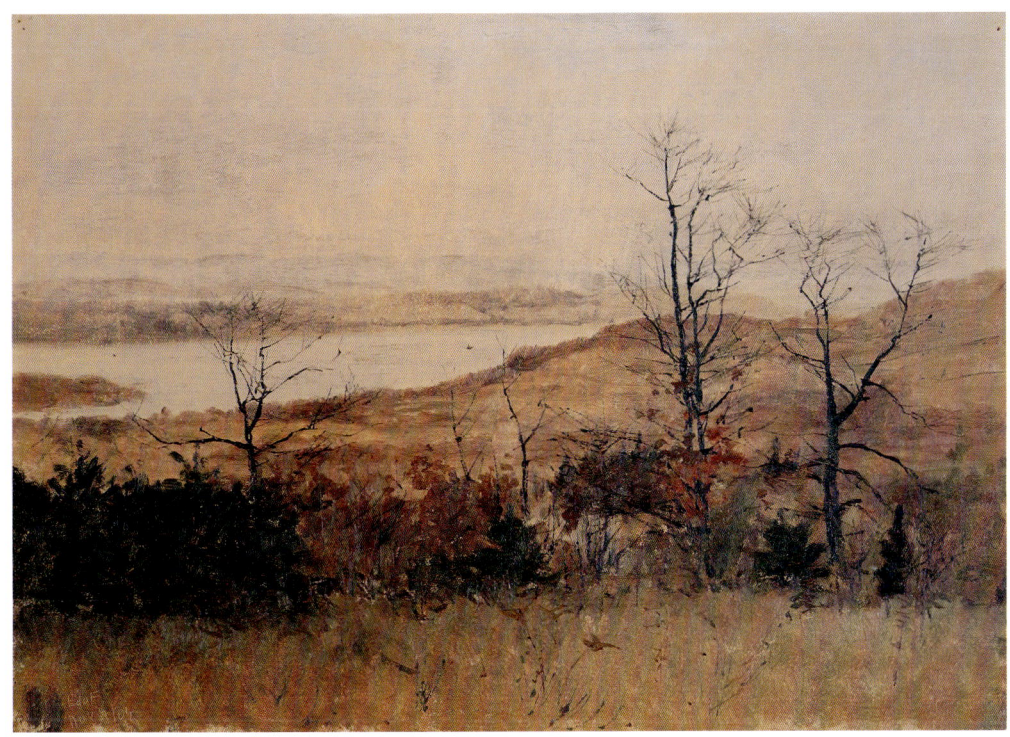

Fig. 63. Lockwood de Forest, *View North over the Hudson*, November 4, 1904, oil on cardboard, 9½ × 14 in., OL.1999.128

Church, nearing his sixty-sixth birthday, required assistance managing the property. In December 1891, Isabel reported the decision to hire their youngest son, Louis, to "be head, of our place . . . your father thought he needed one of his sons, to take charge and <u>Louis</u> dear boy is <u>the</u> one."[131] Louis had already exhibited his willingness to help his aging parents by accompanying them on winter trips to warmer climates. Traveling with his father to Mexico, Louis photographed scenery and natural wonders.[132] As the care-taker of Olana, Louis might have paused in his duties to capture the fleeting sky effects that had always fascinated his father, in a photograph of the sun breaking through the late afternoon clouds over the southern Catskills and Hudson River (fig. 62). The work is inscribed "March 1898."

In May 1899 Isabel Church died, and Church followed eleven months later, on April 7, 1900, in the New York City home of Virginia Sturges Osborn, widow of his close friend William Henry Osborn. Their son Louis married his longtime betrothed, Sally Good, in January 1901, and the couple resided at Olana until their own deaths in 1943 and 1964, respectively.

Throughout their residence, Louis and Sally continued to welcome many old family friends to Olana, among them Susan Hale, the Osborn family, and Lockwood de Forest, Church's former student. On one such visit in the autumn of 1904, de Forest painted *View North over the Hudson* (fig. 63).[133] The oil sketch is executed in the soft

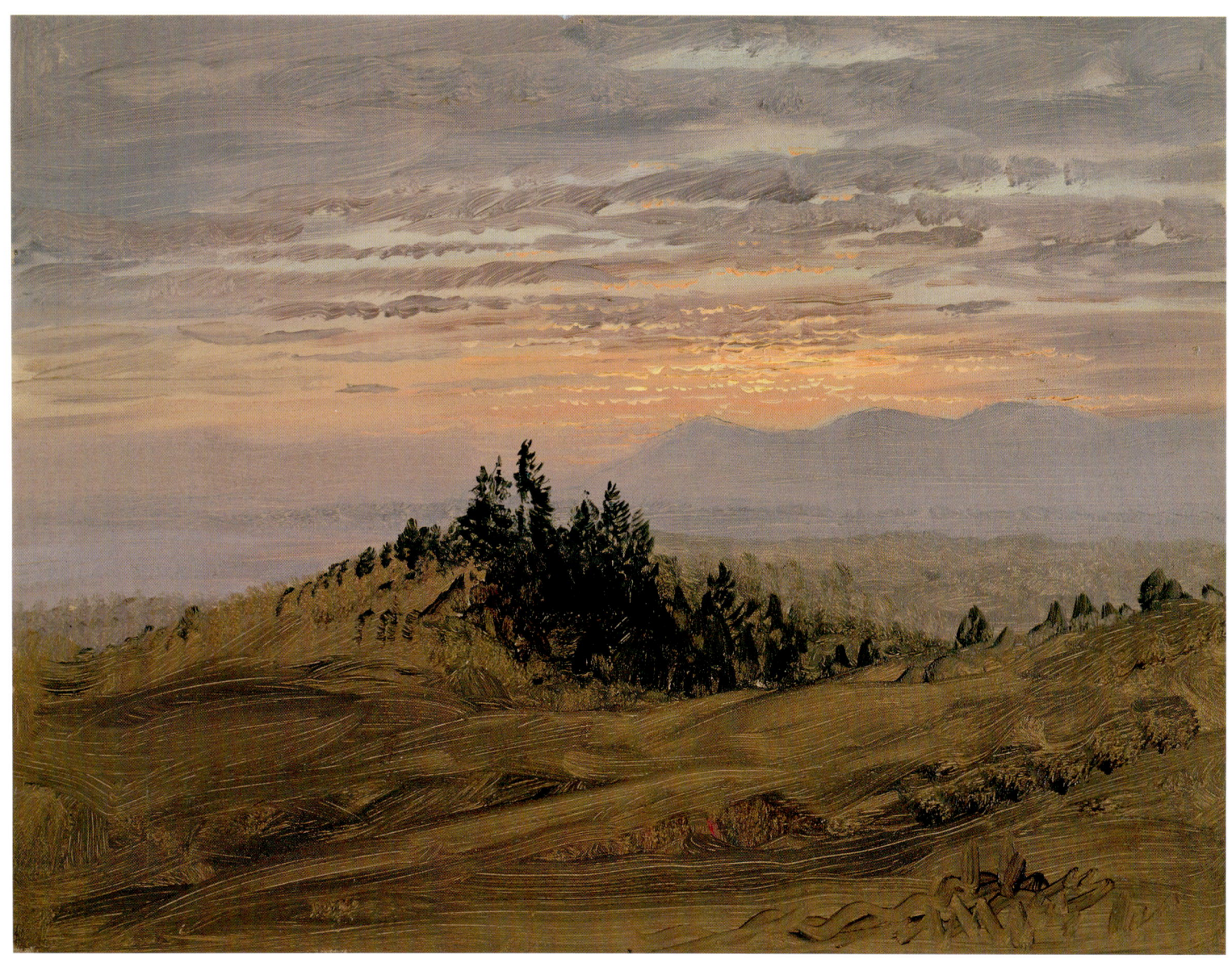

Fig. 64. Frederic Edwin Church, *Winter Sunset*
from Olana, c. 1870–72, oil on heavy tan paper,
10⅜ × 13⅞ in., OL.1976.7

browns and charcoal tints indicative of a bleak day late in the season, when the vivid colors of fall foliage in the Hudson Valley have subsided. The larger trees are bare and some dry, brownish red leaves still cling to the underbrush. The northern tip of Rogers Island is visible in the far left corner of the work, and the mountains appear as a faint outline in the far distance, the river a silver pool disappearing behind the hill. The subject is most likely taken from a northern spot on Bethune Road; the low vantage point and gently sloping hill in the far right indicate this location versus the much higher escarpment of Ridge Road.

The sketch represents de Forest's mature style, influenced more by the intimate vision of the Barbizon than by the Hudson River School. A quiet stillness and melancholy pervades the work, due in part, certainly, to the time of year, but perhaps influenced as well by de Forest's sadness about the loss of his mentor Church.

Church traveled the world and his successful art career made it possible for him to live anywhere he chose. Yet he returned to the Hudson Valley, almost directly across from the home of his teacher, Thomas Cole, and built a home not once, but twice on the property he continued to perfect for close to forty years (fig. 64). The creation of Olana was Church's life work; he spent more time in the planning and building of the house, landscape, and collections than on any of his major canvases. For Church, his Hudson River Valley home was his locus, where he returned again and again despite extensive traveling; where he raised and nurtured a family; where he gained respite from fame; and where he pursued his most personal artistic project, one on a par with any of his landscape paintings. There is no doubt about Olana's singular importance for Church.

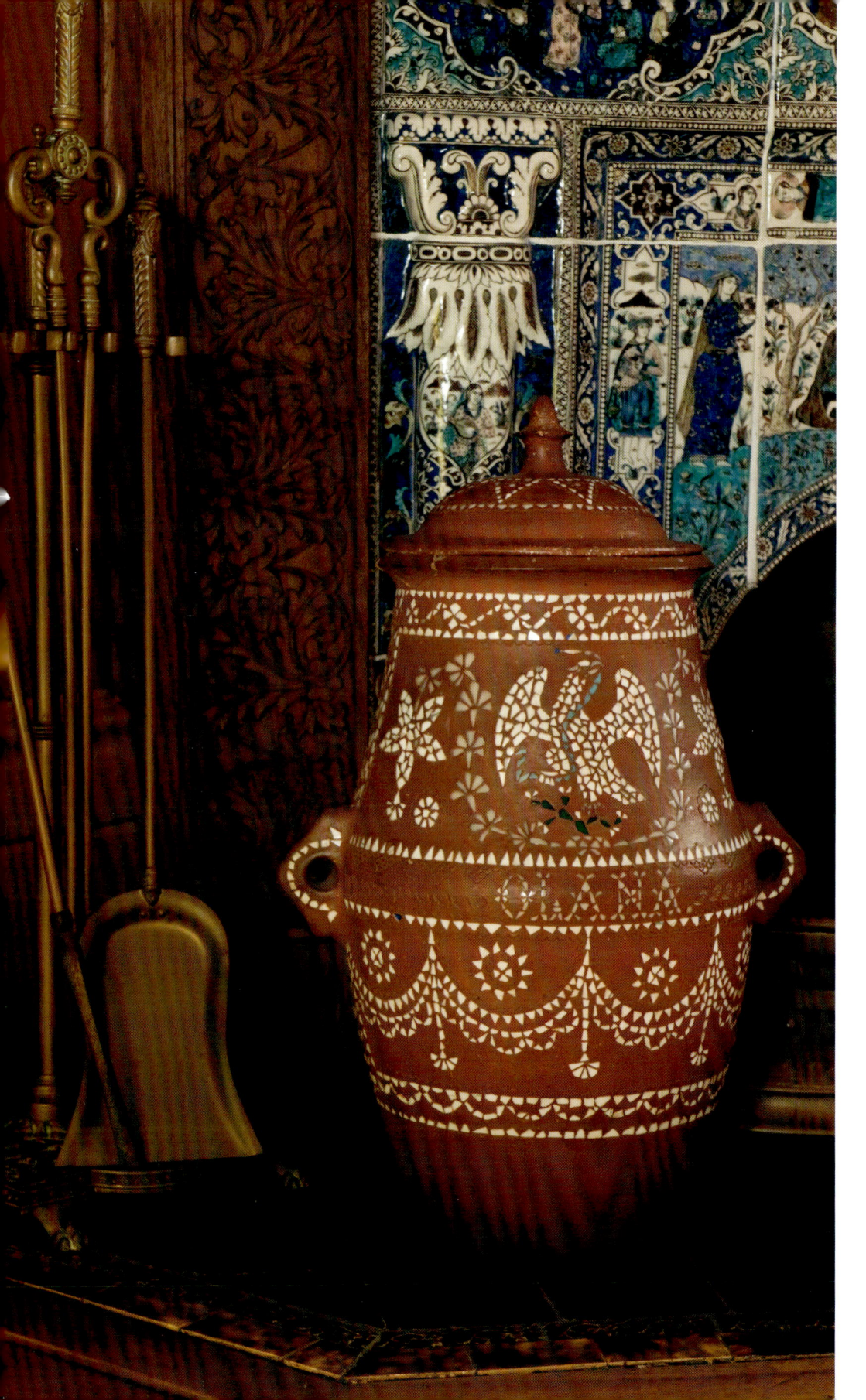

NOTES

In writing this publication, as well as in our daily work at Olana, the authors rely on the existing scholarship on Frederic Edwin Church and Olana. Any work on the collection of Church material at Olana is greatly facilitated by Gerald Carr's *Frederic Edwin Church: Catalogue Raisonné of Works of Art at Olana State Historic Site*. It is an indispensable resource. Other works on Church are also of great importance in our understanding of Church as an artist: David Huntington's *The Landscapes of Frederic Edwin Church*; John K. Howat's *Frederic Church*; Kevin Avery's *Church's Great Picture: The Heart of the Andes*; Franklin Kelly's "A Passion for Landscapes: The Paintings of Frederic Edwin Church," in *Frederic Edwin Church*; and Eleanor Jones Harvey's *The Painted Sketch*.

Of equal importance to this project are the wonderful publications and reports on Olana: James Anthony Ryan's *Frederic Church's Olana: Architecture and Landscape as Art* and Karen Zukowski's *Historic Furnishings Report for Olana State Historic Site*. The collections and research material at Olana would not be so intellectually accessible were it not for the efforts of the Olana staff both past and present, especially Richard Slavin, James Ryan, Linda E. McLean, Joel Swimmler, Laura Kline, Karen Zukowski, Dorren Martin, and Ida Brier. The landscape at Olana has been thoroughly researched by Ellen McClelland Lesser and Robert M. Toole, and the fruits of their labor appear in the *Historic Landscape Report for Olana State Historic Site*. The work of Sara Cedar Miller, *Central Park, an American Masterpiece*, and Morrison H. Heckscher, *Creating Central Park*, gave invaluable context for landscape work at the time.

For information on tourism and artists in the Hudson Valley, the authors are indebted to the work of John Sears, Roland Van Zant, Raymond Beecher, Kenneth John Myers, and William Rhoads. Francis Kowsky's *Country, Park & City* provided insight into Calvert Vaux and his work at Olana. For their generous assistance in our research, we wish to thank Ida Brier; Alyson Mazzone; Jackie Killian, Gail Davidson, and Floramae Cates at the Cooper-Hewitt; John F. McGuigan Jr.; Ellen McClelland Lesser; Georgette Turner; and Diane Shewchuk at the Columbia County Historical Society.

Our readers have been thoughtful and encouraging in their comments: Robin Campbell, Ida Brier, Ellen McClelland Lesser, Kevin Avery, and Bill Trebilcock. We are thankful for the generosity of our lenders Marshall Field and the Vedder Library of the Greene County Historical Society. At the latter we benefited from the assistance of the late Raymond Beecher, Debbie Allen, Bob Hallock, Harvey Durham, and Steve Pec. Our editor, Lory Frankel, and proofreaders, Fronia W. Simpson and Barbara McGill, have given thoughtful suggestions and careful attention to the manuscript and proofs. For the production of this book, we continue to enjoy working with John Ackerman at Cornell University Press and Ed Marquand, John Hubbard, and Marie Weiler at Marquand Books.

This project would not have been possible without the support of the New York State Office of Parks, Recreation and Historic Preservation. In particular we wish to thank Director of New York State Parks Taconic Region Jayne McLaughlin; Olana State Historic Site Manager Linda E. McLean; Interpretive Programs Assistant Carri Manchester; Bureau of Historic Sites Acting Director John Lovell; Curator Robin Campbell; Curator Susan Walker; Collections Manager Anne Cassidy; and the Collections Management staff, Ronna Dixson, Mary Zaremski, and Erin Czernecki; Conservators Joyce Zucker, Eric Price, and Michele Phillips; and Photographer Rich Clauss. We are also very grateful for the support of The Olana Partnership President Sara Griffen; Vice President for Development Robert Burns; Director of Administration and Public Affairs Nelson Sterner; and Executive Assistant Mary Curran; and the advice of the Olana Curatorial Committee, which has been encouraging and helpful. To all, our gratitude.

1. H. W. French, *Art and Artists in Connecticut* (Boston: Lee and Shepard, 1879), p. 130. Church owned French's book. This quote describes Church's home within the context of an artist's biography, which includes descriptions of several of Church's well-known works. There are two letters by Church to John D. Champlin Jr., an editor at *Scribner's*, that reference the book directly. "I have been hunting for a work entitled 'Art & Artists in Connecticut' by H. W. French— The merit of the work lies in the facts partially collected by the Author. I thought it might be of use to you for it includes the names of most of our prominent Artists including Cole." F. E. Church to John D. Champlin, September 6, 1885, Archives of American Art, Smithsonian Institution, Washington, D.C. (hereafter A A A). "I mailed as you requested The Book of Conn. Artist—pray keep it as long as you desire...." Church to Champlin, September 11, 1885, A A A. Copies of the book remain in Church's historic library at Olana, OL.1983.235 and OL.1990.70 (which belonged to Louis Church's wife, Sally).

2. F. E. Church to Erastus Dow Palmer, July 7, 1869, Albany Institute of History and Art Library.

3. John F. Sears, *Sacred Places: American Tourist Attractions in the Nineteenth Century* (New York: Oxford University Press, 1989), p. 56.

4. Cole's 1825 sketchbook, Detroit Institute of Arts, 39.558B, quoted in Ellwood C. Parry, *The Art of Thomas Cole: Ambition and Imagination* (Newark: University of Delaware Press, 1988), p. 23.

5. F. E. Church to Thomas Cole, May 20, 1844, New York State Library.

6. Gerald L. Carr did this initial research on works by Frederic Edwin Church in Olana's collection, culminating in a two-volume publication, *Frederic Edwin Church: Catalogue Raisonné of Works of Art at Olana State Historic Site* (New York: Cambridge University Press, 1994). The authors wish to thank him, as without his groundbreaking research this

current effort would not be possible. Every work by Frederic Edwin Church in Olana's collection, including those reproduced in this catalogue, has a corresponding entry in Carr's comprehensive publication.

7. Gerald L. Carr is to be credited with first identifying the location this sketch depicts. See ibid., p. 64.

8. Ibid., pp. 64–65.

9. Ibid., p. 64.

10. See Frances F. Dunwell, *The Hudson: America's River* (New York: Columbia University Press, 2008), p. 124; and Peter H. Stott, *Looking for Work: Industrial Archeology in Columbia County, New York* (Kinderhook, N.Y.: Columbia County Historical Society, 2007). While information is not always consistent in respect to precise location, several sources make clear that there were several foundries in Hudson by 1851, that Elihu Gifford owned one and was a trustee of another. The pamphlet *Hudson 1851 & 1871* (Hudson, N.Y.: [The Author], 1985), compiled by Barbara Mazur, which reproduces the *Directory of the City of Hudson for the year 1851–52* (Hudson, N.Y.: Parmenter & Van Antwerp, 1851), and Hamilton Child's *Gazetteer & Business Directory of Columbia County 1871–72* (Syracuse, N.Y., 1871) show that a Gifford foundry existed in 1851 (Elihu and William Gifford) and continued to exist at the same address, 31 Columbia, in 1871, although under the name of Wm H and James Gifford (sons). According to Mazur, there were apparently three or more ironworks in Hudson by 1871, the Gifford shop being the earliest: Hudson Iron Co., Columbia County Iron Works, and the Hudson Foundry and Machine Shop (Gifford's), as well as Hunt & Miller's Stove Foundry. "The Hudson Foundry and Machine Shop, under the charge of Gifford Brothers, . . . was for many years the only foundry between New York and Albany."

According to Ruth Piwonka in *Mount Merino: View of Mount Merino, South Bay and the City of Hudson Painted by Henry Ary and His Contemporaries* (Kinderhook, N.Y.: Columbia County Historical Society, 1976), 7th unnumbered page of text, and recounted in Ila Weiss, *Poetic Landscape: The Art and Experience of Sanford R. Gifford* (Newark: University of Delaware Press; Cranbury, N.J.: Associated University Press, 1987), p. 48, Gifford's father, Elihu Gifford, became a trustee of the new Hudson Iron Company in 1844 and a few years later built a plant on South Bay. The Gifford Foundry was built in 1851 on piles in South Bay adjacent to a new rail line. It received hematite via rail from West Stockbridge, Mass., and the slag, cinders, and other waste were used to "reclaim" ten to twelve acres of water lots that they had purchased. There is an image of the ironworks in Benson J. Lossing, *The Hudson, from the Wilderness to the Sea* (1866; reprint, Port Washington, N.Y.: Kennikat Press, 1972), p. 148.

11. For Church's trips through South America, see Kevin J. Avery, *Church's Great Picture: The Heart of the Andes* (New York: Metropolitan Museum of Art, 1993).

12. Ibid., p. 9.

13. For the Carnes family histories, see Karen Zukowski, "Building a Marriage," in *The Historic Furnishings Report for Olana State Historic Site: A History of the Interiors, Thoughts on Their Significance, and Recommendations for Their Restoration,* 3 vols. (Hudson: The Olana Partnership and New York State Office of Parks, Recreation and Historic Preservation [hereafter TOP, NYSOPRHP], 2001), vol. 1, pp. 7–10; and John K. Howat, *Frederic Church* (New Haven: Yale University Press, 2005), pp. 103–4.

14. John I. H. Baur, ed., *Autobiography of Worthington Whittredge 1820–1910, Brooklyn Museum Journal,* 1942, p. 29.

15. "Correspondence of the Transcript," *Boston Evening Transcript,* January 10, 1860.

16. Virginia Osborn to Lucy Wheeler, January 14, 1860, quoted in Zukowski, "Building a Marriage," p. 10.

17. Several articles written over the decades following the construction of Olana mention that Church had been looking for property years before his engagement. Martha J. Lamb, "The Homes of America," pt. 5, *Art Journal* 20 (August 1876): pp. 245–48, OL.2000.166, explains, "The site for the residence was selected by Mr. Church after a careful study of the river-shores." "The American Rhine: Interesting Facts about the Country around Hudson," *World,* July 21, 1889, p. 8, OL.1980.1993.1–.6, mentions, "This spot was selected by Mr. Church after a three years' diligent search along the Hudson and a careful study of other river shores, which he explored in hopes of finding a spot that would combine the greatest number of nature's beauties." Frank J. Bonnelle, "In Summer Time on Olana," *Sunday Boston Herald,* September 7, 1890 (OL.2001.19), states, "For three years he explored the territory on both banks of the Hudson, until at last his artistic eye selected a location unsurpassed by any of the numerous charming places on the river." See also Robert M. Toole, *Historic Landscape Report: Olana State Historic Site* (Hudson: NYSOPRHP and Friends of Olana, now TOP, 1996), pp. 35–37.

18. Thomas Cole, *Essay on American Scenery* (1836), in *The Collected Essays and Prose Sketches,* ed. Marshall B. Tymn (St. Paul, Minn.: John Colet Press, 1980), p. 13.

19. Thomas Cole, "Lines Written after a Walk on [a] Beautiful Morning in November," Catskill, 1838, in *Thomas Cole's Poetry,* ed. Marshall B. Tymn (York, Pa.: Liberty Cap Books, 1972), p. 63. One section reads: "The Hudson lies below, a mirror'd heaven; / Stainless, save where the joyous hills are given / With grassy slope, dark rock, and breezy wood / In purple beauty to the wooing flood— / Yon sails unruffled now, by torturing storms, / Like swans enamoured of their own bright forms; / Or spirits that have left the sky to gaze / Upon the earth's clear mirror, in amaze—." See also "Lines Suggested by a Voyage up the Hudson on a Moonlight Night—," in ibid., pp. 174–75.

20. T. Addison Richards, *American Scenery Illustrated* (New York: Leavitt and Allen,1854), pp. 16, 258–59.

21. For example, ibid.; and Lossing, *The Hudson*, p. 152.

22. Washington Irving, "The Catskill Mountains," in *The Home Book of the Picturesque, or, American Scenery, Art, and Literature, Comprising a Series of Essays by Washington Irving, W. C. Bryant, Fenimore Cooper, et al.* (1852; reprint, Gainesville, Fla.: Scholars' Facsimiles and Reprints, 1967), p. 72.

23. The authors wish to thank Ellen McClelland Lesser for her assistance with this passage.

24. For a more complete summary of this relationship and the property development under Theodore Cole's tenure, see Toole, *Historic Landscape Report*, pp. 36–51.

25. Theodore Cole to F. E. Church, November 29, 1868, OL.1998.1.176.

26. The sketch is not dated, but the inclusion of a wing added later to the left of the house indicates it was painted after September 1869. The authors wish to thank Ellen McClelland Lesser for identifying the foliage on the front of the building.

27. F. E. Church to his patron Ramon Paez, September 4, 1862, AAA.

28. F. E. Church to his father, Joseph Church, May 13, 1864, written from "The Farm," OL.1998.1.7.1.

29. F. E. Church to Gifford Pinchot, May 12, 1866, Gifford Pinchot Papers, Library of Congress.

30. F. E. Church to William Henry Osborn, May 16, 1870, OL.2003.29.

31. Carr, *Catalogue Raisonné*, pp. 348, 378–80.

32. F. E. Church to John F. Kensett, July 13, 1863, Morgan Collection, New York State Library.

33. *Boston Evening Transcript*, November 29, 1865, and a check for seventy-five dollars dated October 6, 1864, OL.2000.1147. The initial publication and discussion of this work appear in James

Anthony Ryan, "Frederic Church's Olana: Architecture and Landscape as Art," in *Frederic Edwin Church*, by Franklin Kelly et al. (Washington, D.C.: National Gallery of Art; Smithsonian Institution Press, 1989), pp. 130–31. For more information on Arthur Parton and his artist brothers, see Maureen Johnson Hickey, *Natural Truth: The Landscape Paintings of the Parton Brothers of Hudson, New York*, exh. cat. (Kinderhook, N.Y.: Columbia County Historical Society, 1998).

34. A check to Arthur Parton for twenty-five dollars dated July 24, 1863, OL.2000.1081.

35. F. E. Church to Joseph Church, May 13, 1864, OL.1998.1.7.1. For further discussion of the purchase of the Bethune lot and the building of this road, see Toole, *Historic Landscape Report*, pp. 42–44.

36. N. Parker Willis, "The Highland Terrace, above West Point," in *The Home Book of the Picturesque*, p. 108.

37. Grace King to May King McDowell, June 7, 1887, Special Collections, Hill Memorial Library, Louisiana State University Libraries, Baton Rouge, La.

38. Benjamin Bellows Grant Stone, diary entries, January 10, 1867, ". . . Mr. and Mrs. Church called[.] Church made quite a long stay and looked over drawings. He likes the 'Fawn's Leap' very much"; March 6, 1867, "In a.m. Church came in and helped me on 'Fawn's Leap'—"; March 30, 1867, "Letter from Church"; April 20, 1867, "In p.m. went over the river and called upon Church, saw Mrs. Church and baby (a little beauty) Very pleasant visit, returned at 6"; November 3, 1867, "Heard today that Mr. Church's brother-in-law had rec'd a call and accepted as pastor of the church here, I am quite delighted." The authors wish to acknowledge the late Raymond Beecher for identifying and transcribing the Church-Stone material in the collections of the Greene County Historical Society, Vedder Library, and for facilitating access to this material. For additional information on Stone, see Catherine Campbell, "Benjamin

Bellows Grant Stone: A Forgotten American Artist," *Historical Society Quarterly* 62, no. 1 (January 1978).

39. F. E. Church to Joseph Church, May 13, 1864, OL.1998.1.7.1. Until this point, Church was painting from a building in the farm complex, most likely Cosy Cottage. See Charles L. Fisher, *Archeological Discovery of Frederic Church's First Studio at Olana State Historic Site, Columbia County, New York* (Peebles Island, Waterford, N.Y.: NYSOPRHP, Bureau of Historic Sites, February 1994).

40. Emma Carnes, diary entry, August 9, 1884, p. 39, OL.2000.285. The "seat" was probably similar to the seat built onto Jervis McEntee's studio in Roundout and depicted in Calvert Vaux's *Villas and Cottages: A Series of Designs Prepared for Execution in the United States* (1864; reprint, New York: Dover, 1991), p. 168.

41. F. E. Church to the explorer Cyrus Field, April 22, 1865, Henry Huntington Library and Art Gallery, San Marino, Calif.

42. F. E. Church to Paez, September 11, 1866, AAA.

43. Frederic Edwin Church, *Cedar Grove, Catskill*, sketch dated October 1848, OL.1980.1413. The color note 5 on the studio building corresponds to the notation "5—Warm Neutral— / roof orange brown ornaments / light—green blinds." See Carr, *Catalogue Raisonné*, p. 149.

44. Church took down the studio in 1888 and it is known only through a photograph, references, and maps. See Fisher, *Archeological Discovery of Frederic Church's First Studio*, pp. 4–5; and Jervis McEntee, diary entry, July 18, 1888, Jervis McEntee Papers, 1850–1925, AAA: "[Church] has torn down his [old] studio."

45. F. E. Church to Osborn, January 1, 1866, OL.1983.1013.

46. Ibid.

47. Ibid.

48. There are numerous oil and pencil sketches in winter done from the studio location. Many are

undated, but a pencil sketch, *Wooded Hilltop, Hilly Valley, Sun*, 1917-4-1082a-recto, is dated January 1866 and is annotated with the word "brilliant" to describe the snow. This sketch is one of several works referenced and illustrated from the collection of the Cooper-Hewitt, National Design Museum, Smithsonian Institution, New York. The museum has the largest collection of oil and pencil sketches by Frederic Edwin Church, numbering more than two thousand. These works were given together in 1917 by Church's youngest son, Louis, who inherited them and Olana after Church's death. During Church's lifetime all these works were among those he kept at Olana for his private reference and pleasure. Olana has the second-largest collection of these types of sketches, which also includes Church's architectural sketches relating to the building of Olana. The combined oil and pencil studies (701), architectural sketches (500), and documented missing sketches (300) at Olana, taken together with the collection at the Cooper-Hewitt, constitute a fairly intact representation of what was in Church's possession at the time of his death.

49. Kate Bradbury to an unknown correspondent, December 25, 1889, location unknown, excerpts from transcripts compiled by Dr. Brenda E. Moon.

50. F. E. Church to Palmer, October 22, 1867, Albany Institute of History and Art Library.

51. "Hudson Revisited," *New York Observer* 45, no. 33 (August 15, 1867), Collection of Greene County Historical Society. The authors wish to acknowledge the late Raymond Beecher for compiling this research and generously donating transcriptions to Olana.

52. F. E. Church to Osborn, November 30, 1868, OL.2003.17.A – .F.

53. F. E. Church to Osborn, from "Beyrout," January 13, 1868, OL.2003.9.A. – .H.

54. Petra lies in a valley between two barrier ranges. One way of entering the city is by way of the deep and sometimes very narrow gorge, called the *siq* or *sik*.

55. The identity of the architect cannot be firmly attributed, but it is possible that Church studied with Richard Morris Hunt, who was his neighbor in the Tenth Street Studio Building. References to Church's study with an architect are mentioned years later when Church's student Lockwood de Forest was setting off for his first trip to the Middle East: "[Church] pass[ed] a few weeks in an architects office. . . . Before he went to Syria," Julia de Forest to Lockwood de Forest, August 15, 1875, microfilm roll 2730, frames 137 – 39, AAA. See also Anne Suydam Lewis, *Lockwood de Forest: Painter, Importer, Decorator*, exh. cat. (Huntington, N.Y.: Heckscher Museum, 1976), as quoted in Carr, *Catalogue Raisonné*, pp. 309, 311. On the same day Lockwood's father, Henry Grant de Forest, wrote to his son, August 15, 1875, ". . . I have come to the conclusion to take passage for Europe during the latter part of October and I I [sic] write you as promptly as I can so that you may confirm your arrangements. I announced my decision to Mr. Church. He repeated to me what he had (he says) already suggested to you, that it wd be well for you to study Architecture. . . . He named Eidlitz as one who perhaps knows most of Oriental architecture and if you wish . . . I will introduce you to him in person, as I have known him a long time"; AAA. For Church's sketches related to his architectural tutelage, see Carr, *Catalogue Raisonné*, pp. 303, 307 – 11, nos. 451 – 63. For more on Church's preparation for his journey to the Middle East, see Howat, *Frederic Church*, pp. 133 – 34.

56. F. E. Church to Palmer, March 10, 1868, writing from Jaffa—Palestine, Albany Institute of History and Art Library.

57. F. E. Church to Osborn, January 13, 1868, OL.2003.9.A. – .H.

58. F. E. Church to Osborn, July 29, 1868, from Berchtesgaden, OL.2003.12.A – .E.

59. F. E. Church to Osborn, November 9, 1868, OL.2003.15.A – .F.

60. George William Curtis, *Lotus-Eating: A Summer Book* (New York: Harper and Brothers, 1852; reprint, 2008), pp. 17 – 18.

61. Frederic Edwin Church, *Landscape View of Rome from the Banks of the Tiber River, with Distant Views of Castle Sant'Angelo, Claude's Villa and Saint Peter's Basilica*, March 18, 1869, Cooper-Hewitt, National Design Museum, Smithsonian Institution, 1917-4-594-b/c. The sketch shows the Tiber in the foreground and the view across to St. Peter's. The authors wish to thank John McGuigan for his insight on this sketch.

62. F. E. Church to Osborn, May 1, 1869, from Rome, OL.2003.24.A – .G.

63. F. E. Church to Osborn, April 14, 1869, from Athens, OL.2003.23.A – .D.

64. *Boston Evening Transcript*, December 3, 1869, quoted in David C. Huntington, "Olana: The Center of the Center of the World," in *World Art: Themes of Unity in Diversity; Acts of the XXVIth International Congress of the History of Art*, ed. Irving Lavin (University Park: Pennsylvania State University Press, 1989), p. 770.

65. F. E. Church to Osborn, February 4, 1869, OL.2003.21.A – .E. Church wrote to Osborn from Rome about boxes that had been shipped from Constantinople to Church's New York studio. Church asked Osborn to go through the boxes, as they contained some gifts for him and his wife.

66. "When I build again I intend to have one old room—with old furniture and old pictures—everything toned down to 400 years back"; F. E. Church to Osborn, November 4, 1868, OL.2004.14.A – .D. Later, from Rome, Church wrote to Osborn, "I expect you will quiz my collection when you see it—but wait until they are hung in a suitable room well toned down, in keeping with the venerable brown canvases, and then you will see much beauty gleaming

out from the film of centuries"; January 1, 1869, OL.2003.18.A – .G; and "I have been busy to-day packing my old masters. There are 59 in all and cost $1353 for the lot. I shall send them off in a few days"; February 24, 1869, OL.2003.22.A – .D.

67. Church at one point hired Hunt to make a proposal, and it is not known when or why Church switched architects. Vaux's involvement at Olana is covered in James Anthony Ryan, *Frederic Church's Olana: Architecture and Landscape as Art* (Hensonville, N.Y.: Black Dome Press, 2001); Francis R. Kowsky, *Country, Park and City: The Architecture and Life of Calvert Vaux* (New York: Oxford University Press, 1998); and in Zukowski, "The Furnishings of Olana: Creating a New Eden," in *The Historic Furnishings Report for Olana State Historic Site*, vol. 1, pp. 107, 111, 118.

68. Vaux, *Villas and Cottages*, p. 67; and Kowsky, *Country, Park and City*, pp. 206 – 15. The location is referenced specifically on page 207.

69. Frederick Law Olmsted to Charles Loring Brace, November 24, 1871, Frederick Law Olmsted Collection, Library of Congress, published in Olmsted, *The Papers of Frederick Law Olmsted*, vol. 6, *The Years of Olmsted, Vaux and Company, 1865–1874* (Baltimore: Johns Hopkins University Press, 1992), p. 493. The letter goes on to define why Church was chosen: "There is, I think a peculiar propriety & significance in it. A quiet, retired man—a model of rank and file citizenship—but who in his special calling has earned the respect & regard of the community, called at last to serve the public in an office where his special training will be of value, in place of a professional politician . . . is one so much the opposite in his qualification—. . . . The appointment of Church signifies more— That offices (for the present) are not for sale to those who want them, but are to seek and draw in the best men—and that they are expected to serve whether convenient or not. We were anxious on a matter of propriety that the art element should be recognized—that the public utility of devotion to art & the study of nature in a public service of this kind should be recognized & Church seemed on the whole the most appropriate & respectable man to express this." For more on Church's involvement with Central Park and the Metropolitan Museum of Art, see Howat, *Frederic Church*, pp. 160 – 61. For more on the relationship between Church and Olmsted, and other contemporaneous professional landscape designers, see Toole, *Historic Landscape Report*, pp. 9 – 31.

70. The collection at Olana includes more than 500 architectural sketches and almost 300 stencils. In addition, 330 architectural sketches and stencils have been documented in photographs, though the location of the originals is currently unknown. See Ida Brier, Karen Zukowski, and Kris Gibbons, *Missing Architectural Sketches Documentation Project*, Research Report of Olana State Historic Site, Olana Research Collection, 2000. In all, there are more than 1,100 architectural sketches and/or stencils.

71. Charles H. J. Smith, *Landscape Gardening, or Parks and Pleasure Grounds* (New York: A. O. Moore, 1858), pp. 55, 63, 191. The authors wish to acknowledge the late Jim Ryan for making the initial connection between the philosophy of Charles Smith and Frederic Church's ideas for the landscape and house placement at Olana.

72. Lockwood de Forest, undated manuscript, microfilm roll 2730, frame 20, AAA.

73. Calvert Vaux, OL.1986.64; Charles H. J. Smith, OL.1984.3; Jules Bourgoin, OL.1986.377.1 – .83; and Pascal Coste, OL.1989.4.

74. Vaux, *Villas and Cottages*, pp. 110 – 11.

75. Virginia Osborn to Mary Sturges, Christmas, c. 1874–76, New-York Historical Society. This letter is undated but the text suggests it was written around the Christmas holidays of one of the first few winters in which the Churches were in residence in the new house.

76. F. N. Zabriskie, "An Artist's Castle, and Our Ride Thereto," "Old Colony" Papers, *Christian Intelligencer*, September 10, 1884, p. 2.

77. Grace King to May King McDowell, June 7, 1887.

78. *Garden and Forest*, January 20, 1892, p. 26, quoted in May Brawley Hill, "'For the Scent of Present Fragrance and the Perfume of Olden Times': The Domestic Garden in American Impressionist Painting," in *Visions of Home: American Images of Suburban Leisure and Country Comfort*, ed. Lisa N. Peters and Peter M. Lukehart (Carlisle, Pa: Trout Gallery, Dickinson College, 1997), p. 53. The authors wish to thank Ellen McClelland Lesser for providing this source. Vaux discusses the growing of vines and "creepers" for the exterior decoration of buildings in *Villas and Cottages*, pp. 77, 83.

79. Bonnelle, "In Summer Time on Olana."

80. F. E. Church to Osborn, July 22, 1871, Princeton University Libraries.

81. Grace King to May King McDowell, June 7, 1887.

82. Fanchon, "The Kaatskills: Their Attractions Enthusiastically Set Forth; Prospects of the Present Season; Artists among the Mountains," undated [c. summer 1871], unattributed clipping marked No. 141-vol. V, copy at the Vedder Library, Greene County Historical Society. Zukowski, "The New House: Public and Private Reactions," in *The Historic Furnishings Report for Olana State Historic Site*, vol. 1, p. 30, writes that the "source of this clipping has not been established, but by comparing it to the chronology of the construction of the main residence, the article can be dated to the summer of 1871. The article not only describes the home at an early stage in its construction, it reveals Church's enthusiasm for his new home—and his propensity to narrate its virtues to visitors."

83. Zabrinski, "An Artist's Castle," p. 2.

84. F. E. Church to Osborn, January 2, 1870, OL.2003.28.A – .C.

85. Carr, *Catalogue Raisonné*, pp. 378–79.

86. F. E. Church to Osborn, February 22, 1871, Princeton University Libraries.

87. F. E. Church to Martin Johnson Heade, February 8, 1871, Martin Johnson Heade Papers, 1853–1904, AAA.

88. F. E. Church to Palmer, May 26, 1870, Albany Institute of History and Art Library.

89. F. E. Church to Heade, May 26, 1870, AAA.

90. F. E. Church to Palmer, May 13, 1870, Albany Institute of History and Art Library.

91. F. E. Church to Palmer, June 18, 1872, Albany Institute of History and Art Library.

92. F. E. Church to Palmer, June 7, 1870, Albany Institute of History and Art Library.

93. F. E. Church to Charles de Wolf Brownell, June 28, 1888, copy from an unknown source, transcript in the Olana Research Collection.

94. F. E. Church to Osborn, July 22, 1871, Princeton University Libraries.

95. F. E. Church to Heade, October 24, 1870, AAA.

96. Tim Barringer links the brushwork of this particular sketch to Thomas Cole's style, in Barringer and Andrew Wilton, *American Sublime: Landscape Painting in the United States; 1820–1880* (London: Tate Publishing, 2002), p. 171.

97. The pencil drawing *Rogers Island and the Catskills from Olana* (OL.1977.125) might have served as a topographical template for the middle ground and background.

98. F. E. Church to Jervis McEntee, December 21, 1890, AAA.

99. Visible in a nineteenth-century photograph in the Olana Archives are seven objects excavated by F. N. Otis (OL.1992.37). The handwriting below the photograph reads: "From the Indian 'Huaco' at Bugolitas Province of Chiriqui—New Grenada—Main piece of wrought stone {weight 25 lbs {length 20 inches {width 8 inches {height 8 inches} —Exhumed Feb. 1860 F. N. Otis—Remaining Articles Pottery."

New Granada was a former Spanish viceroyalty in northwest South America that comprised present-day Colombia, Ecuador, Panama, and Venezuela. By 1830 Venezuela and Ecuador had seceded, and the remnant (Colombia and Panama) was renamed the Republic of New Granada. This became the Republic of Colombia in 1886, from which the present Panama seceded in 1903. Chiriquí is a province in present-day Panama, in the west bordering Costa Rica.

100. Jervis McEntee, diary entry, Monday, July 22, 1872, Jervis McEntee Papers, 1850–1905, AAA.

101. Isabel Carnes Church to Gertrude McEntee, August 30, 1878, AAA. See also discussions of this by Ryan, *Frederic Church's Olana*, p. 46; Gerald L. Carr, *Frederic Edwin Church: Romantic Landscapes and Seascapes* (New York: Adelson Galleries, 2007), pp. 118–23; David C. Huntington, *The Landscapes of Frederic Edwin Church: Vision of an American Era* (New York: George Braziller, 1966), p. 114; and Zukowski, "The Furnishings of Olana: Creating a New Eden," vol. 1, pp. 111–13. For the relationship between the naming of Olana and the painting *El Khasné, Petra*, see Gerald L. Carr, *Olana Landscapes* (New York: Rizzoli, 1989), p. 2.

102. Zukowski, "The Furnishings of Olana: Creating a New Eden," vol. 1, p. 112, writes, "It was shortly after the gift of Strabo's *Geographica* that the couple started using the name Olana, and by 1890 Bonnelle reported that the name had been chosen by Isabel Church, because it was 'the old Latin name for a place in Persia, to which the artist's home bears a resemblance in situation.'"

103. Strabo, *The Geography of Strabo: Literally Translated, with Notes*, trans. H. C. Hamilton and W. Falconer (London: Henry G. Bohn, 1854), OL.1984.430.1; and James Morier, *A Second Journey through Persia, Armenia, and Asia Minor, to Constantinople, between the Years 1810 and 1816* (London: Longman, Hurst, Rees, Orme, and Brown, 1818), OL.1986.92.

104. Lamb, "The Homes of America," p. 247.

105. The home of poet William Cullen Bryant, Cedarmere, was the other house featured in this issue; it depicts his home but not the view. Lamb, ibid., p. 247, wrote, "As we have viewed at length the summer home of one of the foremost poets in the land, we can now do no better than to glance at the new residence of one of our most distinguished landscape-painters." Other issues in the series discuss the homes of Albert Bierstadt, Thomas Gold Appleton, and Miss Louisa Kellogg's Claverhurst, and while the views are discussed, they are not illustrated.

106. F. E. Church to Amelia Edwards, September 2, 1877, Sommerville College Library, Oxford.

107. F. E. Church to Palmer, October 18, 1884, Albany Institute of History and Art Library.

108. Sara Cedar Miller, *Central Park, an American Masterpiece* (New York: Harry N. Abrams, 2003), p. 111; and Frederick Law Olmsted, "Description of the Central Park," January 1859, published in *The Papers of Frederick Law Olmsted*, vol. 3, *Creating Central Park*, ed. Charles E. Beveridge and David Schuyler (Baltimore: Johns Hopkins University Press, 1983), p. 215.

109. Toole, *Historic Landscape Report*, pp. 63–64.

110. Emma Carnes, diary entries, August 23 and August 28, 1884, pp. 42, 43.

111. Emma Carnes, diary entries, August 31 and September 4, 1884, pp. 43, 44.

112. Susan Hale to Lucretia Hale, July 6, 1884, in *Letters of Susan Hale*, ed. Caroline Atkinson (Boston: Marshall Jones, c. 1918), pp. 141–42.

113. Miller, *Central Park, an American Masterpiece*, p. 111.

114. Emma Carnes, diary entry, July 2, 1884, p. 32.

115. F. E. Church to Brownell, September 4, 1889, copy from an unknown source, transcript in the Olana Research Collection.

116. Jervis McEntee, diary entry, July 18, 1888, AAA.

117. Jervis McEntee, diary entry, Wednesday, September 17, 1873, AAA.

118. See Ita G. Krebs [Ita R. Gross], *Charles De Wolf Brownell: Explorer of the American Landscape*, exh. cat. (New York: Kennedy Galleries, 1991), fig. 43.

119. Emma Carnes, diary entry, August 3, 1883, p. 38.

120. Louis P. Church to Sally B. Good, January 11, 1894, OL.1998.1.1503.1.A – .B.

121. *Hudson Register*, September 11, 1896, p. 4, col. 3.

122. Frances F. Dunwell, *The Hudson: America's River* (New York: Columbia University Press, 2008), p. 182.

123. Elizabeth Mankin Kornhauser and Amy Ellis, *Hudson River School: Masterworks from the Wadsworth Atheneum Museum of Art* (Hartford: Wadsworth Atheneum; New Haven: Yale University Press, 2003), p. 11.

124. F. E. Church to Brownell, July 19, 1888, copy from an unknown source, transcript in the Olana Research Collection.

125. F. E. Church to Charles Dudley Warner, July 23, 1888, OL.1985.36.A.

126. "The American Rhine: Interesting Facts about the Country around Hudson," p. 8.

127. Grace King to "Nan" [King], July 4, 1891, Special Collections, Hill Memorial Library, Louisiana State University Libraries, Baton Rouge, La., and Samuel Clemens to Frederic Church, June 11, 1887, Twain Papers, UCCL no. 03582, Bancroft Library, University of California at Berkeley. For identifying Olana as a "Garden of Eden," see Zukowski, "The Furnishings of Olana: Creating a New Eden," vol. 1, pp. 118–20.

128. The album is titled "In Mexico: F. E.C. and W. L. P. Jan – Feb 1895," OL.1992.52.1 – .46.

129. F. E. Church to Palmer, April 19, 1891, Albany Institute of History and Art Library.

130. F. E. Church to John Ferguson Weir, October 25, 1891, AAA.

131. Isabel Carnes Church to Downie Church Black, December 12, 1891, OL.1998.1.1148.1.2.

132. "I took many photographs of Orizaba with my Kodak," Louis Church to Sally B. Good, March 21, 1897, OL.1998.1.1709.1.A – .H; "We took a few photographs had the guide go below [into the crater] and get some sulphor [sic]. . . . ," January 26, 1900, OL.1998.1.1753.A – .F.

133. This work was purchased for Olana by The Friends of Olana (now named The Olana Partnership) in 1998.

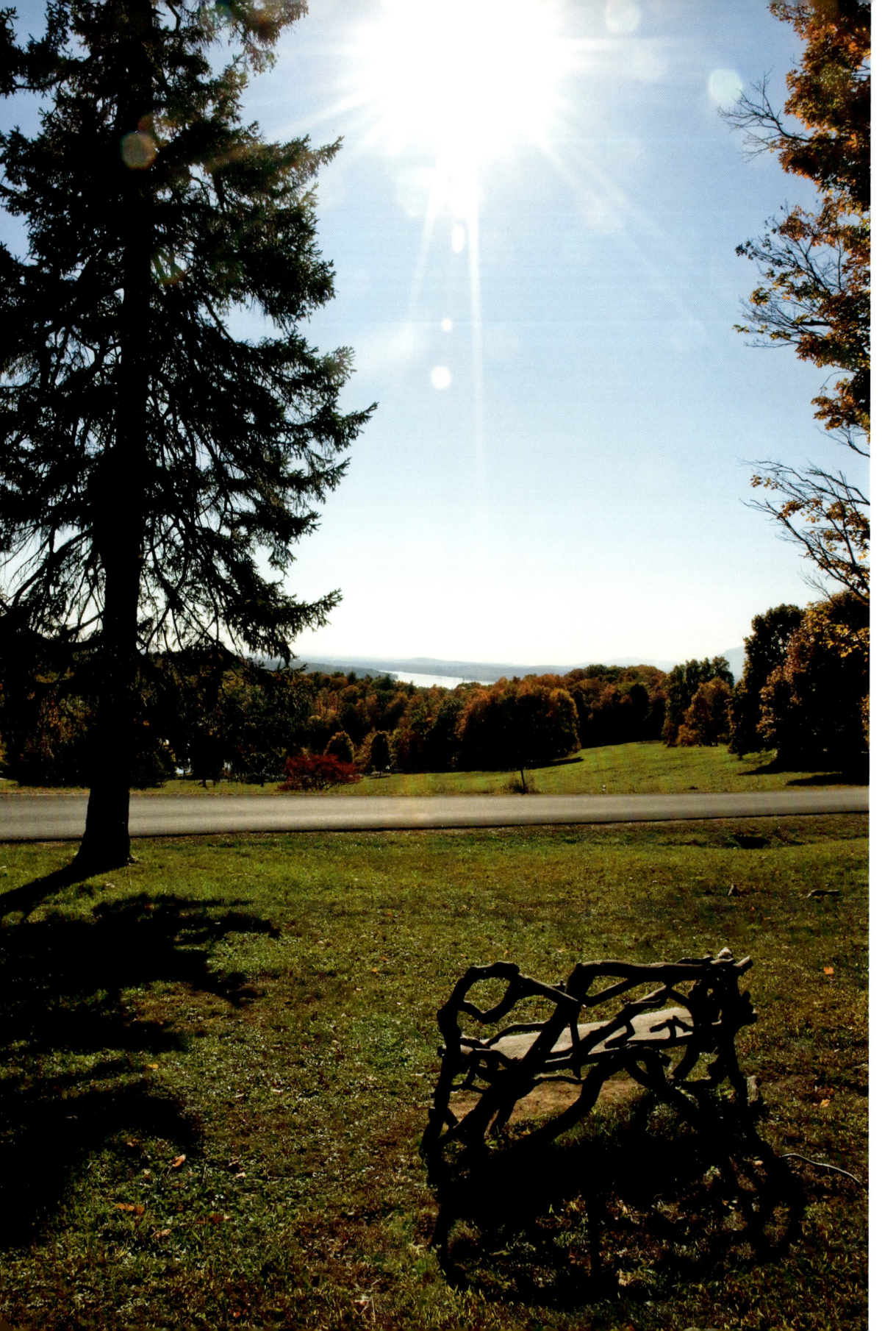

This book and the accompanying exhibition were made possible in part by generous gifts from the following:

Anonymous
Furthermore: a program of the J. M. Kaplan Fund
Mr. and Mrs. Brock Ganeles
Frederick D. and Eileen Hill
Hudson-Fulton-Champlain Quadricentennial Commission
Mark LaSalle
Chas A. Miller III
The Lois and Charles A. Miller Foundation, Inc.
The New York State Council on the Arts Museum Program
Open Space Institute, Inc. Barnabas McHenry Award
Eileen Patrick and Jeffrey Ervine
Lou Salerno, Questroyal Fine Art
Richard T. Sharp
Susan Winokur and Paul Leach

We are particularly grateful to Henry and Sharon Martin, whose early contribution was a catalyst in our fundraising effort to mount this remarkable exhibition.

The Trustees and staff of The Olana Partnership also wish to recognize the support of Governor David A. Paterson; New York State Office of Parks, Recreation and Historic Preservation Commissioner Carol Ash; Deputy Commissioner for Historic Preservation, New York State Office of Parks, Recreation and Historic Preservation J. Winthrop Aldrich; Regional Director, Taconic Region, Jayne McLaughlin; and Olana Site Manager Linda E. McLean.

The Evelyn and Maurice Sharp Gallery was made possible by a generous gift from

Richard T. Sharp

Additional gifts were provided by:

Wayne and Karen Aaron
Adam D. Amsterdam
Mr. and Mrs. Eliot H. Brown
Ann Cotaj
Robert M. De Michele
Milbank, Tweed, Hadley & McCloy LLP
Stacey Rappaport
The Peter Jay Sharp Foundation
Andrew Tomback
Mr. and Mrs. Donald Weeden
Weeden & Co. L.P.
Susan Winokur and Paul Leach

We are most grateful for their support.

Supporting Olana

The Olana Partnership was founded in 1971 to assist and support New York State in the restoration and preservation of Olana. We rely on a large number of supporters—individuals, foundations, companies, and public sector sources—to fund our work for the enhancement of Olana and its integral viewshed, to sponsor educational programs, and to foster scholarly research on the artist and his property. This support is essential to Olana's education, outreach, and public programs, to care for the collection, and to support lending from and exhibitions of the collection. Your donation will make a real difference and enable others to enjoy Olana both now and into the future. For more information on how you can help, please contact The Development Office, The Olana Partnership, PO Box 199, Hudson, NY 12534 or visit us at *www.olana.org*.

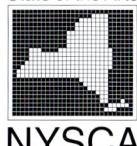

State of the Arts
NYSCA

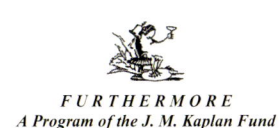

FURTHERMORE
A Program of the J. M. Kaplan Fund

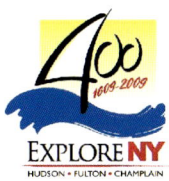

EXPLORE NY
HUDSON · FULTON · CHAMPLAIN

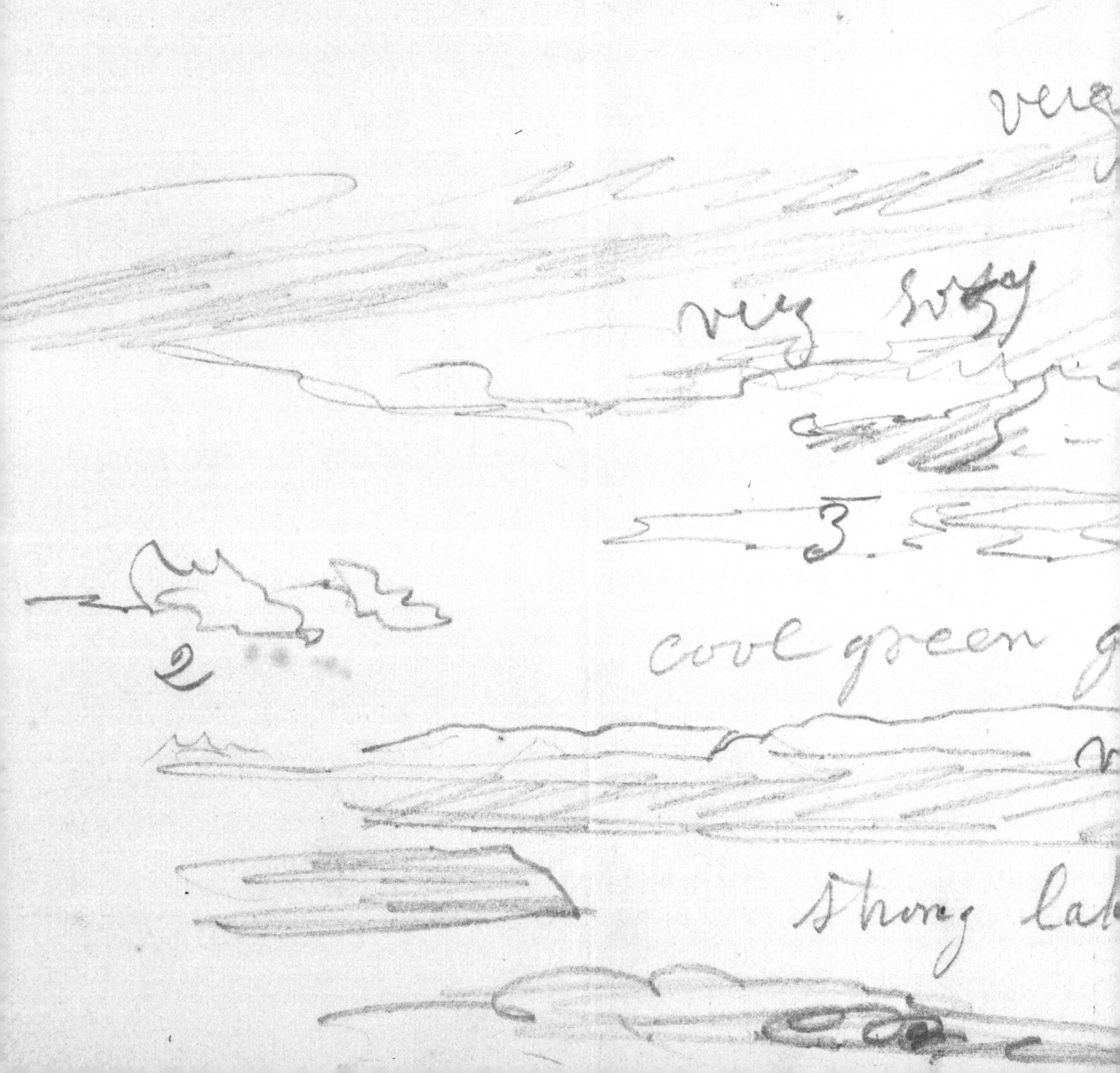
very
3
2
cool green
Strong